THE ADVENTURES OF JOY CHRONICLES **BOOK 1**

PATH *of* SWEETNESS

JOURNAL OF GALACTIC ROMANCE AND GLOBAL EVOLUTION

By Joy Elaine

www.JoyElaine.com

Path of Sweetness:
The Path to Earth's Evolution and Beyond

Second Edition

Copyright © Joy Elaine 2015

Published by Joy Books

ISBN: 1728821045
ISBN-13: 9781728821047

Cover design by Erica Dale with Ambrose Design & CKL Studios

Copy edited by George Verongos and Proofed to Perfection Editing Services

DEDICATION

This book is dedicated to Earth and all those who love and honor her.

ACKNOWLEDGMENTS

Through the support and inspiration of my friend Jill Marie, founder of SVH, I am remembering and embracing my master abilities.

I also wish to personally thank the following people for their contributions to my inspiration, knowledge and support in creating this book:

My parents, Ralph and Vivian Tedrow, and my brother Ron

Erica Dale, project coordinator

Masters of Light and my guides

Tonas, my partner in this work

Liponie, a friend and magical assistant

Commander Ashtar and the Ashtar Command

Gaia

Native Americans and other indigenous peoples of Earth

Sheliah

Council for Earth Vigilance—CEV

NOTES TO READER

Read this book start to finish and enjoy the journey. Enhance your personal evolution and the elevation of Earth by participating in the transmissions that Tonas and I send to Earth from his spaceship. Turn to the back of the book (page just before the glossary), read the Mission Participation Directives and join the greatest adventure of your life.

Explanations for some unfamiliar terms may be found in the glossary at the back of the book.

PROLOGUE

I was past middle-age when I first found myself. Actually, you could say I was on the verge of becoming *old*. And for a long time I had been totally disinterested in having any kind of intimate relationship with a man.

Rewind back to 1969, when I married my complete opposite, and through the course of our twenty-two years together, we continued on our separate paths, never quite understanding or accepting each other. I finally realized I could never be the traditional wife that my husband desired, and so I asked for a divorce.

Since I still didn't know much about who I was or who I could be, I almost immediately jumped into ten years of an on-again-off-again relationship with an alcoholic. It was a miscapade of epic proportions.

By 2001 I'd had enough drama to last me the rest of my life, so I was finally able to walk away from that unhealthy relationship. I knew it wasn't going to be enough just to avoid men. I had to fix myself, but I didn't know how.

I began the search for myself by embarking upon an intense exploration of various healing modalities and esoteric studies— angelic healing, past life regressions, Reiki, acupressure and acupuncture, shamanism, Akashic record reading, and many others.

During this time I also began recording what I liked to call "the nightly news." Throughout the course of my sleep, voices would speak to me, but when I would wake up in the morning, I could never remember what they had said. I began keeping a small digital voice recorder under my pillow and as soon as I heard someone speak I would awaken just enough to record what I'd heard. I wasn't really sure who kept speaking to me, but they certainly shared some interesting information that touched my heart.

One message in particular confounded me: "Teach the world the evolution of man by living it."

What did that mean? I didn't have a clue about how to undertake such a lofty injunction, but when I began studying Serenity Vibration Healing (SVH) in 2003, I quickly realized I had hit the self-improvement jackpot. That modality, unlike everything else I'd studied, fit me perfectly. I could *feel* my body shift as I worked to release old belief systems and programs that did not empower me.

February 2014:

I'm still not interested in an intimate relationship; instead, I am interested in humanity in general and in improving our relationship with the Earth in particular.

My work with SVH and my investigations into all matters pertaining to our elevation led me to put together an "energy package" to assist the Ashtar Command. I knew that they were "good guys," dedicated to assisting Earth, but I'd never worked with them before. Although I was quite comfortable with the idea that there were other life forms out there—after all, I'd been getting advice from some of them for years—it was time to converse with one of them face to face.

Now that I have the capability—using SVH—of moving my energy body to different positions in time and space, my unsuspecting self stepped aboard an Ashtar Command spaceship. It's a journey you'll never believe, and one I'll never forget ...

CHAPTER ONE
February 10, 2014

"My dear, I am Tonas."

This strikingly handsome man's greeting was simple, but it sparked the beginning of what I consider to be the greatest adventure of my life.

I first met Tonas a week ago when my friend Jill Marie and I visited his spaceship. I had received information from another energy worker about a package they had put together to assist the Ashtar Command. Since the work didn't feel complete to me, I invited Jill to help me put some of the missing pieces together. Despite the fact that she and I were meeting someone from another world—maybe even another galaxy—I naively expected this to be just another day's work.

Jill and I translated our energy bodies into a large room in an Ashtar Command ship, and I sensed a man standing in front of several huge windows. (At this stage in the development of my master abilities, I perceived objects around me in a unique manner I call "feel/seeing.") Jill whispered to me, "The commander is handsome."

I was startled by this news and surprised at how appealing her description of his appearance—fair-skinned, dark, soulful eyes and shoulder-length black hair—was to me. It seemed fitting that he was dressed completely in black except for a cape trimmed in gold.

There went my expectations of just another day on the job.

As I stood there gape-mouthed and glassy-eyed, contemplating the stunning figure before me, Jill noticed that Tonas couldn't seem to take his eyes off me. She felt his intense focus gave her the right to ask him, "Are you *smitten* with my friend?"

I was horrified by her boldness, but also fascinated to hear what he would say. He replied, "Very much so. And if you should desire to visit my ship again … we could hold hands."

Before I could decide whether or not I was *ready* for holding hands, he asked permission to kiss my hand! This was such a gallant request that I couldn't refuse.

After I handed Tonas the energy package—templates for Earth's cities of light—to assist the Ashtar Command, he guided me to the large wall of windows on his ship so that we could gaze at the Earth below us and the stars all around us. I remained for a little bit longer to enjoy seeing the night sky.

I concluded our meeting by saying, with more confidence than I felt, "Thank you for speaking with me." Then, having had all the out-of-this-world experience I could handle at that time, I left somewhat precipitously. I suppose you could say I fled.

#

A week later, I am back on the spaceship. Meeting a tall, dark, and handsome stranger proved to be too intriguing for me to settle for a one-time visit; plus, I have a sense that the commander knows much about Earth that he hasn't yet had a chance to share with me.

After Tonas greets me today, he informs me that there is more between us than the connection we have with a council that is supporting Earth's evolution.

"You and I also have a deep heart connection," he says.

This is intriguing news to me, but I'm definitely not yet ready to discover more about a heart connection—it feels far too intimate. To cover my unwillingness to delve into that topic, I change the subject. "Tell me about your work."

Tonas explains that his work became his all-encompassing passion and that his dedication to assisting Earth began some 25,000 years ago. "In the last 2,000 years or so I have been a presence on Earth—not embodied as a human, but as myself. It was a great honor for me to have the privilege to become the commander of this vessel."

"What is this vessel's name?" I ask.

He replies, "In my language it is called *Inishimora* which means 'The Night Sky.'"

I smile. This is the most perfect name I can imagine! I love looking up at the stars, and how much more wonderful it must be to view the night sky from a spaceship by that name.

Bringing my focus back to the present, I ask Tonas to describe what his normal day is like.

"My days are quite typical, except for times when I am visited by a beautiful blonde; you are quite fetching. I am considered to be of the highest rank on my ship, and yet all of us are of one mind. And because we are of one mind, upon the moment of your arrival, it is always known that I will be giving you 100 percent of my focus."

"I appreciate that," I reply, shyly.

"I am one that enjoys *being,* and I focus all of my consciousness on what it is that I am most passionate about. There will be a time when you will have the ability to transmit your physical body to my ship rather than visiting me as an energy transmission."

"I yearn to master that ability," I admit. It sounds incredible, but the galactic masters who have been teaching me have assured me this kind of travel will be part of my future.

Currently, my body is still on Earth, sitting on the sofa in my front room while part of my energy presence is in Tonas's spacecraft. But the thought of my physical body joining my essence up here ... well, I almost can't imagine it, it's so mind-blowing.

"I will enjoy holding your hand and gazing at the stars, our eyes looking out at the night sky together," he continues. "The ship is our connection to the universe and the universes beyond this universe that you exist within."

That there are universes beyond our universe is news to me. Wondering if his duties will take him to other worlds, I ask, "Will you be leaving soon?" Now that I've met such a fascinating man, I'm not ready to give up speaking with him so soon.

"My ship has not moved from this sector since our first connection. I will never leave it until you can leave with me. This is new for you, but it is not new for me." His voice is so intense, I feel mesmerized.

"We have been together now for many years," he says, and seeing my confused expression, he adds, "You have come to visit me when you sleep."

Although this is a surprise, it feels true. I *have* visited him before, but the specifics seem just out of my mind's reach. My inability to access the memories of our previous encounters puzzles me.

"I wish I could remember," I say, with frustration.

"That *will* come. It is our destiny to see the stars in every universe together."

I can think of no way to respond. I am thrilled at the possibility of traveling to other universes—but is traveling with him really my "destiny?"

"What we've had over these years has been priceless to me," Tonas says. "There is nothing I would exchange for even one of our moments together. This is what you must know in your heart. I found you—and you finally found me."

I'm still feeling off-balance because of the depth of his emotion and the ease with which he shares his feelings with me. Since my passion, at least in regards to intimacy, has lain dormant for years, I find that now I can't come up with any sincere reply.

I move our conversation to explore more neutral territory. "Can you tell me more about your body? Do you eat food? Do you sleep? Do you wear different clothes?"

"I look handsome in black," he says with a smile. "It enhances my dark eyes and hair. I always know when you will come to me. The way your eyes sparkled when you first caught sight of me … it was in that moment I knew I must always see that same sparkle, that same look in your eyes. And so, I have changed nothing since we first met."

"Nothing—really? Not even your clothes?"

He chuckles. "Yes, I have changed my clothes. There is the desire of bathing and anointing. Of course I have skin, I have a body. Human beings are designed in the same mold as us. And so, we do have arms, legs, heads, and stomachs. We enjoy consuming foods, drinks, tasty treats, and essences of the most delicious nectars. It is not necessary for us to do so. It is simply a pleasure."

I'm intrigued by his words and by the physical similarities between us. I gaze out of the spacecraft window where inky blackness full of sparkling white dots surrounds us. Below us is my home world, a planet where I have experienced much joy and also much pain. And yet I love it so.

"Your awareness and acceptance of our desire to assist Earth gives us the opportunity to be of great service," Tonas says. "Without an incarnate such as yourself asking for our assistance, we are unable to provide it; the door to your world remains closed and has been for many thousands of years."

He is saying that Earth could have benefitted from the Ashtar Command's help long ago. It upsets me that we lost so many years of assistance … all because humans didn't know to *ask* for help. It's time to change that—I hope this book will help!

"You have incarnated, my dear, at the most pinnacle of times for Earth," Tonas continues. "Your experiences in life have perhaps not reflected the great importance of your presence, because you have an impression of those experiences that is less than ideal. You are in a transition now in which you are learning your valuable position on Earth. You have had the belief that you are less than your true nature—which is, of course, seen and valued by all of us."

I'd like to hear more about my true nature, but before I can probe for more information, Tonas goes on. "What you and I will experience one day will be the seed that all humanity can learn from."

I shake my head. "What can I … what can *we* … teach mankind?"

"They will learn what it is to be fully in heart and have the union of presence. They will master the coupling of physical and energy, the blending of the essence of being—which, my dear, we will one day know."

"I'm confused," I say, and I look away until his voice draws my attention back.

"You will find that you love me," he says simply. "This feeling is still unknown to you, but when you allow yourself to open your mind and heart to what we have meant to each other these years—it will be a great awakening to you. Then you will understand what is present within you as a seed that is ready to germinate and grow into a flower, the flower of our passion. This is truly your greatest desire, although you are not yet fully aware of it. You must realize that you and I speak with each other endlessly in our minds. Throughout many years, we have shared our hearts and our joined hands as we looked out into the night sky."

I feel overwhelmed. There is so much information for me to assimilate that I feel the need to bring our time together to a close.

"Thank you, Tonas, for speaking with me today."

"We are always talking," he replies. "You are *joy*, and through that joy you will experience the greatest union of heart and mind, of spirit of essence, of consciousness. The first moment of this union will create a sun so bright that all human beings will witness and understand from your brightness what is possible for them."

As I stand next to him, feeling the comfort of his form next to me, I still have questions about who I am. But I realize I've found something bigger than myself, a purpose greater than anything I could have imagined.

And for the first time in my life, I'm ready for it.

CHAPTER TWO
February 14, 2014

"Hello, my dear Joy," Tonas greets me. This is our 'holiday of the heart' connection."

"You know about Valentine's Day?"

"I have immersed myself in many Earth cultures. It is a tender decision that you made for us to have this union of minds and hearts on this day of St. Valentine."

"I'm glad that you know about this holiday, because I've decided to celebrate it by giving myself the gift of speaking with you today."

"Your presence is also a gift to me." He gives me a small but gracious bow.

"So," I ask, "are you ready to be interviewed?"

Tonas finds this comical and laughs. "Yes, if it will help you to know me better."

"I suppose you already know all about me, since we've been together for so long. When did we first meet?"

He reveals something that shocks me. "I first met you *millions* of years ago. You and I were both initiates at the ancient academy of Imphere, and one day I saw you step through a gate of light into that space."

Seeing the look of astonishment on my face, he hastens to further explain our first meeting.

"The first time I saw you was quite shocking to me. When my eyes met yours, you stopped not for even a second, but I was frozen in the moment … and I knew. At the time, I was in a committed relationship with a woman named Sironea, but we had been growing apart. She had different ideas. Once I saw you, it became impossible for my heart to see anyone *but* you. To honor Sironea, I told her of my feelings for you, and she celebrated with me, knowing that the heart of my heart had entered my life."

"What made you notice me?" I ask.

"You stood out among the rest of the initiates. I looked upon you and I followed from afar; I made it my focus to understand your future academy. I witnessed you each time you entered into the academy tutorials, both subterranean as well as above Terra, with Osiris, with Isis, and with all of the different instructors. It was an easy matter for me to make my way to each of those positions."

Tonas, noting the look of puzzlement on my face, immediately explains that he spent thousands of years on Earth visiting the ancient academies. "It is not that I was one of the stalkers that you have in your modern world; however, it is true that at every tutorial you ever implemented, I made most assured that I would be in that position where you would step through into that academy.

"I was so taken with you; obsessed could be another word. For you must know that I was not chasing the entry points of other initiates. I knew that you were my destiny. This is not to put undue pressure upon you, of course. You are my destiny even if you fail to ever visit my ship in the future. I will accept and honor your choice."

"You did all this without ever saying hello?" I ask.

"I did not approach you. It was you who approached me, *finally.*"

I am stunned by this revelation and the length of time Tonas has known of me. I wish I could talk with him about his pursuit of me for eons of time, because I'm really flattered; however, the depth of passion and commitment he says he feels for me is unnerving. It seems to me that I've only known him for a few days!

Since my feelings are too jumbled to make an honest reply to his disclosures, it seems best to say nothing more about "us"—at least for a while. If he's waited for me for millions of years, he's certainly not going to be upset about waiting a few more months or even years for me to know my own heart!

I now know what it means to "gather your wits about you," because that's exactly what I do. With my wits firmly in hand, I ask a question about which I have been curious. "What dimension do we exist in, when I visit this ship?"

He explains that we float within a 10th dimensional field—that news thrills me—and that the 10th dimension is a much higher dimension than the blend of 6th and 7th dimensional energies that my physical body currently exists within on Earth.

"My dear, you are blond and youthful—and even if you were a crone, you would be as delightful to my heart. It is not necessary for you to come into partnership with me, though that is the greatest desire of my heart. It is enough for me to be in your presence. It is enough for me to love you."

I am relieved that Tonas is not asking for any commitment from me now. But I do want to acknowledge his declaration somehow, so I say, "I love talking with you. Recently, I did hear you through telepathy say, 'I absolutely *adore* you.' I was delighted that I could actually experience a little bit of communication that way."

"This is the ultimate," he says. "It is more to our liking to sit for long hours in each other's presence with no need for words and allow our thoughts to flow and our wishes to be known."

He gives me a glance. "I know some of your passions. You have been coming to me for a long time, and I have witnessed all of the stages of your—as you might call it—'frustrating life.' I have been a constant ear and I have also been a support to you."

This surprises me. Have I been complaining to this man for *years?* Without chasing him away? His level of acceptance seems astonishing. Why haven't we met until now? As if he can hear my unspoken questions, he responds.

"I have not entered into your life; it would have been a breach of decorum. The councils would have slapped my fingers. You are someone who longs for love, even more than I do. And yet, your words speak of how you are satisfied being free of that entanglement. I believe that a relationship can meet all of the needs of an individual."

"And what about your own needs?" I ask.

"You must know, I have no needs. So it is simply your needs that must be met in order for you to feel comfortable."

This is such a radical idea to me. I wonder what it would be like to be in a relationship where I wouldn't need to "fix" my partner. Could I manage that, or would I always be trying to find something wrong with him? And even more to the point, how can I develop a serious relationship with a man when the only one of my five senses that works perfectly *all* the time is my hearing?

Then Tonas surprises me again by saying something few men in this reality would ever say out loud.

"I am beautiful."

"Can you change your appearance by thinking about it?"

"Yes, but I have no reason to do something like that. I have enjoyed my presence for millions of years. I am quite pretty."

Hearing him claim that he is pretty makes me want to giggle, but I don't. Instead I say, "I have been told that we will have the option of living hundreds of years, which is completely unheard-of on Earth."

"Not *unheard* of. There have been long-lived people."

"Well, maybe in the past. With the body that I currently inhabit, I don't want to live hundreds of years here. What I really want is to regain those feelings of resiliency and vibrancy I had when I was younger. That's why I asked if you could change your appearance."

I can feel his sympathy. "There is an energy within each cell that determines your degeneration or regeneration. It is difficult for an individual, even in the dimensions you exist, to drive the body into the youthful measure that you wish. Yet, as you move the energies of your physical presence into the higher dimensions, my dear, it will be your choice how you appear."

While I contemplate—and long for—this, he continues.

"Here, let me show you the vision of yourself. You will fall greatly in love with your appearance and agree with me that you are most beautiful. Your hair is long and blue and it flows down your back like a waterfall. There was one time that you had the most unique violet eyes. Each time you laughed, they would become radiant with little golden sparkles. Your skin is sometimes violet; sometimes it is blue, of the azure. You are someone who enjoys changing your appearance as often as your clothing."

I find myself delighted by the mental image he creates with this description, because it fits exactly the kind of appearance I'd like to try…at least for a day or two…and then try something else! The masters I'm working with have told me these kinds of abilities are possible, but it's great to hear his confirmation that I've already actually been changing how I look on the 10th dimension.

Tonas explains that this ability to change my appearance occurs within the 8th dimension. While I'm grateful to be where I am, everything that Tonas has told me so far has only strengthened my determination to reach Earth's 8th dimension as soon as possible. The galactic masters I've been studying with have explained that this dimension is Earth's first non-dual dimension—there is no resistance to creation.

Tonas continues. "Now is the time for you to develop your abilities so that you have the enjoyment of visiting me, of course. And in your 10th dimension, which exists on my ship, you will be able to experience these parts of self."

"I'm looking forward to that. That sounds lovely."

As if reading my mind, Tonas states, "It gives you hope."

"Yes," I reply. "Hope."

"You are buried in the 6th and the 7th dimension. Buried. The world and many of the people on it are entrenched in their belief systems that are still linked to the 3rd dimension. It is such a prize to be in the 4th and your 5th dimension, and an even greater prize to be existing in your 6th and 7th. And yet, there is such tremendous resistance. In this entrenchment, you are waiting."

I sigh. The sense of endless waiting *has* been with me all my adult life.

"Yet when you are with me there is no waiting," he continued. "This is why it is important for you to develop your abilities now, so that you have another reality to remind you of where you are going. Your journey will be long. You will live many hundreds of years."

He sees the wide-mouthed grin on my face because I can feel the smile in his voice as he assures me, "This is reality. There is no death for you, and there is no reason for aging beyond the slower pace of those who are still resistant to moving into the higher planes of awareness. There is nothing to stop you."

# # #

Our conversation continues for quite some time. When Tonas senses I can no longer manage the intense intimacy of these revelations, he switches to a more neutral topic by saying, "I have something for you. I gathered orchids from Andromeda and placed them in the observation room on the ship in your honor."

I am so delighted, I almost clap my hands. "Wonderful!"

"I want you to see them. I know that the love of orchids has been in your heart for a long time."

He's right; I've loved those remarkable plants since the first one I saw, perhaps forty years ago.

Tonas doesn't really need to tease me with orchids. I know that these are a "golden carrot" he's using to tempt me to improve my inner vision. I'd love to see them, and even better, I'd love to see him standing surrounded by them.

#

"You know," he says, "It is the feminine which rules all universes. To be led by a queen is to be led by your heart."

"I am glad to know that women are considered worthy to be leaders of other worlds, because they don't always have an easy time of it in this world," I reply. "I can't picture what form of government we will evolve into on Earth. At some point, I hope no government will be necessary. But in the meantime, I dream of when women and men will honor each other as equals."

For a moment I wonder if Tonas has seen that become a reality in our future. I know he won't tell me, but surely that equality must happen.

"Are your parents from Earth?" I ask.

"Oh no. But you've met them. My mother, Firona, who is from another universe, and my father, Emmon, were here when you were visiting my ship years ago. My father was an ambassador on Lyra but is now a high-ranking starship captain. In fact," he added, "that is how I gained access to this ship."

Hearing about his parents and how he became a commander helps Tonas seem more real to me. I'm interested in learning more about his society, so I ask, "Do children have school like they do here?"

"It is unnecessary. At birth, we take on all the knowledge of those who came before us. We are aware upon the moment of the spark of ourselves. There are many in our family. I am one of forty-six children."

"That's incredible!" And then I envision a tired-looking woman surrounded by forty-six children. Perhaps some were adopted? Of course, they are long-lived, so this brings to mind my next question. "How do you age?"

"We develop to the age that we find pleasure in."

I nod. It all seems so fantastic, like the science fiction books I've collected. "I've spent years and years reading fantasy and science fiction novels," I admit.

"I understand. The information I've shared does sound like science fiction, but it's simply how we live."

I realize that I want this kind of life too! Well, probably not the forty-six children part—but being a youthful, never-dying, golden-haired goddess is infinitely more appealing than the life I used to think loomed in front of me … aging, infirmity, and death.

"Earth is the most important world in *the everything*. You incarnated in this time for a reason. You will be showing others the important roads that lay before them. You will not wait for those who are dragging their heels in third-dimensional mental focus. You will continue. I will help you, of course."

Again, Tonas seemed to be reading my thoughts. He knew I had trouble accepting that I held an important role on Earth. "You are a light onto Earth," he said. "And though you have not held within your mind the vision of your importance—because you were taught that you were not important—you will come to accept the sacredness of your presence on Earth. Every experience that you have had in your life has been part of the evolution of this greater experience. You are not, even for a moment, considered to have lesser value because of your experiences. I hope you allow yourself to release your judgments about yourself and your life, because you are perfect in my eyes."

I'm still conflicted. I don't know that the perfectionist in me will ever acknowledge the perfection he sees, at least in this dimension. Perhaps, as I move into the higher dimensions, I will see and accept that I am perfect. I hope so, because I know the judgments I have about myself are disempowering. His words have been a gift. "Thank you for sharing your feelings with me."

"Be playful," he reminds me. "You are most perfectionist."

"Yes, very much so."

"That perfectionism leads you *away* from the perfection of you."

"Do you know that the first time I spoke to you was on my birthday?" I ask.

"This is a sacred day."

"I came to you with the work to assist the Ashtar Command a little before my birthday, but the first day that we spoke was my birthday. I'm assuming you don't have anything like our calendar or the months of the year? Do you have a way of designating time that way?"

Tonas answers, "Although time is a streaming flow to us, we associate with your time to better assist you."

He goes on to tell me that on the American calendar, his birthday is April 4 and I make a mental note to somehow help him celebrate it.

# # #

I have another question. "When I'm communicating with you, is that telepathy—and does everyone hear what we're thinking to each other?"

"Yes, it is telepathy—and no one else hears."

"How does that work?"

"When I have communication with you, the communication is directed to your mind. If I wish to communicate with everyone on my ship, then each receives as if I were individually speaking with them. It is a balanced system."

"It seems better than how we humans communicate."

Tonas explains that, "Others can hear words and perceive what they do from the words you use on Earth. There is room for error. But telepathy, as you would call it, is a pure transmission."

# # #

Since I've been wondering if Tonas has other "superpowers," I ask him if he can teleport and levitate. I'm not surprised when he admits that he has those abilities. "I could even, if I chose, move to another universe in an instant," he says. I'm even more intrigued about these skills when he mentions that I will develop the same abilities in my academy training.

(As Tonas has known me for so long, he is aware of my active participation in the AMS—Academy of Mastery Studies—and he refers to this simply as the academy.)

I realize there is so much more I want to understand about the situation I find myself in and dive into more questions. "How does your ship move? Do you just think about where you want to go, and then you're there?"

"You would call it 'light propulsion.' Light is instant, and yet we are in presence above Earth."

"I looked up at the sky the other day, and I was wondering where you were up there."

"It is not possible for you to see the ship until you are within the 10th dimension."

This reminder of how remote in time and space that Tonas and his ship are from me—who knows how long it will take me to reach *that* dimension—spurs me to blurt out, "I really do want to see you."

"If you wish, I can bring my ship above you. I can do this, of course, whenever we are in our communication," he says, sounding pleased that he has figured out a way to be closer to me. "There are many rules that must be followed, and though I did follow you to each of your positions in the ancient academies—knowing that you would be present in specific time frameworks of millions of years from this moment—it was only for me to catch a glimpse of you."

"When I said that I wanted to see you—please know that I don't want to interfere with the activities on your ship that you are responsible for or the positioning that you are designated to be in. I don't want to intervene in any of those kinds of affairs. Do you understand that?"

He reassures me that it would not be possible for me to interfere with his life and work. Everyone on his ship knows me, he says, and they are delighted when they see me there. "They are happy for me when you are present because they know that my heart is raised to such joy when I am in your presence."

"How many people do you have on your ship?"

"More than what you would call nine hundred."

"It must be a large ship then."

"It is, but it is not even one of the larger ships in this quadrant, as you would call it. My father's ship is five times bigger."

Tonas must sense that I'm almost ready to leave because he says, "You are my valentine, Joy."

Without hesitation, I reply, "And you are mine, Tonas."

As if reading my thoughts again, he says, "One day you will mean that even more. I know this. I do not rush you. You can take hundreds of years and even then decide that I am not for you. It is simply my desire to be in your presence. Love is more; it is more. A third-dimensional image of love is a fraction of what true love is. Like a paper valentine compared to ... a kiss."

I've been unhappy with some of the versions of love I've witnessed and experienced in my 3-D life. I find myself hoping he's right and that I will be able to experience this higher-dimensional version of love.

"I don't like to say goodbye," I tell him. "I would like to talk to you for a longer time, but I have to leave."

"Soon, we will have the opportunity to make our communication endless within our minds."

"I'll look forward to that. Thank you for our conversation today."

"You are a treasure to me," he says, adding in a whisper, "I adore you."

CHAPTER THREE
February 27, 2014

"Dear greetings, Joy!"

"Hello, hello, hello, Tonas!"

"This is quite a surprise … an enjoyable one."

"Good. I just wanted to talk to you again. I still have lots of questions."

"I will be all ears—all ears for you."

I'm so excited to have made this connection again that I give myself a few deep breaths to calm myself before continuing. "I want to know more about you. But first of all, is this a good time to talk?"

"It is an excellent time for us to have communion."

"Okay. This is a comment rather than a question. When you said you saw me millions of years ago, that was difficult for me to comprehend."

"It is a bit of what you would call a *stretch*." He chuckled.

"Yes."

"You must imagine that my first vision of you would be a stretch, for you did not yet exist. And then for me to wait millions of years for even your species to be created is another stretch. Then for me to wait most patiently for you to be born and to grow to the being who would know me, this would be another stretch. For you, all of this happened within a small framework of time. For me, it is millions of years of stretching."

My head is swimming with this information. I've never thought of myself as being patient. As a matter of fact, I'm not patient at all. If our positions were reversed, I wonder if I would have waited that long.

I need some context for these "stretched" time frames, so I ask Tonas how old it is possible to be in our universe. He seems reluctant to give me a straight answer.

"There is no stigma about age or longevity. Non-dual individuals acknowledge that great wisdom is developed through the ages."

"Okay, so how old is our universe? Do you know these kinds of things?"

Again, he seems to find it difficult to reply. I realize that it's not his reluctance, but the use of numbers that holds him back. "Everything was created sequentially from a point of entry," he explains. "It is beyond numbers' calculation. The important history is really felt within the culmination of all of it, the same way it is felt within the collective of your being. You possess the full measure of the memory of all that has ever existed within your presence—and yet you also are a witness of all that has ever existed."

"Are you saying that I can remember events and happenings from times *before* I was born? Do I have memories that aren't really mine?"

He nods, acknowledging my confusion. "At this time, it is not as necessary for you to fully understand as perhaps you might imagine. Simply know that this information is registered within every framework of your geometries that exist as the elements that make up your physical presence."

As soon as Tonas mentions geometries, I lose interest in continuing the conversation. Memories of my struggle to understand math and related subjects in school are still with me. Thank God he hasn't said anything about logarithms.

# # #

Another important question occurs to me. "Have you experienced death?"

"Oh, there is no death for me. I have what you would call a fantasy—that at some point you and I would make our choice to ascend together."

"Ascending? What does that mean to you?"

"It would be quite different from anything that is typical within what you call a dual world. On a non-dual world, there is no aging, unless someone wishes to experience aging. It is then, of course, never taken to the full measure of the last breath. There is always a time for returning to the most ideal presence. We've all experienced desires to have an experience of someone, like you, on the dual plane. It is most desirable for individuals to feel hunger. Of course, those of the academies of Earth felt hunger—but for the first time, you see. They came from non-dual worlds to learn and to experience Earth's duality. Let us imagine that my father at one point might have wished to experience what hunger felt like, and so, he would allow this experience."

Although his words describe something far outside my realm of experience, he speaks with total sincerity, and I find myself believing him.

"Ascension, because it is not typically a part of our experiences, will be a moment of great splendor for us. We now are in full measure of our understanding of the ascension experience. When it is met at the highest point of its potential, we would have the opportunity to move into an energy which then allows us the greatest desires of our hearts—and our greatest desire is always to understand the full measure of all that is to be understood."

Until this moment, I have never consciously realized that a complete understanding of all that could be understood was also one of *my* deepest desires. I want to *know* the "who, what, where, when and especially why" of everything! Well, maybe not everything.

"That is the only reason ascension seems to be, at this point, sponsored by the human. Ascension is revered by those of us who are seeing it now as the prize nearly in front of us."

This fits with something I have learned recently. "One of our academy instructors said that in the next three hundred and fifty years, Earth and humanity will reach the 25th dimension."

Tonas agrees that is possible.

"What happens with you as the human Earth contingent moves to that dimension? Do you move with us or do you just sit there and watch what we're doing?"

"It would not be advantageous for us to remain in the 10th dimension when you are in the 12th. It would be easy for us when you are on the 8th or 10th dimension for us to make our presence known to you and then rise with you as you make your motions—your sweeping, swimming motions into the higher planes."

I picture legions of human beings swimming upwards into the sky and it makes me smile. "Swimming into the higher planes sounds like a lot of fun."

"It will be a great deal of excitement for all of us, and it will be especially fun for the human beings of Earth, because they will have the experience of those of us who have been present— and yet cloaked or invisible—to save them from the nervousness that would be caused from the awareness of our presence."

# # #

I have been attempting to remember all the information Tonas has told me. And even though each of his words seems burned into my memory, I know my memory is fallible. "In my sixty-eight years of life, there are lots of things I don't remember I've done, or experienced or said," I tell him. "Sometimes I don't even remember what happened yesterday! Do you … have complete memories of everything that's happened to you? Because if you do, that seems like it would be overwhelming."

Tonas affirms, "I remember everything, except perhaps how many times I swallow or breathe."

Normally, I'd be tempted to make some kind of smart remark, but since nothing is normal about the conversations I have with this fascinating man, I simply ask him for a specific example. "Can you remember something you said several thousand years ago?"

"Certainly. These memories can be brought to my attention immediately. Remembering everything is not overwhelming to me, although it may appear to be so to you."

A thought flashes through my mind: I could never win an argument with this guy if we had differing views on a past occurrence, because he remembers *everything*. That makes me wonder: Are there even arguments in the 10th dimension?

Tonas explains his ability to remember everything by saying, "It is compartmentalizing that allows the present moment to be the most efficiently directed. And yet, the memory of all that exists—even in the future—is in my mind."

"You can see into the future?"

His voice is solemn and certain. "I have witnessed some of the evolution of the great expanse of all that is in the future," he says. "It is not because I need to evaluate what is to come, so that I may know how to react or respond. It is simply for my own amazement. It is gratifying to watch the progression of what is implied in this moment and then witness how that interfaces with all that it evolves to be in the future of time."

I want to know what he knows! But my desire is based more on a wish to be prepared for the future. I'm not so much one of those "go with the flow" kind of people.

"I have carefully been strategic about this so as not to dishonor your free will of choice," he reassures me. "I have not witnessed much more than a tiny little fragment of that which could be considered *our* future."

His knowing even a tiny bit of our future is more than *I* know. It's frustrating. "I'm not going to ask you because I know you can't tell me about it, but you know how curious I am about my future, *our* future."

"I am also curious, of course. And yet it is important for me to honor your progression and your ultimate choice."

I sigh. Can't he see how eager I am? "I'm interested in experiencing the 8th dimension as soon as possible," I say, understating my excitement.

"You have this within the palm of your hand."

"I know it, and you know I intend to be one of the first to step into that dimension. It's frustrating for me that no one can or will give me any information on *when* it could happen."

I remind myself not to dwell on "when." The explanation I've been given is that time is fluid and setting a date for a future occurrence might prevent it from happening sooner than "scheduled." So I choose another topic that focuses on my more immediate problems.

# # #

"My challenges right now are my parents. My father is ninety-six and my mother is eighty-nine; both are frail. It has been difficult for me and my brother to witness their deterioration during this last year. I know that many of my peers have already experienced the death of their parents, but that doesn't make this any easier. My dad was an active, healthy farmer for most of his life. Now he spends his days in a wheelchair. My mother has mild dementia. The contrast between what they can do now and how they used to be is ... dramatic."

"It is a pity," he says. "And yet it is also a celebration that *you* shall have no experiences of these things."

"I'm never growing old?" I ask, delighted that he is confirming what the masters have told me.

He chuckles. "Your parents are part of the last generation, it would be hoped, to choose to experience the degrading of the physical body."

Thinking about my family brings my children to mind. "I have two sons in this lifetime," I tell him. "I told the younger one that I don't plan on dying. He said, 'Mom, everybody dies!' I told him that's not entirely true. If this is a concept that's difficult for my thirty-two-year-old son to grasp, it's something that is likely not even on the radar for people my age. At this age, we have watched classmates, friends, and parents die. People my age perceive death as inevitable. I have a deep desire to show them there is another option."

"It might not be as easy as you imagine," he warns. "People who witness your life might, at first, deny what they see. Eventually, they will reach a point where they can't ignore your experiences any longer."

"And what about the people who just don't get it?"

Tonas's voice is kind as he tries to reassure me. "Even in the latter of years, if your children were to surpass your aging, they would at some point be compelled to recognize that it is perhaps faulty thinking causing them to age in the energy fields of the dimensions of Earth. They will have that same opportunity to reverse aging, just as individuals who wished to experience white hair on, let us say, Lyra or Andromeda. It is not unheard of for individuals to experience this aging process, but only for the blink of an eye in the timing of their life experience."

Before I ask my next question, I consider all the years I have disliked my stubbornly curly hair. Maybe my energy presence has beautifully wavy hair. "What did I look like the first time you saw me at Imphere?"

Naturally, Tonas doesn't comment on my hair. Instead, he asks me to, "Imagine yourself as ageless and stepping into that arena with great excitement," he says. "You were, perhaps, frustrated at not being able to see everything, even the cobbles beneath your feet, clearly. And yet, I must say, that there was a sparkling in your eyes. There was a delight in your step. And, being ageless, your energy presence is always representing your ageless value. This is what I project."

"You were attracted to my ... agelessness?"

"It is not that you would be rejected if you came to me or I saw you in an older version of yourself that is associated with some of the Earth heritage of our lineages. The essence of you is still the same, and that is what we witness for one another ... although you love my hair."

"I do!" Long hair on a guy has always appealed to me.

"I will never change it," he promises.

#

Tonas's bearing is so stately and confident, I can imagine him twirling me around a dance floor as some classical waltz music plays. But is that even something he would recognize? I decide to ask Tonas if he or his people dance.

He answers with enthusiasm. "Yes! We dance and we move to energy and we love music, the sound of singing and of the instruments that make sound. There is a sound the universe makes that is as sweet as any instrument. That is the sweetest sound; I could dance to that forever. You and I dance in our room overlooking the stars."

This is thrilling news to me, and I leap at the chance to ask if he has a way to learn my favorite dance, the Argentine tango. I've taken some lessons but never became good at it. Maybe in a higher dimension, I will be more graceful, and surely he would be an elegant partner.

"I make this vow," he says. "I will understand this dance before our next meeting."

To tango with Tonas! Dancing with this man in a setting like he describes is beyond anything I've ever dreamed possible.

# # #

I remember that Tonas has orchids growing on his ship and think of my greenhouse where I struggle to keep those exotic flowers alive. "Do your orchids age and die?" I ask.

He confirms what I expected. "The flowers die, but the plants do not—and I don't even have to water them."

I gulp. "No water?"

He laughs at my bewilderment. "They take care of that themselves," he assures me. "These orchids are sentient and creating their own reality."

"You supply them with nothing?"

"I give them the only thing they need from me. Love."

My orchids need to take lessons from his orchids! I give them love every time I step into my greenhouse, but they still get sick and die—and losing one of my precious plants makes me sad.

"Just remember that, in the future, there is perpetual regeneration for all plants, all animals and all beings of Earth."

# # #

Even though I've only consciously visited Tonas three times now, the subject of love feels like an elephant sitting in the middle of the room that we—or rather, I—have been steadfastly ignoring.

My life has not been without love. I love my children with all my heart, but the love that I want to experience is much bigger than anything I've experienced so far in this lifetime. I want a relationship in which I have no need for the other person to be any different than they are, and so far I have been unable to do that.

I don't want to reveal my doubts about my ability to love. Instead, I find myself sharing a vision of the love I hope someday to experience. "When you talk about loving a person's essence through the millennia and all dimensions of separation—that's what I have always sought. That matches my vision of the love I've been longing to know."

As soon as that admission leaves my lips, I realize that I'm not ready to hear his views on this, so I quickly add, "Can we speak about this later—much later—when I know myself and you better?"

He is amenable to a change of subject—I knew he would be—and I quickly review the things I don't yet know about him. "Are any of your brothers or sisters adopted? Because forty-six children is a mind-boggling number to give birth to."

"Not if you begin to count the days of the life experience of my mother and father," he explains. "They are most long-lived."

"How long is a pregnancy? Nine months, like here on Earth?"

"Certainly not. It is almost immediate from the conception. The child is conceived as a spark of light, and then the development between their two hearts creates what can be considered a nest—an energy of golden light that floats between the hearts of the father and mother."

I learn that while the baby is developing in this nest, the mother and father saturate it with their excitement, their love and their hopes and desires. The baby looks similar to a human baby, but without an umbilical. Gestation takes about six hours, and throughout that experience, there is an imprinting of all of the knowledge of both parents, which is carried from the lineage of their own heritage.

"So you have ancestors?"

"Of course, and they are all still alive."

All still alive? I think briefly about asking how many generations that might be, but my mind is still trying to digest the news that *all* his ancestors are alive. How many "greats" could that possibly be?

Finally, I ask, "When you say an imprinting of all the knowledge, does that mean if the mother had read or studied some material in books, or however you learn things, the child would know all that was in those books?"

"Indeed."

"What an incredible gift for their child."

"It is a beautiful thing to watch the beginning of life from the seed that comes from the union of spirit between the two. It becomes brighter and brighter as it gestates, right in their presence. The loving parents look into the eyes and into the heart of that little one who is gestating. It is a full immersion of loving spirit."

My eyes fill with tears imagining it. "It sounds so lovely."

"It is beautiful. It is the beginning of a life. The human gestation is also quite beautiful. It is unfortunate in the dual worlds that there is the feeling of separateness from the father, you see. It all occurs within the feminine womb, and if there are troubles in the relationship or in life experience, this is imprinted on the genetic makeup of this little one. That is why your SVH is so important."

Tonas is referring to the fact that, with SVH, it is possible for babies to experience a process called Angelic Rebirthing. I realize how glad I am that he understands the great work I am involved with. Then I remind myself that not only does he understand the work we are doing—he is my *partner* in it!

# # #

Of all the animals on Earth, I'm especially fond of horses. I ask Tonas if they exist on other worlds and if there are other animals similar to the ones we have here. He tells me something surprising; many Earth animals were created by initiates of the ancient academies as part of their homework! "Students would take an animal they were familiar with and change it slightly. That's one reason there are so many different types of birds," he says.

I also learn from him that some flowers, including the lotus, orchids, and even some woodland plants were brought here by Isis. She wasn't an academy initiate but she spent much time on Earth and liked to surround herself with the plants she loved.

"Where are you from, Tonas?" I ask.

He tells me that his home was Andromeda but he was born on Lyra, which he describes as quite beautiful. "All of the buildings are crystalline, and it is well-inhabited, both inside the planet and on the upper terra. And there are villages floating in the sky."

This intrigues me. I know that this is something I *have* to see and, joy of joys, he promises, "We will one day travel there together."

Further questions about Lyra reveal that it was the beginning point for all existence in this universe, and it encompasses *all* dimensions. Lyra is like a time portal, and everything that enters into existence is brought through that space. But it's more than just a portal—it is the "first thought."

I ask him if his homeland is a world in the constellation of Lyra, and he says, "You may call it that. It is in that space of light and it pulses. You can feel it with your heart, your mind."

# # #

Then Tonas reveals a delightful surprise to me. "My primary directive for being in the atmosphere of Earth is to support her advancement—and yet you must know that my *true* mission is to be near you. I have, of course, moved my ship to your location. I am directly above your abode."

I have goosebumps all over at the thought of his ship being right above my house.

He continues, "There will be a small period of time before you can see me standing before you in your world. I promise you that it won't be too long."

Although I am wondering what a small period of time means to him, I know he won't or can't tell me, and so I simply answer, "I hope so."

He reassures me, saying, "I don't believe it will be long for you because you're so motivated to enhance your abilities."

I *am* motivated. I want to see Tonas standing in front of the window where together we watch the stars. Will he really be as handsome as he says? Will I feel the same heart connection that he says he feels for me? I remind myself that I am doing all I can to move to his dimension. But then I must bring my mind back to our conversation, before I become frustrated at my inability to do so *right now*.

# # #

"You must understand that, if we wish to experience something, we are able to do so. This is our 10th dimension. We are able to move to higher dimensions. We will never lower our dimensions to be visible to you. It is simply energetically unfathomable for us to have untidiness or dirt on the ship."

"There's nothing like war?"

"Never."

"Do you ever experience anger or fear or those kinds of emotions?"

"These are unnecessary emotions; it would not be in our desire to experience them."

As he says this, I realize the dynamics of this relationship will be like nothing I've ever experienced. This could take some getting used to, but in a good way!

"Do the Andromedans and Arcturians look like human beings?"

"Different. I am more human-looking than the Andromedans. They are tall."

"Yes, I wondered about that. How tall are *you*?"

"I am just a little bit taller than you."

"How tall am I there?"

"You are nearly as tall as I."

I'm tempted to laugh about our circular conversation, but when I want to know something, I don't give up easily. After I explain that I'm 5 feet, 6 inches tall, Tonas takes a moment to calculate the equivalent and says he would be 6 feet tall.

Then he tells me that he believes he is in perfect shape and form and that, although most on his ship are quite slender, he has chosen to be more muscular for me. He relates that his capes hang over his body most beautifully.

Previously, when I visited Tonas, he asked to greet me by kissing my fingertips. Now it occurs to me that it might help me to know how muscular he is if he hugs me; accordingly, I request that after he kisses my finger-tips, I would like to have a big hug.

"May we make this our standard?"

"Yes, I would love that!"

"There are many hours for us to wait—unless, of course, you wish to make a journey to see me sooner."

"I can come during the day?"

"That would be most exciting for me, because I will have that opportunity to kiss your fingertips and give you that hug. It will be a long hug that becomes dancing."

I'm excited by the thought of dancing during the day instead of waiting to visit him when I go to sleep or during one of our scheduled meetings.

He sounds excited, too, and asks if I will come to him now.

Without bothering to reply, I hop through the gate to the ship.

Joy Elaine

CHAPTER FOUR
March 7, 2014

"Ah, we are together again!"

"Hello, Tonas, do you have a minute to talk?"

"I was not observing to 'snoop,' as you would say. It has been in my awareness that we would have this conversation, and so I have been waiting patiently, very patiently indeed, for our moments of connection. Of course, I have minutes for you. I have a lifetime of minutes for you."

The first question on my list is to find out if he can see into the dimension I am within.

"It is a product of sensing. My dimension is present within me, but I can see through my feeling, as well as my inner vision, all of the dimensions of Earth. This is something you will be developing yourself."

"When you refer to your inner vision, are you talking about clairvoyance and things like that?"

"Something like that. I was born with the ability to select a specific dimension and have a full vision within me of all that is before me. I can easily connect with any dimension of Earth."

"That's interesting. Can you tell me when we will reach the 8th dimension?"

I know he won't tell me, but maybe he'll give me a hint. He replies: "Beings in many universes are wondering the same thing."

He explains that all of Earth spent millions of years in the third dimension and now some of us (including me) are existing in a blend of the 6th and 7th dimension. He estimates that the pinnacle moment when all of the consciousness of Earth moves into the 8th dimension could be as much as ten years from now.

"Ten years?" I cry.

"I don't believe it will be that long for you."

He adds, "It is like waiting for the sunset and finally the

colors begin to present before you. Your eyes are watching it and you are drinking it in and then it is gone. But then, of course, the display of stars, as you know, is an even greater wonder. Imagine what your 8th dimension will present for you."

"I would like to know more about it, but I guess I'll just have to wait until I get there."

"The most important aspect of this, to me, is that your 8th dimension will be a portal between us where I will be able to physically manifest. It is easy to move from the 10th dimension to the 8th. It will be easy for me to manifest in physical form in your 8th dimension."

This information is thrilling, but it's also a bit unnerving. Tonas will be here in person! What will he think of me? Will I feel shy? Maybe ... Will I leap into his arms? Probably not...

I allow thoughts of future possibilities to flow through me for a moment before asking something I am deeply curious about. "Do we need money in the 8th dimension?"

"This is another topic of great consideration. *What will they do?*"

Although I really would like to know the answer to this, I am able to laugh at the tone of his voice as he asks that question.

"There is a tremendous ... not so much an excitement as a *connection* to monies. There is a feeling for it; there is great joy. At this time, it is a valuable asset which has much energy. I am sure you are aware that there is little of the intrinsic that is physical, touchable money. Most money that is spent is spent through energy, the use of plastic cards, and the use of computers to transmit the monies from place to place. It is considered to be a great excitement to spend the money as well as it is to harbor it. Individuals gain great pleasure in this."

"Do you folks on the 10th dimension use money?"

Tonas laughs as he assures me that they certainly do not. They wouldn't even know what to do with money, since their thoughts form their desires.

I've heard for years that everyone creates their own reality, but this takes that concept to a completely new level. Further discussion with Tonas confirms that he creates his clothing by thinking about what he wants. Apparently, in the 8th dimension, it will be easy to manifest a piece of popcorn or a diamond on your hand.

"Learning how to direct elements of energy that form objects is easy to do in the 8th dimension—because there is no resistance."

I love the idea that when you can create anything you desire, making money—in every sense of that phrase—will just be a waste of time. Even so, I think I'll create a bunch of beautiful diamonds and other jewels before I manifest popcorn.

# # #

I've been thinking about some of the things Tonas has told me about himself: He is physically perfect, he never gets angry, he manifests with thought, he never forgets anything he's said, and he has all the memories of his entire genetic lineage. This prompts me to ask him why he is interested in *me*.

Before he can answer, I add, "Human beings are so primitive compared to you and others like you. The things that you are capable of doing, the vision you have and the *way* that you are amazes me. This part of me that's talking to you is not all sweetness and light, Tonas. I get angry. I have doubts and fears."

He pauses to make sure my thought is complete, and then says, "Let me give you a vision. Imagine that you would take a sturdy sailing craft out onto the ocean and you would find a beautiful island. You would bring your boat to that shore, step onto the sands and find a beautiful being like myself who is, in this illustration, quite human and yet quite beautiful, as I am. Having been born and lived on this island, I would not have had an education. I would know more about fishing with crude implements. I would not have the forks and the knives, would I?"

"No."

"And yet, I believe that one look into my eyes and you would be sold on the beauty of my heart and the beauty of my spirit. And you would, of course, never judge this beautiful one for killing the fish to eat, for this would be the means to sustain the body. You would see this as just another of the experiences of this being."

I nod, intrigued.

"The first time I saw you, I saw the essence of your being. I felt the resonance of your purity of heart and being. It was this first vision of you and your beautiful eyes, your lips, and your spirit that brought my heart into the greatest expansion. You must realize that, in each opportunity to witness your presence in the academies of the ancient, as you would call them, I could feel my heart expanded as it had *never* been before. How would *I*, or any being such as I, release from the mind such a flavor of love? It would be impossible! And so, it is not your experiences of living that entice me. It is the spirit of your *being*. You are who and what you have created yourself to be in this incarnation. Will you let yourself understand?"

I don't say a word. I *cannot* say a word. My mind wants to reject what he has said, but my heart longs to embrace it. In the midst of this internal battle, I ask myself—can I begin to see myself as he sees me? The only answer possible is that I must try.

# # #

Tonas surprises me by asking if I would like to tango.

"You have been able to find out about that dance?"

"Indeed, I have witnessed every move. I am fluid, as you might say."

"Did you learn by looking into the dimensions and watching

people dance?"

"Ah, yes, I identified the motions, the movements, and the music. I identified how my body would respond to such movement and I became the music. I became the vehicle that will move your body. It is *my* position to move your body."

I like the way he said that and quickly agree. He leads and I follow. "Are there set patterns of steps for the dances you do?"

"It depends on the music. There is music that tempts the heart to express itself through movements of the body that are quite acrobatic. There are also means for moving as if one. It is a unity of the body. You and I have danced in this way. We have moved our bodies against each other and simply moved to the sound of the stars."

I stop for a moment to try to imagine any kind of dancing that could compare to an experience like that. Absolutely nothing comes to mind and now I really want to consciously experience dancing to the sound of the stars with him.

# # #

"We have people who write music. Are there composers in your dimension?"

"There are artistic individuals who create music, of course. These individuals can, in their mind, in their heart and spirit, feel the movement, color, and vibrations of all that exists. From this, they can tap into the essence of an individual who is listening to the music. And so, each individual can be hearing the same song in a different way. When individuals in my dimension join in body and move to the music, they hear and experience the same music in all parts of their being."

"Do people still write books, or are they outdated?"

"This is an interesting question. There are places where there are books, or what you would consider to be books. They would look different from your books. There is pleasure in integrating information through this means. Great insights are brought forth in this means of transmission. Of course, some of these ideas have excitement within them. But love stories and stories of adventure are not in books; instead, they are transmissions that can be received."

"Where would they be received from? Who would send such a transmission?"

"These are all archived. If a parent has been associated with such a memory, it would automatically be transmitted to the children of the parent. Something new that was inspired from the point beyond conception would be something that would be accessible. If one was interested in the history of an unknown concept—or a new idea about an experience that was in the mind of someone who had great adventures—they could bring this story forward for others to invent along with. It was and is as if you are all of the players in the story. It is experiential to, as you would call it, 'read.' It is experience and thought in the mind of one, and the thought is then able to be transmitted to the minds of others, if they wish. These are all archivable as well."

I appreciate the information he has given me about artists and the arts, but I don't think I'll be able to grasp how this works until I experience it myself. I'm comforted by the information that books still exist, even if they look different than our books.

We're almost at the end of our conversation today, but before I leave, I implore Tonas to help me remember more.

He makes this sound easy to do when he simply says, "Indeed, let us."

"Goodbye, Tonas."

"Until our next meeting, our next tango."

"Oh, I love you." I am amazed by what just slipped out of my mouth. It felt so natural to say—but could I really have meant it?

"Ah, you are my dearest heart. It is a love that lasts forever between us. You have given me a gift today, one that I will cherish forever."

CHAPTER FIVE
March 11, 2014

I've come to realize that the part of me that would have accurate information about many of my endless questions would, in fact, be my future self. I have received information from that part of me in the past; however, I've never spoken directly with my future self. Now seems like an opportune time to do so. The following conversation is with the part of me who exists in the year 2294.

#

The first important question I have is, "Do I have a guardian angel?"

"You have more than forty angels and guides who have been part of your entourage over the years," comes the reply.

This number is a total surprise to me! It must mean that everyone has several angels assisting them.

My future self continues, "It's because of the stature of your presence of being and also because of the times that are coming. Right now, in 2014, you have seventeen guides who are assisting you. Their names are: Teressa, who always wants you to play more; Markon is Andromedan, not human; Shera; Michael; Chamuel, who is an archangel who is also your birth angel; Tamara, who has a goatee; K; Lomar; Saundra, who projects strength to help you stay safe; Archangel Michael; Metatron; Esthra, who was influential in your childhood; Init; Kyler, a human who lived about two hundred years ago; Laressa; Kaffe, who is an angel who's been assisting you your whole life; and Zomat who is androgynous and not from this universe."

I don't know which of these interesting-sounding individuals to speak with first. Then it occurs to me to ask which one would be the most helpful for me to speak with now.

My future self replies, "Esthra."

I direct my attention towards Esthra and ask what he would like to tell me.

He advises me to be at peace with myself. While that is a lovely sentiment, and also good advice, I'd like more specific information; accordingly, I ask him what else he would like to tell me.

"I have many volumes that can be filled with all that I would wish to tell you. There are lifetimes of experiences that are linking into your present at this moment. Many are of great importance to you because of what you will design for your future. You have the ability to integrate from your soul lineage these attributes that will assist you to smoothly move into the higher dimensions. We desire these elevations for you, and yet you desire them even more because of your commitment to the man, Tonas."

That's the kind of input I was hoping for, and I eagerly request, "Can you help me with that?"

"We can all help you. We are simply waiting for you to give us the dedication for such a task. You must understand, I am not collaborating to assist Tonas in any way. I am here for you. It is your desire that has brought this to the forefront. What we are designing at this moment, you and I, is something that will catapult your advancement of consciousness forward much more swiftly."

Swift advancement is definitely what I'm looking for. Since it seems that Esthra might be able to furnish me the "how to catapult forward" information that I now desire, I ask him, "What do I need to do?"

"This is a creative process. It is possible for you to immerse within fields of your lineage of soul that have the same mindset as your future self. I have witnessed you, my dear, all of your life. You have been building bridges, preparing in the last nine years—and more fully preparing in the past four—for this moment."

I think back to the past several years, and this feels true. He continues: "This moment is an awakening of that part of yourself that is a *true* representation of that part of you who associates with your man. You want to become that beloved of his who has been in his presence for these many years. You are that being, yet you believe that you are different when you are with him—that you are somehow more evolved. And this is true. There is *that* Joy, standing on his deck, looking out at the stars with him for many years. That part of you is truly enraptured with this Tonas. Knowing that he is in love with that 10th dimensional presence of your being, you must think that he couldn't possibly be in love with you. And so, you are wishing to evolve into a being of great stature in order to meet that value of your own personage that you have reached, as you might think, ahead of yourself."

Esthra has perfectly expressed my desires to be more than I am. I *know* the 10th dimensional version of me is more evolved than the part of me living on Earth.

"Tonas says that in the 8th dimension, it is possible to start doing some of the things I want to do, like rejuvenating my body."

"Be patient with this; this is all part of your destiny. These physical matters will right themselves. The timing would simply be to bring the greatest *joy* to your being. The way to do this is to make a connection with these of your lineage. We can reflect these attributes to you. It will be as if you are a computer receiving new programs. There are specific lineages of the soul that have attributes you would wish to imbue."

I say, with confusion, that I thought I had already done that using SVH.

"This is different; you must request correctly."

"Can you please tell me the exact way to ask?"

"Request that this connection—the one I'm bringing to your awareness—become a conduit connecting you with those of your soul lineage who can assist you. It is something like putting a pink sweater on top of a yellow one and then a green sweater. These higher values, which are associated with non-duality, will saturate your presence."

# # #

Before we move to the area where Esthra plans to help me put on "soul sweaters," I have a question that I can't wait any longer to ask. "Can you tell me anything about my destiny?"

Instead of giving me even the tiniest hint, he says, "No. You will become angry if I tell you of your destiny. You will stomp your foot."

Now he's really got me curious. I try to persuade him that I *might* not get angry.

"We are all in agreement that you will be angry. It is easier for you to reach that point of destiny and in that awareness of the sweeter values of non-dual, you will easily recognize it for yourself and move gracefully into that destiny. You are a speaker of one who reaches into the deepest recesses of the many—and of course, this would require for you to step into the forefront of the public."

"And how would I do that?"

"It will come; be patient. In the moment that you are aware of this, it will bring you joy instead of making you angry."

Since Esthra seems to know me so well, I reluctantly admit that I do occasionally get ticked off.

"Indeed, my dear, sometimes your feet stomp even when they are not stomping."

"Does my destiny involve writing? I used to dabble with writing, but I just haven't felt like there's anything to write about. You know this has been a source of frustration for me for a long time."

"That is another point of anger. You will work through this

dissatisfaction. I wish for you to have no concern, because this will take care of itself."

# # #

Esthra is almost as stubborn as I am; I can see this line of questioning is going nowhere, so I change subjects. "Can you help me to play the violin much better than I'm currently playing?"

"Dissatisfaction with the beauty of that which you create is another source of your anger. We are all in awe of your great abilities, and yet they sometimes seem to have no value to you. I am always whispering to you that you are magnificent. We all do. We are always bringing this to your attention. You are gifted."

I'm coming to realize that my guides and Tonas must see only the perfected version of me, and I assume that the music they hear me play must also seem as if it is perfect. Unfortunately, my music doesn't sound that way in this dimension! I used to be a good violinist in this reality, although never what you could consider a virtuoso. Now I might be considered somewhat above average, but not nearly as good as I'd like to be. In college, I used to sit "first chair" in orchestra; now I sit in the back of the first violin section in our local symphony.

I remember periods of depression—repressed anger—I experienced in my middle years, and I realize that Esthra's observations about my anger are true. I resolve to do more SVH work to release this emotion.

It occurs to me that Esthra might really be able to help me with an area of my life that is immensely dissatisfying. Trying not to sound like I'm complaining, I explain to him that I feel all alone. "I used to hear and see more than I do now. Why?"

He answers with a question. "Will you bring me up in

stature?"

"What does that mean?"

"Choose for me to be in your vocal presence. There are others that push to the front; when you choose me, you've brought me forward. I am most generally witnessing and pulling strings in the background."

"Do you mean … I should just ask you to talk to me and tell me things?"

"Indeed. I wish for you to know that I am neutral about this fellow, this man of yours. It is important for you to focus on your experience, and if that experience is enjoyable with this fellow, then how wonderful for you. It is not necessary for you to make proclamations, and yet you must know that when the higher part of your consciousness is with him, it proclaims much."

I'm astonished that the other part of me is making proclamations. What is she proclaiming? What if she's making commitments that I don't want to honor? I share with Esthra that I don't want to get into trouble—and I certainly don't want to cause Tonas any distress.

"This is a conversation you should have with Tonas."

I know he's right, but it's a discussion I'm not looking forward to. After a moment, I let go of my worries about how to broach this subject and ask Esthra to do the work we were planning to do.

Esthra asks me to join him in a special room in the Library of Akashic Records. He's already selected ninety-four books from ninety-four aspects of my soul lineage.

"As you walk up and put your hands on the books, information will begin to stream up through you and move into your levels of consciousness. This will be graceful for you, because you have connections to these beings and some of them have already imprinted attributes into your genes. I am weaving the stories of their non-dual lives into the stories of your life. It will perhaps feel that you are wearing coats of many different colors. Be patient. This process should assist you to be happier and not so angry all the time."

"Thank you, Esthra. More happiness and less anger sounds wonderful."

# # #

At the conclusion of my work with Esthra, I feel drawn to ask Isis if there is anything she can help me with, and she comes into my consciousness.

"Indeed, my beloved, I am here for you. There is much that I can do to assist you; I believe that you will enjoy this."

I *know* I will and give her an eager and affirmative, "Yes!"

She directs me into a different chamber. Instead of working with any books, Isis brings me the vessel of a goddess from Lyra who is in my soul lineage. Her name is Sheona, but she prefers to be called Sheera. Isis calls her one of the "golden."

Isis places the vessel in my hands and we lift the lid off. She instructs me simply to breathe in the sweetness of Sheera's essence. "It will assist to awaken the goddess essence within you."

She explains that although we each remain ourselves, this work will assist us to benefit each other. "Sheera feels your presence, and there is a connection between you. And now, you will take on the attributes of the *golden one*. Remember this in your heart, remember this in your mind, and remember this in your stature. Stand taller, my dear. You are a goddess, a great priestess of Lyra. You also are a great goddess and a priestess of Earth. Remember this with all parts of your mind, essence, and being."

Remember my stature ... as I reflect on her words, I feel my love for Isis deepen. I realize that, even though I've only felt her energy a few times in my life so far, she has always been with me. There is no goddess I admire more. I am determined to remember what she said. Instinctively, I stand taller.

CHAPTER SIX

March 20, 2014

"Hello, I am Melchizedek."

"It's lovely to speak with you," I reply in awe.

"It's more than a pleasure; it is a reunion for us. There are few who call upon me; it is quite delightful that we should have this dear connection."

He asks how he may be of service to me, and I can feel his sincere desire to assist me.

"I have four areas that I would like your help with," I tell him. "The first area is my artistic ability, especially my skill in playing the violin; the second area is increased intelligence; the third area is being rejuvenated physically; and the fourth area is assistance with any of my 'clair' abilities." I'm laughing as I finish this ambitious list. "That's it!"

Melchizedek agrees that this is an impressive list, but at least he doesn't say it's impossible. He asks me if I remember that, years ago, he gave me a great blessing. I know he must have done this, but I am embarrassed to admit that I do not remember.

Melchizedek is kind enough to describe the event. "I placed oils of great purity upon the crown of your being. I placed my hands above your crown and I began to bring in the tones of wonder. I did this to attract that which would elevate you greatly into a spirit of release for everything associated with veils of forgetting."

#

Addressing my requests today, Melchizedek begins by reminding me, as others have, that my "pickiness" and "scrutinizing" have been holding me back. Ouch! That assessment is painful to hear, especially since I feel my tendencies toward self-criticism are deeply embedded.

He offers words of encouragement, saying he's going to help me to release my rejection of self. "This will make you happy, and also it will spark within your spirit the greater intelligence that has been your desire to achieve."

I find it interesting when he says he kept his white hair to remind people of his age and wisdom. I'm glad he adds that it's not necessary for me to do anything like that and that he *will* help me with rejuvenation. When he asks me if I'm going to be watching for every wrinkle to be removed, I promptly reply that I'm ready—however my rejuvenation happens.

"I know that you are or you would not have called upon me. These 'clairs'—as you call them—will be another matter. They are not hidden from you; I must admit that you have each of these honed to their greatest perfection. They are simply in another reality. We must draw those together."

"Yes, definitely," I agree. "I really want that to happen in this reality."

He then suggests I call upon my inner awareness and pretend that I am wearing gold and ruby robes of "great presence." I almost shudder at the word "pretend," because I've never felt I was any good at imagining myself in other situations. But I definitely am not going to say anything to him that might be construed as "scrutinizing."

He also tells me he believes that more laughter and humor in my life will bring about the transformation I desire. "When you are laughing, it is not possible for you to be angry."

I agree that's true.

"You have a history of anger, but that is the past. Are you much attached to the 3rd dimension?"

After I assure him I'm not, we begin discussing ways that will help me achieve my goals. "If you take pleasure in your endeavors instead of being critical of them, you will release your artistic abilities," he says.

I know he's right—but I also know it is going to be really

difficult to do. Of course, I don't tell him that. I'll bet he knows anyway.

He tells me that for the next thirty days, for thirty minutes each day beginning at one o'clock, he will be "laying roses before my feet." This is his way of telling me he's going to assist me to take the easy, scented road.

Melchizedek continues with, "Now, let's address your intelligence. Take your finger and touch it to your forehead; allow those fingers to become the conduit of light that I bring now through your crown. I am driving a wedge of light, something like a lightning bolt, to bring the spirit of your inner spark of genius into the energy flow of your being. Let your fingers be the conduit; bring two fingers and then three to your forehead. As your fingers are placed, the flow of your life essence—which carries the essence or spark of your future self—will move through your fingers and into your brain. Your right and left hemispheres and the center will feel the cracking, the opening of the two pathways, followed by the unity, the openness of the mind. It is about being open-minded. Continue to keep your fingers in this place. May I touch your shoulders from behind you, my dear?"

"Yes, of course."

"It is my pleasure to bring you a burst of presence. I will do this every day at your one o'clock. You will bring your fingers to your forehead, your brain, and I will bring the spark into your crown. Now, as I am transmitting through your shoulders into your being that which moves to your arms, feel as if you are becoming a rubber band. This is how I wish for you to paint, to play your instruments, to live your passions. As if you are dancing with the flow of light, with your arms, your body moving as if you are a rubber band."

I try to imagine dancing as a rubber band, and he continues.

"In this way, I will bring you the rejuvenation, as well. The rejuvenation is a reminder to the body of its true perfection. This is what, each day, you and I are remembering together. Allow your body to move as if you are a rubber band. Imagine the bow in your hand moving as if you are a rubber band. Envision the dancing of your body, free of consternation. Don't condemn the sounds that come from the vessel that you play with your bow."

#

At this point, I share with Melchizedek my admiration for the master violinist, Heifetz. I also explain that the concept of flowing and flexibility that he's been encouraging is a challenge for me, because of my struggle to play the written musical notes correctly.

He assures me that within all great artists, "There is a flow, a movement, and there is no constriction; there is simply the bliss of the movement. This should not be confused with playing the notes, for the flow is within this Heifetz. It would be impossible to bring through his greatness if this were not so."

"I get tangled up in the notes. I'm trying to play what's written and I get frustrated when I can't do that as well as I would like."

"I know. Our exercise is pretending and envisioning that you are making the sounds of this Heifetz. You are setting the stage for fluidity of movements like he had."

"Will my muscles be able to do that?"

"As you pretend, you will tone your muscles and mind to an even greater degree. You have more of an advantage than Heifetz. You have an encodement within yourself that is most interesting. How is this possible?"

"Perhaps you are seeing the work that Sananda and I have done to help me embody the genetic attributes of geniuses and violinists."

"Well, it is present and valid that you have these genetics. Oh, we must extend for at least another thirty days. I will be pondering on this; we will be building many patterns of response. This should excite you, my dear—for indeed, it excites me."

I enthusiastically agree to this new plan. Perhaps I really will be able to become a virtuoso violinist!

"Now, in our joining together, you will be *pretending* that you are using your 'clairs.' You will release your frustrations and your pickiness and begin to bring more joy into your passions. See that which is, that which can be."

"Thank you for your assistance."

"It will continue."

# # #

A few days later, I question Esthra about Melchizedek's suggestion that I become "like a rubber band" when playing my violin. That description still doesn't make much sense to me.

Esthra advises me to pretend that my entire body is fluid. "What Melchizedek wants to do is unwind you and make it so that the music is actually coming through as a feeling, more than motion and movement that's rigidly directed. Because of the way you were taught, you believe you need to move the bow in a particular way. The bow actually will come to life in your hands if you will let it; moving in that way takes you out of your rigidness, and that's when your music will change."

He asks me to think of a leprechaun. "They are like children in that their motions are fluid. This is what you are to pretend."

"Esthra, that's an interesting suggestion. Thank you."

CHAPTER SEVEN
March 25, 2014

I begin this session by calling Esthra forward to thank him for assisting me to imbue certain attributes of my soul lineage the last time we worked together, saying, "It did help me feel more serene, at least for a while."

"There are more stages of this braiding, if you would allow it."

"I would love that. I'd like for you guys to 'go for the gusto' when working with me."

He chuckles at my enthusiasm. "Let us move then to the Akashic Records; there is another library I wish to visit. This is what I would consider to be a higher-value group of records. I wish for you also to understand that I have a vision of you from your future self that this particular chamber will assist you to rise quickly to meet its measure."

"Wonderful!"

"I have handpicked each of the volumes of your lineage in this room that are quite relevant. Let me move you to the center of the room. It is as if the winds of Karea begin to blow in their circular motions, lighting up all that they touch upon."

"What is this word 'Karea'?"

"Karea is a world in another universe; it is what I would consider to be a place where the breezes carry the song of the presence of everything in the surroundings, the birds, the leaves, the moisture of the air, the perfume of the flowers.

"If you were to visit this world, you would be bathed in the beauty of these 'songs.' As you step into a region and you wish to become a part of what is all around you, the wind rises up around you to immerse you in the flavors of all that exists in that particular place. Many of us have gone to this beautiful space on Karea; it was an academy not unlike the Earth academies."

"Sounds wonderful to me."

"It will be, my dear. In the volumes I have selected, instead of the leaves and the flowers, you will find the attributes of more than four hundred and less than seven hundred individuals in your soul lineage."

"You know how much I like to know all those details."

"These are the winds of change for you; we are carrying the visions of perfection. Open yourself to this as the pages of these books begin to rustle, and from them will come the elements of that perfection. Soon you will exist in a non-dual plane of reality. There are all of these in the rustling of the pages of these volumes. It will be as if musical tones are lifting from the pages and meeting in the swirling breeze. This is creating a cocoon that will inscribe into the flavors of your energy. Your energy is so delicious today."

"That's probably because I love visiting libraries. They have been one of my most favorite places to go to since I was a little girl. The type of libraries you take me to are the most special of all!"

"This particular library is one that I believe carries the song of your heart. Rather than braiding, we are immersing; those notes of the true song of the sweet experiences resonate with you because you have many of these stories already in the libraries in your consciousness."

"I would like to be able to better access my levels of consciousness."

"This will assist you. Also, I have an idea the great Osiris has plans for you. The books are wishing to dance; let us allow them to fly from the walls and dance in your circle. This would be as a 'cartoon.' I am looking at this breeze that carries them, and it is as if they are immersing and melting into the pools of energy that the winds of Karea allow. They are streaming and they are now liquid. This is the sacred record which has been dedicated specifically for you. It is a copy of a copy. Now, as if you are a sponge, open yourself up to the full receiving. As you do, you may now feel as if little vaults are opening to receive."

I try to imagine this as he goes on. "You are being prepared for something quite magical. You are being prepared to be the carrier of the vision of what is to be considered the perfection vision—and, of course, you are the perfection vision. The full measure of your receiving is now complete. What would you wish now?"

I'm feeling rather "floaty" after this work, and I forget to ask Esthra about this "perfection vision" he mentions. I do come back to it on another day, however.

# # #

"Esthra, I would like to know more about some of the other guides." I ask. "Who are the two new people? The other night I heard someone say, 'Can we join your club?' I'm assuming they were two new guides."

"It is Gerah who is always in the presence of Yarnick; Yarnick is very much about playfulness. There is a little bit of tightness about you from time to time; this is moving on. Yarnick is jovial and could become 'over the top' but Gerah balances him."

"Who was the little girl with black hair and almond-shaped eyes who blew me a kiss?"

"That is Shera. She is a young one from an old lineage of human, a mixture of Lemurian and human. She ascended over seven thousand years ago and is from your soul lineage."

"What about K?"

"He is quite studious, serious and a thinker."

"And Init?"

"Init is Venusian; what would you like to know about him?"

"I have a general question about all of my guides. When I only see or hear them briefly, how do they assist me? Do they each have a special *thing* they like to do?"

"All of us have our areas of expertise, as you would say."

"What would be his area of expertise?"

"Init is always looking for gopher holes; he is always watching out for the possibility of a disaster. It is in his nature to be a great protector. Dogma schools would consider him to be a guardian angel. It was an interesting choice for Init to become of angelic protection for an Earth human. You are the *only* one he oversees. Many of us oversee multiple individuals. There are those of us who are singularly dedicated; I am yours."

I prod Esthra a little bit by mentioning that Jill Marie thinks he's good looking. He agrees that's true and says he believes she loves his "gams."

This statement tickles me and I have to stop and think for a moment what "gams" are. Maybe Esthra experienced an incarnation on Earth when that term was in common usage?

"Do you have any idea when I might be fully in the 8th dimension or is that up in the air?"

"It isn't so much in the air as it is in the hearts and minds of those of your collective. *You* will be in that dimension well before they; you are speedily rising. Osiris has what you would consider an ultimate agenda to assist those of you who are academy initiates. You are thought of as the forerunners for all of humanity. This must seem strange to you."

"It does. I just feel like I'm diddling around with my orchids."

"You are not ever diddling; what you do in a day is more than many do in a lifetime. You must witness what occurs on so many different levels of your being during one day of your life."

I still don't get what I could be doing that would keep me so busy. Maybe I'll have a better idea of that as I continue to work with Esthra and Tonas. At least, I hope so.

# # #

"What would be the most advantageous thing for me to do now?"

"I believe that you will know when you are ready to speak with Laressa. She knows what it is to be human, not from her own experience but from the Great One of Compassion."

"Quan Yin?"

"Yes, having been of that lineage, she also was the primary guardian for Miss Yin. A lot of people believe that Quan Yin was a myth; that is untrue. I encourage you to find the measure of peace within and find your readiness before working with Laressa. There is some resistance within you to let go of the tug-of-war between the feminine and the masculine. There is still an undiscovered part of you."

"Can you help me with that?" I ask this with frustration because I have worked on balancing the masculine and feminine aspects of myself for a long time.

"Your erroneous belief that the feminine is weak and frail and the male is domineering creates discomfort for you and also pushes one aspect away from the other. There is within you a lack of respect for the teacher of your femininity, although you love her dearly. The role she played in teaching you that strength of the feminine is something that was lacking. It is possible for us, here in the records, to perhaps find you a model who would best help you raise that vision of the feminine, so that it would not feel overpowered by the masculine."

I was happy to hear this. "I was so disappointed, when I was old enough to know, that I was a little girl. It seemed like the women stayed at home, cooked, and had babies while the men made all the decisions. The whole interplay of men and women in our society is not good, in my opinion. Is there something you can do to help me balance the masculine and feminine aspects of myself?"

"The masculine within you does not respect your feminine aspect. But there are many pieces from your childhood that can be rewritten."

That means I need to do more work on this imbalance with SVH—good advice.

I am still curious about my future, so I press forward. "Let's return to a subject that we've talked about a little bit and that I would like to know much more about. Tell me more about my destiny. I promise I won't stomp my foot. Does it involve something I will be able to do to make some money?"

"Money is not as important to you. You will always have money; you'll never be without it. There will always be surprise monies for you. And then one day …" He pauses and reminds me, "you promised not to be angry?"

"Yes."

"One day you will be quite famous. It is undecided by you how you will become so famous."

Famous? This is the *last* thing I ever expected to hear him say. I wonder if this is something my future self will decide to become, because fame has never been on my radar. Esthra's definitely right when he says it's undecided; I haven't even considered it!

"You could create a wonderful story that would give people a dream of what to create," he continues. "You have the vision of this in your mind; you have a million story lines you could grasp. This would be your opportunity to touch those that you inspire. They would call it fiction, yet you and I know that it is the reality of this world to move into the higher harmonic."

I know I am not prepared for this level of achievement. "Let's have some coaching at night or something," I suggest.

"Let us have coaching in the day as well," he agrees. "It is easier to enter the arena of the average person and inspire them to become more than average through the stories of what appears to be fiction. You can do this!"

And with those words, I feel encouraged. Maybe I *could* write a story. "Please thank all my guides for me. You have my permission that, if there's something I need or that will help me, do it! I'm giving all of you the go ahead, 100 percent."

There is excitement in his voice. "This was an important statement, my dear. Can you hear the cheering? There is great noise-making here in your field of energy. I'm with you, and yet I am also in this tiny room."

"What dimension does your tiny room exist within?"

"I am connected to a tiny little dimension slightly off from the merged 6th and 7th dimension you exist within, 7.2 on the dial. If you were to turn on your radio, you could dial it to perfect pitch so that you could hear every one of our words clearly. We are within your dimension; we are simply dialed off a tiny bit. It is important for us to be in the higher dimension that you are a part of. When you were in the 4th dimension, we were in your merging of the 5th dimension. There is no 7th dimension without the 6th. You've stepped into both, and so now it is a merged dimension. It is not for everyone yet."

CHAPTER EIGHT

March 26, 2014

Esthra says, "Ah, I have become your favorite."

I agree that he *is* one of my favorites.

"It feels as though I must be," he says, his voice warm with agreement.

"Please tell me more about some of the guides I haven't asked you about. Do any of them want to say anything to me?"

"They all are present and vying," Esthra assures me. "Many times, I have even felt their incarnations entering into my verbiage. It is not dishonor on their part—they are simply excited, as you can imagine. But what is your agenda for me?"

"In addition to knowing more about my other guides, I also want to work with Laressa today. I did some additional work with my masculine/feminine balance and I hope I am ready to work with her today."

I had attempted to work with Laressa on this subject a few days earlier, but I became too emotional to continue.

"I believe that you will find her most apologetic."

"I don't think she needs to apologize for anything. I just wasn't in a good place that day. I think I would actually like to speak with Teressa first today."

# # #

Teressa enters into conversation with me. "You will find me luscious, just as you are luscious. When you stretch in the mornings and you feel yourself so lusciously and pleasantly comfortable, I reflect that same comfort to you. I encourage you to treat yourself with great honor. This is something that I have helped many to do. The only time I see you nurturing yourself is with the morning ritual in your bed. You truly allow yourself to luxuriate. I am always reminding you of the importance of honoring yourself. I am sister to Laressa."

"Were you ever a human?"

"I enjoy witnessing, but I have never embodied. It is an image of what is possible through you that gives me the greatest pleasure. I reflect to you what is possible for you. When you luxuriate and honor yourself, I reflect this to you to magnetize it, so that you feel extra pleasure. I do so when you enjoy your foods and when you enjoy something of beauty. I magnetize this; it is a good job."

# # #

My next guide steps forward to say, "I am Shera. I am like your little fairy, although I have no wings. I am a guardian; I am not of your kin, and yet I am part human. I am what you would consider a great wonder to a new tribe of Earth. That new tribe of Earth—advanced, of course—existed after the grand migration. My father was here on Earth as an emissary. Being human-looking, he is quite handsome. My mother was not taken with him; it was he who fell into his love with her. She was and is a quite beautiful Jewish maiden. My father had to hide his great powers; he taught me in secret. It would not have been acceptable to do otherwise."

"Where was he from originally?"

"It is known that we are called Lemurian, and that is the name that was given to individuals who came from Lemuria. It is a star we are from. There was a great framework of time in human history that Lemurians were instrumental in balancing the Earth. It was not popular to intermix with the human beings (Lemurians are non-dual and humans were and still are dual); it was important instead to hold the balance of Earth and to keep it safe from falling stars that could damage the ecosystem."

Her voice is small and soft. I quiet myself so I can hear her better. "Most of the Lemurians left during the great migration of human beings into the higher dimensions. It was those of the blended species (when Lemurians mated with humans they created the Atlantean race), human and Lemurian like myself, who created such a lashing back of energies that it set Earth back perhaps fifty thousand years. (The lashing back she is referring to happened when the Atlanteans energetically jumped from the 3rd dimension to the 5th dimension of Earth.) And so it was that my father and ancestors left Earth; it was important to sever the possibility of creating the same experience again. It was not thought to be a bad thing for my father to fall 'head over heels,' as you would say, with my mother. He assisted both of us to ascend. As a human, my mother would have grown old."

# # #

I feel Esthra enter the conversation. "Who now, my dear?"

"Tell me a couple of things about Michael."

"Michael is a good overall worker; he is in constant vigilance. He is most assuredly an angel—an angel who has, like others, never embodied as human. If you were to witness him, you would see him as a tiny, thin angel who can get between the cracks of things. He is one that tries to find order in everything. And then, after finding the order, it is as if his only wish is to bring all of the pieces into place to help you feel that order and attract it, as well as choose it. He is always co-creating balance with you. Michael loves to just *be*. Whenever he sees an opportunity to help, he steps in. It is good for the angel teams to have one such as Michael. He helps where he can."

"And what about Lomar?"

"We will call him a fellow, because he was incarnate. He is kindly and he also is a short individual. He comes from a race of individuals—are you familiar with Betelgeuse? I believe if you were to define him as a being, you would say that he has strength in his mannerism. You might see him as a little person, and you would perhaps think you could overpower him. If he was embodied as a person, I believe you would never have this thought; you would think of him as incredibly powerful. I am not speaking of a world of this dimension. There was no form in the realm of these individuals; it was a consciousness, not a physical reality, that he existed within. He has no desire to present himself as physical. He is such a serious thinker as an angel because he wants to be in a collective of minds."

#

I ask to work with Laressa, but Esthra says, "This will be hard. The great Archangel Chamuel is standing here. It would be difficult for me to push him aside."

"Well then, let me speak with him, please." As soon as I speak those words, I feel drawn to speak some Language of Light. This is a language of the heart that bears the imprints of love and neutrality.

Chamuel answers me in that language and then says, "That, my dear, is my greeting to *you*. I am the great Chamuel and I am *your* angel; that is all I am. You might see me as just your friend. I am your guardian and I love you. To me, you are of the greatest importance. There are others who see you as their important focus as well. And yet, none other can speak as I to the seriousness of that which must be brought through in every stage of your incarnation, simply because it is of the greatest importance to the plan of magnitude."

His enthusiasm is compelling, but I make myself stay focused on his words as he continues. "You shall step into your role of awareness of the *true* magnificence of yourself. It has been hidden for far too long. You are finally, with everyone speaking to you of magnificence, beginning to open your heart to what could be possible and somewhat acceptable to you of that great figure of the one you are."

"I don't *feel* magnificent."

"If one were to take the great Mary, Jesus, Buddha, Quan Yin or any of the others of greatness who were of human species, and they were to state that those beings were less than even the worms in the ground, no one would believe it—nor would they believe that *you* are any less than the greatest of them. It is only in your remembering, and this will come."

"I *will* remember my greatness?" I can feel his affirmation.

"It is my *greatest* passion to bring you this awareness. How fun it will be for us to discover this together, and for you to step into those little recognitions that will lead to the bigger one. We are all so excited, because this is the time! It is the time! Look! You are talking to all of us! It is like a dream for the universes. We are all grateful to you; there will be a time when you understand this. Until then, give yourself some breaks, please."

#

As I bask in these words, Laressa begins speaking to me. "I've been thinking of ways I can bring you more grace in this unity of the masculine with the feminine. There is a place we can go, and I have permission to bring you there. We will travel to the far corners of the Earth to an academy you are aware of. Please allow Archangel Michael, Metatron, and Sananda to guide you. You can restore the divine nature of being there; I will be directing you. It might sometimes feel somewhat sexual, though it is not. It is a release of some of those energies. You are a sensuous and sexual being, and so it will be easy for you to allow this. It is not the kind of releasing that you can never capture back. It is the releasing of sexual energy that binds the servitude of the feminine to the masculine."

This is all quite fascinating. I wonder how she can restore this divine balance—but before I can even ask, I feel her begin to work on me through *light*.

"This is the reflection of unity within the presence of self," she says. "You can feel the energies of release, and the reminding of the presence of your being that this releasing and accepting is all in order. It is in your desires, in your new image of self. Before long, you shall be an emissary for the world for that which is of the most balanced of energies. You will allow yourself and all parts of your being to find freedom from the bonds of the masculine suppressing the feminine and the feminine mistrust of the masculine; the feminine desire to be emancipated from that which is a part of itself. Do you feel the deliciousness of your presence of being? Take within your presence of being the pure vision of unity. You can witness to me what your body feels."

I tell her it feels sleepy.

"It is appropriate for you to feel yourself in deliciousness. It is such a great honor for me to assist you to balance this part of yourself."

"I'm blowing you a kiss," I say, drowsily.

"I am sending a kiss to your heart."

Esthra returns and we speak briefly about Tonas and his upcoming birthday next week. He tells me, "You know, this is a dear one. We are in a deep connection with one another. I have witnessed to you that he is of my lineage and I have had some support of him as well. It is *boring*, as you would say, to guardian those of non-duality."

"Because they don't get into the trouble that we do?"

"Ah, but this is the excitement!"

"Well, I guess exciting is one way to look at it. I've had more of the *drama* kind of excitement in my life than I would wish. That's one reason I've avoided, for a long time, having any kind of relationship with a man, Esthra."

"I wish for you to know that I have been privy to many of your meetings with Tonas for many years. I have witnessed, and if you would like information, I can give some to you as your guardian."

The gesture is kind, and I appreciate his offer. "Tell me anything that would help me. I still haven't seen him. He supposedly learned the tango for me, which is impressive."

"He would not lie about something like this. There is no *supposedness*. I will tell you, he is respectful of you. There are some in the universes who would have taken advantage; he is not one of them. He is of non-dual, so it is in his nature to be honoring."

"That's good to know. I thought about talking to him about this, because I hardly know him, while the part that he has seen for fifty years knows him well. Part of me doesn't know what the other part is doing."

"He is very much aware of your physical being. He desires to be as honorable with that part of the essence of that spark of your consciousness and being as he is with that physical part of you. He is careful never to pry."

"Could he see me in this reality if I asked him to?"

"He could, indeed. Yet he has chosen instead to allow himself to let you learn about him and perhaps to come to enjoy his presence—and then, perhaps, even to feel the same great love that he holds for you. That which is your essence of being is already in great enamorment, and yet he has not 'crossed the lines,' as you would say. It is important for him to honor your privacy."

Esthra's information about Tonas's conduct toward me when I'm not consciously interacting with him is gratifying. I was almost positive it would be that way, but still it's nice to have that confirmed.

# # #

"If it comes to your knowledge that any further library work would be of benefit, I would like to know it," I tell Esthra. "Let me remind you that you have the green light to go, go, go!"

"If you could truly see yourself as you are—and one day you will—you would understand the passion that is within you to reach that understanding."

From the assertions of my beauty I've been hearing from my guides, it will, of course, be delightful to eventually see myself the way they do. However, when Esthra talks about passion to reach an understanding, *that* elicits an immediate longing within me.

To remember, to understand, to *know*—these are my most pressing desires.

CHAPTER NINE
April 3, 2014

"Esthra, can you see me as I'm sitting here?"

"I certainly can. Feeling, of course, is more of the essence of our energies."

"When I'm going through my day, are you all just sitting around watching me? Do you understand what I'm trying to find out?"

He chuckles softly. "This is something that few think to ask. We are in direct communication with you. It is a trance channel connection where our essence, our energy, is with you. There are times when we are called upon to be in your presence, then the essence of our energy can be witnessed. It can be seen as if we are standing in front of you in a physical body."

"I'm wondering what exactly you mean by 'seeing me.'"

"I can see the energy of the essence of your body."

"So it's not like I'm looking around my room here and seeing things?"

Esthra continues to explain in more detail. "This is a bit different. It is not as if I am looking to find if you are wearing green clothing today. It is the essence of you and the transmission of myself from a point where all of us commune as one. All of the angel presences are of one mind, and yet we are individual, just as human beings are individuals. Many of your angels are not embodied in a life experience; they have been merely consciousness. And yet, we are as strong in lifting you away from danger as if we were there with our arms. This is disappointing for some people to hear, although for others, it is quite a relief. I know some people must wonder if we're seeing them have bowel movements and other private functions."

"Right, that had occurred to me."

"This is not an important action that must be witnessed; it is, of course, celebrated always."

I am amused that the conversation has landed on this topic. There have been many periods in my life when that "action" was indeed greeted with tears of relief and great celebration.

"When I'm going through my day and I'm thinking about one thing or another, is it the tenor of my thoughts that you are receiving?"

"I like this word, the 'tenor.' Yes, and it is the energy that we follow. We know what you are creating by the energy you are transmitting with your thoughts and actions. It is quite scientific, as you can imagine."

I wonder just how much he has figured out about my plans for this meeting. "You know that I'm going to ask for a miracle today, right?"

"This was not something that came to my mind, and yet I think sometimes there are imprints of requests for miracles for the simplest as well as for the more expansive. What can we do for you?"

"It's about my violin. I've got a concert—and by the way, you're all invited."

Esthra assures me they will be present.

"On April 26, at one of the high schools here, we're playing Tchaikovsky's Fourth Symphony and a piece by Verdi. I can play these pieces better than when I first got the music, and I know Melchizedek is working with me on this."

"He is tireless in this."

"My playing is supposed to be better eventually, but I want more improvement right now. Can my energy body help me play better?"

He seems to mull this over. "Perhaps it could be the sentience in your limbs, and perhaps the connection of heart to the music, to the instrument, to the limbs of your body."

"What about my Higher Self? Can I incorporate more of that into my physical body?"

"That collaboration is always at its maximum; its

participation in things of physicality is less actively pursued. We would draw this part of yourself into the heart of your being if you will promise me that you will allow the music to flow from you without judgment. It will grow and expand as you play; it will become the great experience that you are hoping for. We can bring the angelic choir so that all in the arena will hear in the deepest part of their awareness. This will drown out anything that is not *perfect,*" he says.

This comment sparks immediate excitement within me, but before I can reply, he fills in, "I am only jesting."

I don't really find this humorous, but I manage a chuckle for his benefit. Inwardly, I sigh.

"I'm hitting quite a few things that aren't perfect in the music; it's called faking. I would like to play more of the notes."

# # #

I begin to wonder if there are other beings who could assist me with my creative abilities and decide to ask Esthra *another* thing I've been curious about. "Do the muses exist?"

"You are speaking of the spirit of the music, of the poetry, the spirit of the lyrics?"

"I only remember Polyhymnia and Terpsichore. Are there such beings? Do they have names?"

"They do not have names; however, they are individuals with great awareness who are held in the collective consciousness. They are considered to be myths, and yet this energy, which is the spirit of the dance and music, is well known in the hearts of many. The myth part is that the nine daughters of Zeus would be the ones who are the muses. This would be a fantasy, and yet it became real for individuals of many times. It is what we would consider to be an energy support; that which is caught on the mind and heart, not only of the player, but of the listener as well."

"How can we weave all these thoughts together to assist me with the artistic areas that I would like to explore—with the violin, with writing, dancing, creating and being joyful when I do those kinds of activities? What can we do?"

"This exists; it is even in Sanskrit as part of a mantra, the thought of the muse. It is the essence of something, and so to invoke the muses is to call for their assistance and inspiration. This should be simple, because the energies are already with you. There is aliveness in the vibrations made by your instrument. There is a vibration that is carried on the mouthpiece of the Earth itself. Catching on the vibrations of all of these, it would be possible for us to call upon these *muses*, as you would say, energetically."

I feel encouraged again that he might actually be able to help me improve my violin playing. "We are working with you to prepare you for an understanding of the steps that you are building. You have built your body into a machine at one point in your life. (He's talking about when I was a bodybuilder.) You were judgmental of yourself, and yet you reached your goal. I can tell you now that you will be able to see me standing before you and I will move and perhaps even dance. I might even take you into the dance.

"You will be of great pleasure at that time, just as you knew when your body had reached its greatest pinnacle. All of the judging and all of the frustrations leading to your goals are part of an exercise that you can partake in or not. We love you in any stead and we are here for you in any stead. I believe that you are working to release these frustrations and to become more at peace with the process."

# # #

"You said you were in the 7.2 dimension—in other words, just a little removed from where I am. Is this a dimension of

Earth that you exist on?"

"Yes, our transmissions come from that dimension," Esthra replies. "It is not known how to describe to you the presence that exists of us except to say that, if you were to pour me as if liquid into a large glass of water, that would be my presence within everything. And yet, my transmission into that point of that dimension is my interface with you."

He seems to sense that I'm confused, so he tries a different approach. "Let me say it another way. Just as you have your position where you are, you are still everywhere, my dear. You are as if a drop in a great sea spread throughout its whole presence. You cannot really be apart from anything."

"I've heard that description. Here's another way to approach this subject. Do you, the guides, have lives? Do you say, 'Well, I've worked my shift with Joy today and now I'm going to go home to my family?'"

Esthra is uncharacteristically emphatic in his response. "No. In no way! We are a constant with you. There are some of your angels who are only drawn in in times of crisis for intervention, but that is simply a mindset. I am one of the angels who is always in your presence. I am a constant with you."

A sigh escapes me, which sends Esthra an incorrect message.

"Would you prefer I not?"

"No, no! Don't leave."

"That was not my intention and yet it is always in our choice to honor you." He switches gears, "Let me speak of Init. Init never stops watching. He is the least-flavored individual that I have ever known because he is of the greatest vigilance. There is little or no personality. You are the *only* one that he guards."

"Init watches over only me?"

"Exactly. There are some of us who are closely guarding those of your important affiliation. Of course, this means that we are in guardianship of Isis as well as the others of those who are even your instructors. They are part of the origin gathering. For some of us, that is our sole duty, a duty that we chose from the beginning. Many of us have had experiences of incarnations. The moment that those of you of Earth began to seed, that is when *all* eyes moved to Earth. Do you feel special? I hope you do, for we *live* for you."

I am startled by the passion in Esthra's voice. I *do* feel such tenderness and appreciation for his constant dedication, and I immediately resolve to share those feelings with him more often.

#

"Did Init choose me, or did I choose him before I incarnated?"

"Init chose to be your guardian. He is one who made his position well-known that, the moment the thought of your existence occurred—this included your parents first meeting and later choosing to be married—he would leave his Venusian life and become an angel."

"That is awesome!" I am deeply touched by the dedication of this guardian.

"It is quite awesome," Esthra concurs. "If only you could fully vision the great importance of yourself and the others of your academy affiliation. Many think of Sananda and some of the others as more deserving—yet to us, all of you are greatly deserving. In fact, you of the Earth contingent are of the greatest importance to all of us, for without all of you, there would not be the great emergence that is to come for all that is."

I can't help but wonder again about my destiny. Fame seems such a distant possibility.

"Tell me one thing, and I promise I won't be angry. When you talked about destiny and me being famous—was that something that I just decided I wanted?"

Esthra is patient with me as he explains. "How can you *not* be? How can you be anything *but* famous at one point? Imagine what it will be like when, after years upon years of existence, you become your ageless self. You'll have many stories to tell about the *ways* to reach the higher vision of consciousness. The reason you will have these stories is because you are living them and you are living even more. And so, you will be in the living history of this world and someone who can be looked upon."

It's hard for me to imagine this, but I let him continue. "There will be no fighting, no wars. There will be peace on your world and there will be those, just as there were followers of your Jesus and your Buddha and others, who will be followers of you. This knowledge is not meant to intimidate you, my dear; it is simply the way of things. If you discover something and others find benefit from learning this from you or witnessing you, is it not a gift to give them the benefit of your knowledge? It will happen most gracefully. There will be no stamping of your foot, I promise."

This sounds like it *might* be possible. In the meantime, I'm just going to keep on "paddling my boat" into the higher dimensions and see what happens.

# # #

This talk of muses and famous people in our past has made me wonder about other, perhaps mythological, beings in Earth's history. "Besides the Egyptian deities, the other gods who have interested me are the Nordic ones. Is there an Odin?"

"Indeed, there is. Does this delight you? Shall we call him into service?"

After a moment, I decide not to pursue working with this Norse deity now. "I spoke with Thor a few years ago, you know."

"Yes, I am aware."

"I assume that if he exists, some of the other legendary gods also do. But I'm going to find out more about them before I attempt communication."

"This is your choice. It is the way of the human to deify those of us from other worlds. It is easy to imagine how that would be possible, for we have what can be considered by these individuals to be supernatural powers. These powers are natural to us."

"And the existence of gods seems natural to us."

"That's because supernatural beings are part of the spirit of this world; they are part of the spirit of the essence of joy, the vibrational elements of music and sound. If you listen to a bird, the beauty of its sound is ethereal. The beauty of a tree also inspires awe."

I contemplate the nature of my own "supernatural" powers. "I've experienced my Ka energy moving out from me. How can I train or access that energy body that I have?"

"It is like a bank of batteries that you can access to more powerfully drive the vehicle of your body."

"But how can we train my Ka? I remember watching it perch on top of my bedpost, so I know it can move independently from my body."

"It is like Peter Pan."

I like this comparison and ask Esthra how I can interface with my Ka.

"Both parties must be willing to interface. To trap a lightning bug inside of glass is a way to get light, but it has less of an impact because the entity is trapped."

"I don't want to trap my Ka. How can we work together?"

"How can you move in collaboration with the Ka?"

"Yes. I think that could help me with lots of things, including my violin playing."

"I think you are wise in this. I believe that it is possible for us to establish that connection. It is connected to all parts of your physical presence; this is the essence of the being. It is so linked to your intention; it is so very much associated with your emotional body, yet it can be thwarted by a single thought. You see, there is the attraction to great positives and the music you make is of great positives. So the essence of that which you call Ka is attracted as if it was a magnet to the positive, to the vibration of that great sweetness. And so, if you have the intention of playing this music as never before, you also have the passion, the emotion, to do so. The emotion will be caught up in sounds. I am working on this quite diligently, and it will be my pleasure to have this ready for you—perhaps even today. Would this be soon enough?"

Of course I want this right now. "What do I do?"

"It is more about your thoughts. I will ask you to monitor your thoughts most closely this day; be positive about your music, thinking about it as the best you have ever played. That is the attraction of the magnetic to the Ka."

"So ... I just think positive thoughts today?"

"Yes, when you play your violin or even *think* about playing your violin, set your intentions to play your best. Picture in your heart and mind that the Ka is within and that it is resonating the vibration of perfected tones of this music that you are creating. I will do what I can to amplify this by placing the energies within the bow and the violin itself. If you can allow me this moment of placing all the pieces together; I am ready. It is for you, my dear. There is nothing for you to do. I have the muses that are in readiness as well. If you play in less than your greatest form that you are anticipating, let not even a single negative thought enter your mind. You have your SVH wordings. This is an experiment for you. Melchizedek is most pleased with what we are doing."

I ask if I should go practice a little bit.

"We are ready for you to begin your playing. You may consider it to be practice, but is it not said that you *play* violin?"

"Yes, and I play viola also."

"These are your instruments of delight. Let them be your delight."

"Thank you for your assistance. Say hello to everybody for me."

"They are all waving their feathers for you, dear."

I can't help but smile at this remark; it creates such a lovely picture in my mind. Before I disengage from our conversation, Estha asks if he may give me a compliment. Of course I say yes.

"The sound of your laughter is truly the ringing of joy that you are named for."

"Thank you. I do like to laugh."

"Laughter is easy for you."

"I love you all."

"And we are in great honor to be of assistance to you for always."

CHAPTER TEN
April 4, 2014

I use my SVH gateway to move to Tonas's ship and say, "Happy birthday!"

"You have a good, kind heart to celebrate a birth such as mine. Of course, I am in great celebration of it as well."

"I didn't know if you celebrated that kind of thing."

"We are associating with Earth at this time. We are living by your calendar year, so I choose to celebrate."

"Before we celebrate, would it be appropriate for me to ask you to assist me with some of the work I'm going to do today? I went to some of the galactic councils of light and received transmissions to assist the Earth to connect more fully with the higher dimensions. If it's not appropriate, I could implement this by myself—but I think it might be interesting for us to do this work together."

"I believe it would be a delight. May I see what you have? Ah, you are connecting with areas where enlightened groups of galactic beings are holding position supporting Earth. These are also habited greatly by your masters of light. The transmissions that I am witnessing seem to be generating from the star council. They are transmitting inward to the ship and to yourself, creating a field of energy around you which is affecting your chakras. Of course, the transmission comes to you, and then you are transmitting outward from yourself, piercing the veils of the dimensions."

I take in this information, but I'm still uncertain if he's offering his help. "Would you like to assist me, or is this just for me to do?"

"This is an interesting set of circumstances," Tonas answers after a pause. "The galactic councils are connecting with you and you are connecting with them. They are again transmitting to *you.* I believe that it is possible for me to join you in this, but only if you would take my hand."

It might be just my imagination, but it seems that I can sense his hand reaching toward mine! "This transmission is of great importance," he continues. "You have just placed me in a new position. You have positioned me with an ability now to support your Earth even more so simply through this connection with you. It is our collective effort. You are receiving a different transmission than myself. This is a delicious experience for me as we share that energy bubble."

"Uh-huh," I say, entranced. "It feels wonderful."

"You have encompassed me; it is most delicious, most delicious indeed."

As we do this work, it feels important for me to enhance our transmission by speaking the Language of Light. I transmit this higher dimensional language until it feels complete, at which time Tonas tells me that we are offering areas of Earth an opportunity to connect with itself at the higher dimensional frequency that exists in this 10th dimension.

He continues, "You are the ideal conduit, for you have your energy in this dimension and all of the higher dimensions leading up to your 25th dimension of Earth. This is creating some kind of a bridging effect; you are becoming that bridge. These galactic gatherings of people who have elevated consciousness are pleased with how you are assisting them. It is a transmission I send back to them that you are quite genius."

I confess that I've had a *lot* of help and add that it feels wonderful to do this work with him.

"This unity that we are—it is as if we are moving into position to assist the whole of the Earth together. I have always had desire for this; I have been waiting until you have reached your position on your 8th dimension, knowing then that you will make your choice to perhaps, on occasion, be more consciously in my presence. I believe that working together to support the greater expansion of the Earth, as we did today, was the beginning of this."

I am delighted that this work is as important to Tonas as it is to me and that we can be together to do it. It seems that I was able to give him the perfect birthday gift!

"Do you know how we celebrate birthdays here?" I ask.

"It is not of my understanding."

Using an Oreo cupcake (something *I* can eat after the demonstration), I explain that there wasn't room for twenty-five million candles on it, so there is only one to represent his age. After singing "Happy Birthday," I ask him to make a wish that he has to keep secret. Then I blow out the candle and let him know that now his wish will come true.

"It was an easy wish. Knowing my heart, you know what this wish must be."

"I can guess, but you can't tell me until it comes true."

#

I decide to mix things up a bit by asking Tonas if there's anything he would like to ask me.

"You came right into business; I had no time to kiss your fingers."

"I know. I'm sorry."

"May we embrace?"

"Yes, I'd love that."

"This is my first experience of a celebration of this kind, and it is quite exciting for me."

"Normally, there would be presents that would be wrapped and you would get a chance to open them, but ..." I hesitate, stumped. How do you convey all the joy and excitement of birthdays?

"Do you mean a gift like your presence here today?"

"I guess that will have to do."

"You are a conduit for me to be in connection with the

councils and these presences on Earth that are of great brightness. You, since you live on this world, have the right to ask for and receive our aid. By asking, you have made our assistance—is the word 'legal?'"

"Yes."

"You made it legal for me to make this great service with you."

"I'm really happy about that."

"It is quite an enhancement of what my purpose can expand to be. Many of the serious works that I have been employing have been instrumental—as have the works of all of the federation, as you might call us. We are in position all over the outer perimeter of Earth's atmosphere; there are many of our ships. I think this would frighten some, if they were aware of it, but there would be no reason for fright, as you know. It is our hope that we can always be of great service to Earth itself. We are here with an agenda to support that which is the brightest of light as the hearts and minds of the populace of this world become more awakened to what is possible. The greatest opportunity for us came at the birth of you and the others of your affiliation. That, of course, was something to be excited about."

"It still seems odd to me, this importance of our little group. I guess eventually I will figure it out. Esthra told me that, at some point, I will be famous. I'm thinking, 'really?' That's another oddity. Maybe you would like my autograph before it gets really expensive."

Of course, I am joking when I say that—but Tonas takes my statement seriously.

"Yes, of course. You are speaking about becoming even more famous than you are now?"

"Well, I don't feel like I'm famous at the moment."

"Imagine what it is for so many to know your designation, your name, your presence. There are *all* eyes on Earth. Imagine what it must have been to be born as yourself, to be in the moment of your conceiving, to have so many eyes, so many hearts hoping and praying that you would live. Hoping and praying that the world would allow those of you in the academy to rise into your greatest power. It is a curiosity, I am sure."

I know I probably should pursue this subject, but I don't even know what to ask. I still find this line of thinking somewhat overwhelming. I hope I will understand, as I do more of this work, why those of us in the academy, as well as Earth herself, are so important.

# # #

I decide to ask another question. "Tell me more about yourself. Do you deal with the physical force of gravity that we experience here on Earth?"

"Well, of course, we have our feet on the ground, and on this ship, on the floor of the ship."

"But is there gravity?"

He pauses, because apparently I've asked something difficult to describe. "We create this, for in space there is no such gravity. Gravity is a funny word. There are planets with atmosphere; the atmosphere creates the opportunity for gravity. There are certainly worlds with no gravity, and the conscious sentience that exists there is simply energy."

"What do beings on other planets look like?

Tonas tells me that all worlds with embodied beings have gravity and that the inhabitants of many worlds look humanoid; however, there are some tall species who have arms and legs but also bug-like features.

I wish he hadn't told me that.

When I ask him if he needs a space suit or another ship to leave his ship, he demolishes another science-fiction scenario by telling me he can exist, unaided, in any environment. (He later explained that, if he wished to step outside his ship, into space, he would simply surround himself with a bubble of air.) He creates his own environment of "pleasureness" wherever he goes. The idea of always being comfortable seems wonderful to me—especially not being cold in winter. This is definitely something to look forward to.

#

Remembering the birthday we are celebrating, I ask Tonas exactly how old he is. He pauses a moment to calculate and then tells me he is 25,489,001 today.

"Wow," is my immediate reaction. "I can't believe a while ago that you felt you needed to impress me. You're a twenty-five million year old starship commander who remembers everything you've ever said. I'm just totally in awe of you. Like, *holy cow!*"

"This is your life as well," he reminds me. "Or at least, soon this will be your life."

"I'm ready for it right now! What kind of timeline can you give me? How much of a peek into my future did you take?"

"I did look at your one-year, your two-year, and your three- and four-year scenarios. I looked into each year leading to the point, simply the point, where you would feel your greatest comfort in your presence and have the abilities that you have desired. For all of your life, you have desired to be able... I have disappointed you. I can tell."

"Why?"

"You are thinking it is all happening in one year. And that is possible, of course."

"No, I didn't think that. I can't see me reaching those goals in a year."

"Your face made a frown; I know that I disappointed you. You are thinking that your hair and your teeth and skin will fall into beautiful place within the next few months—and I'm telling you, it is possible."

"That part of me there may have thought that, but this part of me here—the one talking to you right now—did not think that. That dichotomy between me here and me there is interesting. When you were saying one year, two years, three years, I wasn't thinking about my body being transformed that quickly, though it would be nice."

"There was a frown; indeed there was. I witnessed it with my own eyes, and I will rue it forever. It is our first frown together."

I know it's not *my* first frown, and probably not my last, but I'm not going to mention that. To lighten the mood, I ask him to tell the part of me there to shape up.

"Your frown here is, I think, an automatic response to the great desire that you have within you to experience the true value of your potential. But I live on a longer timeline. I have waited thousands of years for humanity to even be birthed onto this world that we are looking at."

# # #

Tonas changes the subject. "If you wish to come over to the window, you can easily view Earth. From this 10th dimension, it is somewhat more elegant."

"That's what I really want to see. The garbage, the junkyard cars, billboards, pollution, and everything else that's not beautiful—gone."

"These things do not exist on the 10th dimension."

When I ask him if these things exist on the 8th dimension, he tells me "only for those who wish to look back in their memories." He explains, "Earth is transitioning into a new energy and the new children who are born onto this world will have no awareness of the things you have known through the years of your childhood and your adult experiences."

"That will be good."

"Yes. I believe you will be pleased."

# # #

Now I switch gears by giving Tonas information about the symphony's April concert. "I'll be performing, and you are invited to watch," I say.

"There is an opportunity for me to step into that arena of your concert; I will make arrangement for this. You have invited me; there are rulings you see, stringent rulings. We are always falling within the acceptance of those declarations. You come to see me; I have never, beyond my heart, beckoned you here. You made the determination to come to me, which allows this connection between us. You have invited me to witness this great celebration of music, and because of this, I will find a way to be there. Where would you like me to be in presence?"

"Just pick a good seat. Everybody that's on your ship is also invited, if they'd like to come."

Tonas immediately tells me that all nine hundred of his shipmates will be attending. I was concerned that some of them would need to stay with the ship, but he informs me that they can be in both places at once! How totally cool is that?

But thinking of these new nine hundred audience members heightens my concern about playing well. "I haven't quite got all the notes yet, but I'll do the best I can."

His reply that I will be "brilliant" doesn't reassure me one bit.

Then he says something really interesting. "You must also know that the only harmonic we hear is of the highest."

"Oh, that's good." I laugh and then say, "You won't hear it if I play any wrong notes, then."

"You are so comical. Ah, it is no wonder I love you so much. You bring great smiles to me."

Before I can reply, he informs me that I visit him every

night and we dance. I wondered if he would like our dances. He tells me they have become his passion, and that he finds them "interesting and intimate."

It's great to find a guy who likes to dance. Now if I can just begin to feel his body next to mine and his arms around me.

# # #

"I play the viola for a lot of weddings." I offer this information to Tonas since it will give me a sneaky way to ask if this ceremony is part of life in the higher dimensions. "Do they do weddings on the 10th dimension?"

"You are speaking of the commitment?"

"Yes. Here it's a ceremony and the couple promises to love each other for the rest of their lives, until death parts them. But a lot of them get divorced in a few years."

"If they left out that segment of the wording, it would be much easier to make their separation, would it not?"

I smile at his wisdom. "I suppose that it would."

"It is different for us. We make a commitment of heart for as long as the hearts beat individually as one. Many of those commitments last, what you would consider to be, forever. When I shared with Sironea my feelings about you, we released our commitment to each other. It is amicable, and it is accepted."

"Did you have other relationships besides with Sironea? It's okay if you don't want to answer such a personal question."

"It is a personal question that I believe a woman in your position has the right to ask. I have felt only two heart connections. The commitment I make to you is free of your need or desire to commit to me. I made that commitment to you long ago and, of course, to Sironea. So, it is only to the two of you that I have been deeply committed."

"How did you know? How do people know when you're ready to commit?"

"The connection with individuals is as if a fire explodes between them and their hearts know that they are open for that unity. This is a delicious moment and uplifting for both."

This kind of connection sounds like something worth waiting for. I wonder if I will be able to experience this with Tonas…

"As you may have imagined, I have been what you would consider monogamous for you since our first meeting of eyes. Not that your eyes even landed on me for more than a second, but I was besotted with you. My heartfelt message is that I have had no interest in another since our first meeting—which was, of course, millions of years ago. I feel the greatest of pleasure simply being in your presence on this day, in this spark of time."

"I know that one of these days, I'll be able to see you. I just want it to be sooner rather than later."

"It will be. Of this, I speak confidently. It will be."

"Have you seen that? You don't have to tell me when, but have you seen that I actually do get to see you?"

"Yes. I know this to be true."

"That's heartening."

"I know this to be true. I—oh, it is so hard not to tell you things!"

"I know, but please don't. If you were to start telling me about future events, I don't think I'd ever be able to stop asking you questions about what will happen."

# # #

Tonas seems to carefully consider before he begins sharing various truths about our shared future, as if to reassure me that it will be possible. "You and I will have our opportunities for travel; it is no longer wishful thinking. There will be a day, I am sure of it, when we see *all* that is to be seen. And you will still, of course, maintain your energy presence on Earth. It will be easy for you to be consciously with me as we travel and also present in your important position on Earth. I will never consider whisking you away from that which you have spent an eternity planning."

"That's good to know. Tonas … I don't know when I will speak with you again."

"It is my pleasure to have been gifted today. You spoke of gifts being wrapped. I was wrapped in the essence of your presence here."

"Happy birthday!"

"And enjoy, please, the cupcake."

"I will. Goodbye, Tonas."

"Forever you have my heart."

CHAPTER ELEVEN
April 9, 2014

"What a lovely surprise!"

"Hello, Tonas! I hadn't really planned on talking to you today but I feel I should. I am going to approach the star councils to see if we could do more of the work that we did the other day. I feel like I should ask if that would be okay with you first."

"Oh, it would be my delight. It would be an answer to, as you would say, my prayers—something I have greatly wished for. I would enjoy this very much. Thank you for including me in this endeavor."

"You will make it more special. It just felt really wonderful to hold your hand and to be on the ship and do that work. I'd like to do more of that."

"It will be my greatest pleasure."

Thinking about pleasure reminds me of an area I've been concerned about. I decide I might as well bring it up. "It worries me that I'm not aware of that part of me who comes to visit you. I want to make sure that she does not do anything ..." I pause, and then continue, "well, to be blunt, I want to make sure she does not attempt to seduce you. I don't know if she would do that, but I would feel uncomfortable if she did. So beware!"

"Do you mean that all the times that you have seduced me have been incorrect?"

Appalled, I exclaim, "Oh, no!"

Tonas quickly adds that he is just "making a laughter" for me. I'm relieved, but I certainly don't feel like laughing at that little "jest."

"I promise you," he says, his tone serious, "that no part of you shall have any opportunity to seduce me until you, fully and wholly—if it should come to that—desire me."

This does greatly relieve me. Not being consciously aware of what I do on his ship had been worrying me.

He tells me that the part of me that visits him is aware of his all-encompassing love for me, but I need have no concern. "I am longing for the day that you make such an overture," he says, "because that will mean you have come even closer to me in heart, in your physical presence. If that should happen, it would surely mean that you are beginning to fall in love with me."

Again, as so often happens, his words leave me speechless. He continues. "It is your energy that I love; of course, it is also *you* that I love. I am hoping that you will wish to have human coupling of this consummation at some point, if you desire. Yet it is in my great hope also to bring that joining between our hearts, which is something I will show you when you are ready—*if* you become ready. It will always be your choice. But I promise you, it will take you beyond any euphoria that you have ever experienced."

His frankness in discussing sexual matters is a surprise to me. I've been treading carefully around that subject; it took a great deal of nerve for me to even express my concern about seducing him. I decide I'm just going to pretend to take this all in stride and tell him, "That sounds interesting. Obviously, I've never experienced anything like that."

"Nor have I experienced the human coupling act."

This admission is quite a surprise for me, and I'm not sure how to respond. It seems best to answer with a neutral observation. "Human sex can be very … sweaty."

"It will be a curiosity; I will be your virgin."

"Oh, my God!" Never have I had any guy admit *that* to me.

"I will be your virgin, you see, and you will train me, I'm sure—that is, if we have this opportunity. Yes, for you to train me to pleasure you would be of the greatest delight."

Several thoughts pop into my mind about this possible future scenario. The first thought, *Mmm, that sounds like delicious fun.* The second thought, *That could be a bit daunting.* I decide to go, bravely, in the direction of my first thought and say, "We could take the expression 'out of this world sex' to new heights."

Maybe *I* need some tutoring about sex on the 10th dimension, but I'm certainly not going to ask him. I wonder if Esthra could help me.

I realize Tonas has been waiting for me to continue, so I casually say, "Well, thank you. That sounds wonderful. I'm looking forward to speaking with you again sometime soon, because it's a delight for me to hear your voice."

"It will be a great delight for me. You have made my day something extra special. Thank you."

#

I decide that the next step to take in order to assist Gaia is to ask the Creator's assistance in finding the appropriate galactic council with whom to confer. The closest I could come to a name for this council was the Council of Earth Vigilance. They oversee anything applied to Earth by galactic interference—the term "interference" is meant in a good way. I'm calling them the CEV from now on.

"We are at your disposal." The CEV announces.

"Good afternoon. Who am I speaking with?"

"You are speaking with the Supreme Overseer of this council. We are a collective, and so you also are speaking to all of us in the council."

"I did some work the other day with an Ashtar Commander named Tonas. I enjoyed it very much, and I'm wondering if there is additional work that I can do to assist Earth, hopefully in conjunction with him."

"In bringing him into this collaboration," the overseer says. "You have given this one an opportunity to apply this collaborative effort. This would have been un-allowed, as you would say, disallowed. I am not accustomed to speaking English language. We are telepathic."

They do sound like talking is a new experience. The Supreme Overseer's voice is gravelly, and there are frequent pauses between words.

"Did I make an error when I did the work with him?"

"You opened a means for this one, Tonas, to interface applications of Earth assistance from a higher dimensional plane through the conduit of your own energies of the collaboration. It is acceptable."

"Are there more things that we can do to assist Earth?"

"There are millions upon millions of opportunities for you, especially in the collaboration that you are creating with this one."

When I ask the CEV how to begin working with them, they suggest that I simply gate into their council and make my desire known. They will provide something to help me direct the assistance they give me, and, according to them, Tonas will understand what to do. "Someday," the Supreme Overseer adds in a halting voice, "there will be a time when you will also understand. Your presence here today is of great delight to all of us."

I already like these guys, and this sounds like a perfect plan to me.

Further questions reveal that, although there are ninety-four of them in this Council of Earth Vigilance, they are all of one connected mind. When I ask what dimension they exist upon, they tell me that they exist in all dimensions.

"I should have known that. Let me make sure I have this procedure correct. When I desire to do some additional work, I use my gateway to step into your council and speak with you who are the Supreme Overseer of the council. You will know what to give me, correct?"

"Yes. It will be in the form of an energy orb. It will have no means to exist on the dimensional frame of your existence. It will only exist when you make your way into the dimension of this one (Tonas)."

"Very well. I thank you for your assistance today and for all your future assistance. I look forward to working with you."

"It is our great delight."

# # #

Esthra joins me so that I can ask him more about the future. "Is it correct to say that every moment of every day, the future can vary from one possibility to another possibility?"

"Yes, that is correct—and even when something is complete, it can be rewritten."

"Tonas has said that the changes I want to happen to my body will be easier to do in the 8th dimension. But I do not want to wait until the 8th dimension. I want things to be better now. What can we do about that?"

Esthra seems unsurprised by my request, and eager to help. "This is simple. When you focus on what it is that you desire, you hold that focus as the only reality that you will accept. As you do so, never throw cold waters on the heated path that is fueling it."

"I get that I have to keep my thoughts on the changes I desire. But is there something you can do to assist me with this? I'm tired of a body that's not doing what I want it to do. I'm complaining, Esthra."

"I understand. There is something that you can do. It speeds the process if you consciously hold a vision of what it is that you desire. A grand vision of life in which you have white teeth, skin that tightly and lovingly shapes your face, as it did in your youth, and muscles that are long and gently immersing within the skin as well as around the bones. You can speed this by holding the vision of what you desire instead of looking to see if it is there or noticing that it is not. Keep holding a vision; this is what it will be."

I know this is excellent advice. I just have to remember to keep visualizing what I desire instead of focusing on what I don't like. "Is there anything anyone can do to help me rid my breasts of the lumps?" This medical condition has plagued me for some time.

"We would have done this ourselves with interventions if it had been allowed," Esthra replies. "There is no reason for this to be in presence, and so it will simply transform, just as the rest of your body does. Don't be concerned that your body is not yet in its perfection, as it will all come to pass as the dimensional frames fall into place."

"That's what people keep telling me. I'm sixty-eight now."

"You are but a baby."

"Perhaps you are right. Still, I don't want to wait twenty years for my body to begin to rejuvenate. Does anyone know when the changes I desire will begin?"

"They will begin gradually, and they already have begun. And by the way, your dear Tonas is also a baby."

"He says he's a young man, but then I think, twenty-five *million* years?"

"He is indeed a baby, and yet he is a powerful and focused individual who is highly attracted to you for good reason."

"I wonder sometimes if I'm too raunchy for him. Plus, I bet he's never even been sick. Think of all the Earth stuff that I've gone through."

"It is expected. You would expect that someone in an infestation of mosquitoes would perhaps periodically receive a bite."

# # #

My next remark comes because of the delight I feel in sharing the desires of my heart with this guide who is always so supportive. "Esthra, what about Paris?"

"Let us leave today."

I love his witty response, and normally, I'd play along. But I really want his opinion of my chances for visiting that city this year.

"I've been thinking about going in September, but I'm concerned about my parents. I may need to stick around here for them."

"I know your heart wishes to be in presence and to have the benefit of their presence as much as possible."

"They're getting old. I really don't want them to go, but they're not in good shape."

"I know. It is impossible for them to meet the energy exchange that would be required for them to make the motion into the next dimensions. This is difficult. There are not enough numbers to describe the times that we have experienced that great separation illusion of death. You will enjoy them even more so after their deaths. Your mother will be a different woman in the Fifth Realm."

I hope he's right. She has suffered with digestive difficulties for much of her life and has become exceedingly frail.

"It will be a breath of fresh air for you to witness her in that place. The freedom that she will receive will allow you to witness her in that new environment of freedom. It will be a goodly experience for you to prepare yourself to be able to communicate with her by communicating with the frogs, the dogs, and the kitty cats."

"Maybe I'll go to Paris, then."

"You will know. You will either have a comfort in going or you will not, for your destiny on this is linked to the destiny of two others, and they are choosing for themselves. Your destiny for Paris is defined by their destinies."

"If I don't go this year, I can go some other time," I say, feeling a pang of remorse already at possibly missing this opportunity.

"You have your whole life," Esthra says, "and there is a great deal of life ahead of you."

"Esthra … just as I fall asleep, or when I first wake up, I can see or hear my guides and guardians a little. But I want more. That's my mantra; *I want more*. Can you use megaphones or something?"

"Let us practice this."

"How do I practice this?"

"Just be open, my dear, to hearing us. When you do hear us, celebrate and be grateful."

I giggle. "Okay, but step right up and yell in my ear."

"And if the communication stops, celebrate again."

"All right. I love you all. Thank you for your help today."

CHAPTER TWELVE

April 10, 2014

"You surprise me!" Tonas says.

Gleefully, I reply, "Oh, I know."

"We have these orbs to play with today."

"I didn't know if we'd done the work already. That's why I'm checking in with you."

"It requires our collective focus of consciousness. We can apply both of these at the same time."

"Can I hold your hand?"

"Ah, may I kiss your fingers?"

I had forgotten that this is part of his greeting ritual; obviously, he hasn't.

"Yes, you may."

"It is a great pleasure to have you visit me in this time. It is like the doorbell, the telephone ringing that you must experience, when someone that you delight in seeing then comes to be in your collective focus. Please move your presence more closely to me through your gate."

"All right, hold on."

"And now I will smother your fingers." He laughs. "You are a delight to me; I like this word, 'delight.' There is wisdom in this Council of Earth Vigilance; I have gone to meet with them personally."

I didn't think to suggest that to him, but I'm glad he took the initiative to visit them.

"It was, I believe, important for me to state my intentions. My intentions are to support Earth … to support you … and to support *all* who support Earth."

With this reassurance, I start speaking Language of Light in order to ready the grids to receive our transmission. Tonas provides a commentary for me by telling me that there are nine other councils watching what we are doing and there are seventy or more upper atmosphere grids being switched on. Tenth dimensional energies are streaming from both of us! That's exciting to hear. He relays that we are also sending our love for Earth to her and to all of the consciousness and beings who exist on her. I feel that!

He then reminds me we need to find the grids below the Earth's crust and that he will follow my lead. I tell him that I'm going down to the center of the Earth and emanating from that point. I can feel/see bursts of light.

Tonas exclaims, "It is my heart that I give to Earth! It is our joined hearts that are making the piercing through the veils of the dimensions. And so, we are complete."

"That was magnificent!"

He agrees. "It was a delight."

"I decided you needed to be busier."

"It is always my pleasure to be busy with you."

"This has got to be a feather in your cap—the work that you're doing with me, right?"

"It is strictly unheard of. The feather that you have put in my cap is something that is spoken of quite often by those who are in the awareness. They say that you honor me greatly, and they are of truth."

"I think you deserve it."

"You have come to me, though my heart beckoned you. It is my great honor as well as my pleasure to have been so graced by your company and by your presence here."

I assure him that I'll see him again soon.

"May I say my great thanks for your faith in me? For surely your faith in me is what has brought me this feather."

"How could I not have faith in you? You're a wonderful person."

"Well, that is true, and so are you. We are both wonderful people. And it is not so much that we are wonderful as that we are wonderful *together*. For what we have just done for Earth, you and I will be written and spoken about for a long, long time. This is what you call a 'window of opportunity' for us to be able to draw this higher dimension consciousness into the Earth."

"It feels perfect to do this work with you. I look forward to next week."

"I will be waiting."

CHAPTER THIRTEEN

April 17, 2014

Tonas exclaims, "It is you, Joy!"

"Yes, it's me! I'm so excited to talk to you! I've heard you a couple of times lately."

"Ah! You have?"

"This morning, I heard you say, 'My darling.' And then I heard 'My heart.'"

"Mmm, I am whispering to you of my great desire to be of the most assistance to you in every of your moments," he replied. "Rather than wait for the hope of a moment that will make my life the most fulfilled, it is even more important, I think, for me to step into the role of being your greatest champion. I know that you have angels and many guardians. Please be assured that *my* heart also is holding you."

"Thank you, thank you, thank you for your support and assistance."

"It is easy for me."

#

"Tell me now, if you're a youth—which I still find so extraordinary—is that like someone on Earth in their twenties?"

"That would be an interesting calculation. You might consider that I am as a six year old."

"No! I can't believe that!"

"You can see that I am adult, and yet in that calculation, I would be perhaps only six. Not much older than a toddler."

"How old do you have to be before you're considered mature?"

"Many billions, I am sure, by this calculation. It is not the same as for Earth children; you expect for them to make boo-boos and to get themselves into some troubles. This is not part of our heritage story at all. It is only that I have less personal experience than the great wise ones."

"Who do you consider to be some of the great wise ones?"

"Most assuredly, I would consider Isis, of course; Osiris would be the oldest. This 'old' thing is interesting as a description; it is 3rd dimension description. The wisest and the ones of the greatest longevity would be many of the great ones like Metatron and some of the others. Your Melchizedek is one of the great wise ones as well."

"Melchizedek is working with me every day."

"I am greatly aware of this; it is of the greatest excitement. Oh, and we are *all* excited about attending your concert."

"I had a rehearsal Tuesday night; I'm getting more notes. I'm still not playing as well as I hope to, but I plan to do my best."

"You are fastidious in all that you do, and the sweet quality of you is that you are always searching to be even more in perfection. That is sweet, that you would imagine that you are less than perfect in the eyes of any. That is only your own vision of yourself, you see. You can be nothing less than perfect in my eyes."

These kinds of statements about "perfection" and being a "perfection vision" are appealing to me, but they are also something I am still uncomfortable hearing. These people just do not see me as I am here—that's for sure. They all sound so sure of themselves. I guess I'll just have to hope they're right.

In the meantime, I'm still trying to find out as much as I can about Tonas. A series of questions reveal that sleep is not necessary for him. Excretions of any kind are also unnecessary, because everything he consumes is of the purest energy. Yet his body is designed like mine and would work like mine if he were to move into my dimension and consume food here.

Vehicles are not needed—at least not on Lyra—because people just think where they wish to be, and they're there. I love the idea of being able to travel like that, but Tonas tells me the thought of riding in an automobile is exciting for him. He adds, "Airplanes are the closest to my ship in that we are choosing an existence within an environment. So we have created vessels such as this. It is much more convenient than floating in the air with nothing between us."

Laughing, I say, "The thought had crossed my mind that you could probably all just hang around in space."

"It would require more effort, but we would become accustomed to it quite easily."

Tonas goes on to tell me he has many abodes on different worlds that are considered to be great palaces. This is a completely unexpected aspect of his life that is enticing to me. He has underwater homes on Andromeda and Sirius as well as one that is above ground on Sirius. He adds that his homes are part of the "nature wonderlands" on these worlds.

This makes me wonder if there are seasons on the different worlds. His surprising answer is, "We create seasons as we will."

"But people would have to agree upon that—wouldn't they?"

"Ah, my season can be different than that of someone who exists even a short distance away."

I remark that I can't see how that could possibly work.

"We create our own realities, you see; we coexist in a fluid consciousness of creations that are designed to give us pleasure. Imagine I had a thought that I would wish to experience the Earth's snow. I would not have to visit a place where everyone had the same vision and view of that snow. I would just create it for myself, opening the scenario for others if they wished to embrace that same opportunity. It is a wonder to be at your ideal temperature and reach into the snow and hold it in your hand, to feel it against your face, perhaps even to taste the nectar of it." He casually adds, "You will see all of my homes. They will become yours as well, if you wish."

"Wow!"

"No pressure for you, my dear. They are to be yours at your liking. I am requiring no commitment on your part in order to make this a reality." He has sensed my hesitation.

"You are right in that I don't feel like I can make a commitment at this time, but I do like the idea of seeing your homes. Visiting them is something I really would enjoy experiencing. This relationship we have must be extremely unique; are you aware of anyone else who has anything like this?"

"On Earth, this is uncommon. Let us say, many thousands of years ago, someone on Earth caught the eye of a species from another world that is of duality. It would have been considered somewhat ridiculous for them to bring attention to any full commitment. With Earth, it is different. *Earth* is the pinnacle of all that is driving the forces of every universe into its ideal position of evolution."

"Can you elaborate on that? It seems so odd that Earth is important. We see these pictures of the universe and here's this little bitty speck way out somewhere on the arm of the Milky Way, and that's Earth. And yet, you're saying we're so important. It's hard to understand why."

"The culmination happens when you, and others of Earth, make your final leap into that energy field of Earth called the Fifth Realm. When the Atlanteans evolved into the 5th dimension, they brought the energy of duality into it. So the Fifth Realm is the only space where there is no evolution linked to the mind and the action of any species within any reality anywhere. And so, there it sat for you and others like yourself, those in what you call your larger number of 144,000, who are creating that space for all of us to move into for that final phase of the greater understanding of everything."

"We will be able to learn about and understand everything in the Fifth Realm?"

"Yes. And when everyone understands everything, down to the tiniest of particle, based on our greater understanding of each other and the oneness of the particles of everything, taken to the tiniest spark of recognition of understanding, then, of course, it will be our desire to return to the origin. And that could only happen from Earth."

"But can you give me a time frame?"

"Yes. All worlds must meet the timing of Earth, so all of those worlds of dual are stretching their time also. The rubber band is stretching widely for some of them, for there is, very likely, no more to be expended than three hundred and fifty years, we believe."

"You are saying we are within three hundred and fifty years of this transition into the Fifth Realm?"

"That's correct. Cosmically, it has taken as long as the beginning of all that is and the beginning of Earth herself for you to even reach collectively the dimension that you are existing in now. So imagine this tiny little framework—three hundred and fifty of your years, or a few days or years more than that. Imagine these worlds that are nowhere near your readiness, stretching their years, perhaps forty million or forty billion years, and then compacted within that three hundred and fifty years that you and all of us will have in remaining to play. It is all defined from Earth."

"Did you always know Earth would be the key?"

"You AMS initiates traveled millions of years into the past of the present moment of your reality as most focused initiates, and showed us who you are. It was a vision of great wonder. I believe it is our destiny that I saw you and my jaw dropped, as you would say. My mouth fell wide open as my eyes were struck by the great essence of your presence."

I know this is important information, and the passion in Tonas's voice is unmistakable. The concept of Earth being so important is radically different than the way I'm used to thinking of our lovely little out of the way planet. Equally astounding is that Tonas considered those of us of the academy "a vision of great wonder." I mostly think of myself as a woman doing the best I can while hoping to do better.

I don't want to ask Tonas to explain this again; I think I'd just get more confused. Trying to sound like I understood his explanation, I give myself a graceful out by saying, "That is much to ponder."

# # #

"I'm assuming that in your dimension, the 9th and maybe beginning in the 8th, that people don't buy and sell things. Is that correct?"

He pauses and I can't tell if he's amused or confused. "Why would they do this?"

"Well, that's been the whole entrepreneurial and capitalistic force behind our economy, selling things and buying things. But when everyone manifests whatever they want, I can see there wouldn't be any need for that. Is there trade? Do you have starships that travel to other worlds and trade things with people?"

"That would be against the accords, for if there was a need for trade, their technology would not be matching our own. If their technology measured up to ours, they would easily be capable of creating whatever they needed."

He's destroying the premise of many science fiction novels I've read, so I protest. "But they might not think of doing it that way."

"In which case, it would be out of their realm of possibility, and so, it would be against the accords to bring them technology that is less than what they can vision for themselves."

I need to find out more about these accords; another thing to add to my question list.

"You said your dad was an emissary. What would an emissary do?"

"My father was what you would consider an ambassador on Lyra; he is now captain of a much larger Ashtar ship. An ambassador is one who oversees the connection with different species. It is in his greatest interest to support the understanding of all species. Those who have the ability of interstellar travel have visited Lyra and many of these other worlds, so there are ambassadors to assure that the compliance of the accords is met."

There's that word again. But in context, I understand it better now.

"How many ships are there in the Ashtar Command around Earth?"

"There are millions."

"It must be crowded up there."

"Well, they are on different dimensions as well."

"There are Ashtar Command ships in the 8th and 9th dimensions?"

"They are beginning in your 10th dimension; we can move to whatever dimension we wish. We are simply in many eventualities attempting to maintain our presence in dimensions that are supportive rather than coming forward to be seen. For instance, we are also committed to supporting the Atlantean evolution from this 10th dimension; we are slightly askew of the dimension, although it is still considered the 10th dimension."

"The Atlanteans are on the 10th dimension?"

"They are, indeed. This is quite impressive, yet not as impressive, I will be bragging now, as your generation. Look what has occurred simply in the last years. Third dimension is no more, you have moved into the 6th and 7th merged dimensions, and most of Earth is moving in that same direction. Very impressive, and I am proud, of course. The word proud is a sweet word, and we are of proudness of the Atlanteans as well. And yet, it is the focus of your generation. This is our greatest vision for Earth at this time—the accomplishments of the world of Earth in your generation."

# # #

"Did I draw you my little valentine bee pin?" Before Valentine's Day, I had asked Tonas to have the part of me there draw a picture of it.

"Indeed you did. We have something similar on other worlds."

He missed what I hoped he would notice, namely that the bee is cute and it is holding a red heart that says "Bee Mine." But now I'm interested in what he has to say about bees. I learn that Earth is filled with "reproductions" of animals because the ancient academy initiates had to create different species as part of their homework. That certainly took the concept of homework to a whole new level for me. He informs me that perhaps one of the initiates had something similar to a bee on their world, so when they created their homework bee, they made it just a little bit different than the insect they knew. It was important to be original, you see.

"All species of even what you would consider a bee or other insect have the same ability to create, perhaps, as I," he tells me.

The creation abilities of animals is an interesting concept I have never considered. For a moment, I'm tempted to ask Tonas more about this subject, but I quickly decide not to explore how the bees create. I'm having enough difficulty trying to understand how *I* create.

Tonas continues, "On a non-dual world, we experience lives of fulfillment and bliss. You must be aware that every moment is spent in the joy of experiencing it. There is never a reason to be in dissatisfaction. There is always a reason to be in the joy of the experience. Now, there is something that can bring us into the closest of what you might consider to be sadness; it would make me have sadness if you were to be in pain or dissatisfaction. This would bring me some of that same experience."

I attest that I've certainly experienced pain and dissatisfaction. "Not so much recently, although two or three weeks ago, I was ill. I had the flu and threw up and stayed in bed for four days, and it was no fun. I don't imagine you've ever experienced those joys of duality: headaches, fever, digestive issues, and all those kinds of challenges."

"That is expected in duality."

"Well, you're just glad when it's over."

"Ah, so there is a positive side to it."

"Yes, there is a positive side. It's when you say, 'Boy, I'm glad that I'm not throwing up anymore and that I can get out of bed.' It's that contrast thing that we go through here. There have been such extremes in the past for me."

"I believe there is still more of that to come."

"Oh, no! That is disheartening."

"And in the same moment that I say this, I know that there will be less of it than you have ever experienced. There is a transitional phase that some individuals are moving through at this time. With it comes greater understanding, if they can survive."

"My parents are not in that survival category."

"I have been pondering this, and it will be my honor to be in sadness with you on the eve of this experience. I know that it will bring you great displeasure."

"I'm not looking forward to their deaths, but they are old. It's not like how your race lives. My father is elderly at ninety-six."

"Ninety-six of years?"

"Yes, he tells everyone, 'I'm a senior citizen; I'm ninety-six years old.'"

"Ah, he must be a dear man."

"He's vocal and outgoing—he never met a stranger—and

my mother is quiet and reserved."

"And you are that balance in between."

"I suppose so. But being the balance has been challenging."

# # #

"Let's do our work."

"We, indeed, will have a great pleasure today. I will alert you that there is a special 'Easter egg' for you, if it is true that we will be together on Sunday. You have brought to our forefront a discussion of Earth, and it is known that you have received information that would move you into readiness to be a part of something important. May I expound on this?"

With my acceptance, Tonas asks me to imagine the most wonderfully sculptured and artistically beautiful "egg." Then he asks me to imagine something almost incomprehensible: When we hold and activate it, threads from it will connect to *all* worlds of duality in *every* universe. This is so that the timing of the evolution of those worlds will match Earth's completion of its 25th dimension and movement into the Fifth Realm. At that point, all of Earth will have ascended.

Tonas finishes by explaining that, "The greatest desire of individuals living on non-dual worlds is to support Earth until its moment of transition into the Fifth Realm, so that all that exists moves simultaneously through that pinhole of light into their existence within the Fifth Realm."

After more questions, I learn that Isis and Osiris are going to be involved in facilitating this work on Sunday. There is an astrological alignment called a Grand Cross on that day; I don't really know what that means, but it sounds important. I'm to get the "Easter egg" from the Council of Earth Vigilance and take it to Tonas on the ship. After that, we'll play it by ear.

# # #

I've been bringing orbs to Tonas from the CEV, and we decide to activate them. As usual, I speak Language of Light to begin, and then we both intend that the energies within the orbs stream into all positions of Earth.

Tonas tells me that there are many councils of great wisdom within the Earth as well as in the upper atmosphere of Earth; they're a little "off dimension" yet still part of Earth's environment. These councils join us and draw upon the streams of energy coming from the orbs to assist in activating grids that are in alignment with their specific works.

The work today has made me so giddy that I ask Tonas to dance through the orbs with me.

"I believe that would be the greatest pleasure; indeed, let us."

"Whirl me around!"

"Indeed, you are light as feathers."

"I love doing this with you."

"It is our dance, and it is most delicious, mmm. And now we are complete, my dear. Ah yes, of course, I will bring your head to the floor."

"A dip?"

"Yes, I dipped you to the floor."

"I've always wanted a dance partner to do that!"

"I am never reading your mind, and yet I know your desires. It is allowed. This has been such a great pleasure."

"I look forward to talking with you on Sunday."

"This will be a day of great … I wish to use something that doesn't make any sense, so I will not use the verbiage."

"No! Say it."

"This will be a red letter day."

"Oh, yes."

"One day, we will perhaps converse in such manner. It is impossible for me to send you a letter, yet you will one day soon have the ability to hear me as clearly as you did this morning."

"Can you see my house? Can you see where I live?"

"I will combine the geometries to have the vision of your abode. It is an endeavor to witness your concert as well."

"That's the most important, so I'll talk with you after that to see what you thought."

Tonas assures me that I will play as never before.

"I hope so. I'm going to say goodbye for today. I'll talk to you in just a couple of days."

"It will be a day to remember. Perhaps we will write that red letter."

CHAPTER FOURTEEN

April 20, 2014

Osiris begins to speak, "This is a great day that we have ahead of us; there is much to be accomplished. I am most pleased that you are so open to be the conduit. You have your Easter egg?"

"I gave it to Tonas. Should I not have given it to him?"

Osiris says, "Oh, he is unreliable," and then he laughs. "I am only jesting, my dear! It is intelligent of you to position the egg within that dimensional frame."

"May I make a request, Osiris? Tonas has asked to be my champion and I have accepted him as such. I really enjoy working with him, so without stepping on any toes or breaking any of the rules, I would like for him to be involved, as much as possible, in the energy work that I do."

"We will honor him. This will be important, I believe, because of your collaboration. He is greatly enamored, my dear; I believe he would create a world just for you. It is within his power, of course. It is an important day for us. With your approval, I wish to also include my beloved, Isis."

"Oh, yes."

Now Osiris asks me to move my energy into dimensions four through twenty-five and tells me it is important to stay pinned to those dimensions. He jokes that perhaps I could ask my angels to hold my feet on the ground in each of those dimensions, or use a stake to pin my shoes to the ground. I am also to move my energy to Tonas's ship. The latter, I do easily.

# # #

Tonas greets me and lets me know that Osiris and Isis have joined us. "I am humbled that they have brought such distinction to my ship," he says.

Osiris replies, "And we are humbled as well, being in your presence. I wish you could see the full vision of the *excitement* that exists everywhere through the possibilities that are available at this time. Perhaps you wish to make quick use of the orbs that you have brought. Then we shall apply that which does more than your Grand Cross."

"Tonas, can we hold hands?"

"Yes, my dear. Now it is for us to do what we do. Let us bring all of our orbs and allow them again to circulate before us. If I may hold your hand, and give one quick little kiss to your fingers? I cannot miss my opportunity. And now, hand in hand, we activate with our joined hearts."

We follow our usual procedure of streaming the energies in the orbs to Earth. Once we are complete, Tonas suggests we allow Isis and Osiris the privilege of directing us. I agree, of course.

# # #

Isis speaks. "My beloved, it is I. What you are about to accomplish sets the foundation for all lines of time to find their readiness. Many of these worlds will take much longer than Earth to reach their highest pinnacle—and yet time is most elastic for us. The most important step of today is to set the threads in motion so that, no matter how far the elastic is stretched, it still fits within the pattern of the vision of Earth's timing. Your Easter egg is the map for this. Your beloved wishes a kiss for luck. He has witnesses; we are chaperones."

I surrender with a laugh and say "All right."

"Tonas is romantic, like my beloved," Isis says. "It is quite delicious. The spark I see in his eyes, I also see in my beloved's eyes."

Osiris is laughing as he says, "Now that you have had your kissing, I will kiss my beloved; she never pushes me away. Now,

Tonas, if you will bring the egg orb. It is most relevant that it should be the shape of the cosmic egg, and that it should fall on the Pascal is quite extraordinary. You have heard many stories about crosses in the sky and connections to different worlds. This, of course, is all true—and yet it is a small piece of the story. It is impossible for those to have such a big story as that which is known within your consciousness, and that which you are aware of now. It would be impossible for them to hold all of the information within this egg. But it is possible for you, my dear. And so, before this egg is activated, it is important for you to bear witness and hold the imprint of this within your many consciousness levels. Is this within your acceptance?"

"Yes, definitely," I respond.

Osiris begins his instruction by asking Tonas to hand the egg to me. I am to hold it outward and allow it to transmit to me the full measure of all worlds, dimensions, and existence. All of this information imprints in my many levels of consciousness and I *become* the map. The map for "that which is and always shall be and that which shall come into being."

This sounds somewhat intimidating as Osiris is describing what is happening, but I feel fine. He asks if it is acceptable for Tonas to also hold this information. I readily agree, since I really don't want to be the only one holding this map.

I hand the egg to Tonas and Osiris instructs him to draw in all of the encodements and gate keys and everything that sets the stage for all of creation to fit within a "circle of light." This circle will be the entry into our final moments of physical existence. Thankfully, this is three hundred or so years from now.

#

Osiris asks Tonas and me to turn toward each other and hold the egg in our hands, adding that we are "holding the future of all worlds." We are to raise the egg above our heads as if it is a great beacon; at that moment, an activation of cosmic transference will begin. Osiris's description of this transference is that Tonas and I are holding between us the vision of the restructuring of the grids, the circle created, and the opening of gateways that will connect Earth in all of its dimensions.

He adds that, "As the threads of light reach outward from the egg into all dimensions, it is as if the light of existence itself is reforming, re-calibrating, and connecting with Earth as the center point. The connections are made with every particle of matter and energy in all dimensions and all universes and with the sentience of the beings of all worlds. It is done."

Tonas and I are still standing but both of us are dizzy. I am so glad he is a "map" also. It seems like a good idea to have a back-up. I'd like to laugh at that thought, but that would take too much focus to accomplish.

Tonas does manage to say that he is grateful to me, and to Osiris and Isis, for being allowed to be part of this experience. He says he knows it is the most important work he has ever done.

"I feel it wouldn't have been right to do this without you," I tell him.

"It is as if our destinies are interwoven in a way that is unpredictable," he says. "I am sure this is my destiny—and yet how could I possibly have ever predicted such an exquisite possibility?"

"I like to stir things up."

# # #

"My dear, they wish to know if they may take their leave," Tonas alerts me.

"Yes, you may, and thank you both," I say to Osiris and Isis. "My blessings and love to you."

Osiris states that I am the one they are most grateful to.

Isis agrees. "Dear one, what you have offered today is

perhaps considered to be impossible, and yet you have made it possible. You brought the vision; you brought the idea that was linked to the inevitable, which then allowed us to step in to be your guides. Without you, it would have been impossible for us. There are laws, as you might know. We are in gratitude."

# # #

After they depart, Tonas tells me, "I think that there must be much talk of you in all universes after this. Of course, I am in the light of the lime as well, but it is only because of you."

I love those kinds of wordings that he comes up with—"light of the lime" indeed. Then it occurs to me that perhaps Tonas and I are supposed to do something with the maps we hold. He doesn't know, and so I ask for another conference with Isis and Osiris.

Osiris responds. "Right now it is more instrumental for you to acknowledge the important role you are playing and to honor yourself in every way possible. To be the carrier of such a map is, to me, a gargantuan experience. It is almost impossible—in the bigger framework of what exists now, because of you—to even define fully the presence of how you are affecting all that exists."

His words are mind-boggling, but I force myself to follow his explanation as he continues.

"If you imagine a great map that is fluid ... your unconditional acceptance of the timing of all that exists, living in the present moment, loving the present moment and all that unfolds as a result of it, seeing it as simply part of the story that is being written of the progress of all that exists and your role within it ... you are the great adventurer. Simply honor yourself and this will raise the elevation of the radiance that is unquenchable."

"All right, thank you."

"My beloved Isis might have been able to express that to you in perhaps three sentences; she is giving me the eye-rolling."

I am tickled that Osiris will admit such a thing. His speech does tend to be lengthy, but it is always passionate as well as eloquent. If Isis was indeed rolling her eyes, I know she would also have had a lovely grin on her face.

I let them know that I'm still going to be bringing orbs to Tonas for us to activate, and I ask them to let him know if there is additional work we can do. Osiris reminds me that it is through my discoveries that he and the others are able to assist me. "Simply be yourself, and I will make myself available—and my beloved as well. I think Tonas will not be displeased if we enter his great craft."

I tell them that they have my permission.

Tonas agrees. "And you have mine also. Thank you, dear Osiris, and thank you, Great One. (He's speaking to me!) Osiris is correct in saying that you are a great elevated one. It is hard for you, I think."

"It is," I admit. "When I hear those words, I never think they are about me."

"It is difficult because of your smelly feet or your breath or something that you believe is of disaster. But those things are not truth; they are not the defining moment of you."

I want to inform him that I certainly do not have smelly *anything*, and if I did smell, it would be good. Then I decide to just let this slide and move on to the next topic on my mind.

# # #

"Remember that Saturday is our date for the concert."

"We are doing everything in our possibilities. We will be early."

"I'll be there early also, to warm up, get set up, and get tuned before the concert. Will you really be able to hear it?"

"Indeed, we will be able to hear it. We're coaxing our energy into the dimension, but not so much that we will be physically visible to others. We are so beautiful, you see, and our clothes are quite different. May I have permission to be in your front row?"

"Yes. I'll be on the left side of the stage."

"Oh, I will find you. I will be leaning against the stage."

The vision this statement creates in my mind almost takes my breath away. I can see him so clearly as he stands there, listening intently. My heart speeds up as I think about him being so close to me in *this* reality. After a moment to collect my thoughts, I manage to resume our conversation.

"I don't plan on talking with you this week, but I will talk with you after the concert, sometime next week."

"I have this to dream."

"A hug and a kiss before I go, please."

"It is a pleasure for me."

"My blessings to you—and my love."

"It is my blessings and my love, undying for you."

CHAPTER FIFTEEN
April 29, 2014

I intend to speak with Tonas today to find out about his experience of the concert I played three days ago, but first I feel drawn to converse with Thoth. He is considered to be the Egyptian god of wisdom, but to me, he is a wise, good friend. Before I can begin my conversation with Thoth, he informs me that there are those who wish to speak. Wondering who this could be, I agree to listen.

The Council of Earth Vigilance says, "It is the we of us. It is the we of us. We are clamoring for your attention."

"You have it."

"It is most exciting for us to communicate with you."

Their enthusiasm surprises me and proves to be contagious. "What would you like to tell me today?"

"I wish to convey to you that there is another opportunity for you in the days ahead—one similar to that which you completed with the egg."

"Can you tell me more about it?"

"We will enjoy explaining to you now. As you hold the egg in your heart, in your hands—joined, of course, with your beloved—both of you holding the energy of it in your hearts, there is much that can be brought to the universes and all beyond. It is an opportunity that is in close proximity to these days; it is your decision on which day."

For many years I have paid special attention to solstices, equinoxes, and full moons, so choosing days that coincide with those events is a natural choice for me. "I have selected three dates for future work with Osiris," I tell the council. "They are the full moons of May and June and also the summer solstice. I know those are normally regarded as special energy days, but I'm open to any day that you feel would be a good day."

"It is in our consideration that, if you were to bring the

birthing of this same, or a similar egg, into the many dimensions you exist within, the elevation that you desire will come into focus even more swiftly," the council advises. "It is possible that you could be in the conjoined effort with your beloved in these higher dimensions. He is capable."

"I like working with him so that would be great," I say, but then I realize that I need to know the next steps to take. "Are you suggesting that I set a date at this time?"

"When you set a date, we can set the parameters."

I look at my calendar—the one with pictures of legendary heroes and mythological Gods and Goddesses and see that May 5 is the first day I am available to do the work. We set that date with the assumption that Tonas will be able to join me.

#

Thoth's first comment is, "That was interesting."

"Could you hear our conversation?"

"I was with my ear to the door, as you can imagine. There is a plan afoot. I can feel the excitement in the collective already."

"I'm excited, too," I tell him. "I would like for you to be on my team because I've always admired you. May I conscript you?"

"It would be difficult to keep me away from this opportunity."

"I don't know what the work will be on the three future dates I've selected. If you have any clues, I would appreciate your help in figuring out what to do."

"It is your willingness that brings the opportunity to the forefront, you see."

I assure him that I'm willing.

"You spoke the words to me. You spoke the desire, and you see what has transpired. The council immediately made itself known."

"I know, and they're so lovely."

"Ah, they are, indeed. They are quite enamored."

"It's funny, because you can tell by the way they talk that they don't normally communicate verbally."

"I believe this may be the first opportunity for them to speak the English."

"Yes, and they do well. Anyway, that's your homework, Thoth—the full moons and the summer solstice." I enjoy giving him this assignment. I can feel the teacher in me resurfacing.

"This will be delightful. You are finished with me?"

"Do you have anything else that you would like to tell me?"

Thoth explains that the CEV are suggesting applying an egg from each dimension. The last one was applied only from the 10th dimension.

"I'm hoping that this work helps us to move more quickly into the 8th dimension, because then I will likely *see* Tonas."

"Your motivation is love and also your enquiring thoughts, your desire to experience and to understand," Thoth says. "This is most delightful, most delightful indeed."

"And Tonas said that the regeneration of the physical body that I most want to experience is easier to do in the 8th dimension."

"It is the difference between swimming in dirt and swimming in water."

This analogy causes me to laugh and I say, "Okay then, I'm ready for water."

"You are lovely," Thoth says.

"Oh, I'd just like to hug you."

"Well, that will be sooner than later. So it is your Esthra you wish to speak with?"

"Yes."

"The call has been sent out. I understand he is projecting beside you."

# # #

I hear Esthra's distinctive voice announce that he is present.

"Hi, Esthra. Were you able to listen to the concert I just played?"

"My dear, the vision, as well as the sound, the essence, the particles of light that carried beauty that was to be heard and felt—they were carried out to the everything. I know you believe that you were less than proficient. Yet from my witness, you were spectacular."

"Esthra, I want to be able to say, 'Oh, wow, I really can play that piece of music much better than I used to be able to play it.' That's my goal, to really notice that I can play better. That goal is eluding me."

"Not for much longer. You must realize that the dimensional framework of the planet is supporting the higher vision, the easier development and forming of those realities that you desire. Those are your desires. The key element is never to add sawdust to the fire. Only add fuels of positives. When you witness yourself as you are playing—as you hear the beauty you are creating—drink it in. Drink in and see it as positive."

"I have been trying to be less critical of myself."

"You are successing in this, I tell you. I have witnessed your life; you are awakening to the true beauty of yourself at last."

# # #

"Is there anything else you can tell me that I would benefit from knowing?"

"Yes," Esthra says. "I must tell you that, as a child, you had a dream that you were someone of great importance. You knew this. It is only now that you are developing a greater understanding and acceptance of that truth."

I struggle to remember this dream, but it's no use. There

isn't even a hint of an impression. Esthra continues.

"I wish for you to know that there are many who revere you and have taken up position to assist you and those who birthed you. It is difficult for them; they are playing the story that many before them have played. We hold a bright star of hope that this kind of playing is soon to be no more."

These words encourage me. "I am all for that! I want to put the undertakers out of business. I am eager to show people that death is optional."

"They will be most pleased, I am sure—for there is no undertaker who relishes their position."

"I think I would like to talk with Tonas. I give you my love before I go."

# # #

Tonas is quick to ask, "Did I hear *love?*"

I can't help but giggle as I answer yes.

"My beauty, I know that those words were for another, and yet I wish for you to know that Esthra is also assisting me in these days."

"I didn't know that he was assisting you, but that's good. Guess what?"

"Hmm, I am guessing, but nothing is coming to my mind."

"We're going to have another egg!"

"We are having a baby!"

This starts me laughing again. "Oh, you're funny!"

"Ah, tell me more. It is ours, of course."

I let Tonas know that the CEV says we're going to be activating more eggs starting with the 11th dimension and going on up to the 25th. I can tell from his voice that he is excited about this and is already planning to do "homework." He lets me know the ship will easily transmit to those dimensions.

"Oh, and I have added Thoth to our team, since he helped

with the last egg we activated."

# # #

Tonas and I decide to ask Osiris to come to the ship to talk with us about what we will be doing.

Osiris answers, "Indeed, I am in presence. I am most delighted, of course, to return to this beautiful arena. What do you wish from me, my dear?"

"The Council for Earth Vigilance spoke with me, and they have more eggs for us."

"And what is their purpose?" he asks.

"I think Tonas and I are going to apply them from the 11th dimension and then on up."

"Oh, this is genius! I wonder that I did not think of it myself! I am so, so pleased with this opportunity."

His delight is encouraging. "Yes, it sounds really marvelous. May 5 is when we're going to do the next egg, but I'm not exactly sure *what* we're supposed to do."

"Let me find this information; give me a moment."

# # #

The CEV make themselves known, "It is us; it is we again. We are in great gratitude. There is among us the visioning—ah, the vision is here. The collective has the vision."

I learn they are going to give us one egg for each dimension and that we can apply them from Tonas's ship, beginning with the 11th dimension and moving all the way to the 25th. I agree to come and get the eggs on May 5.

"We are in gratitude."

"Thank you, I am also in gratitude."

"Is it appropriate for me to call you, *my dear*? Others apply this same verbiage."

"I like it," I say with a chuckle. "You have my permission to use it whenever you wish."

#

Osiris speaks again, "And so, we have the story! The grand story unfolds before us!" He exclaims, almost yelling. "This is most exciting! I am ready to jump off something high!"

I take a deep breath to calm myself in the face of all this enthusiasm.

"All can feel what is unfolding here," he says. "It is what I call a stream of unity, linking threads of that energy you are streaming from your 10th dimension into all the dimensions. It is something like a 'bonding agent,' as you would call it. Oh, this is most delightful, yes, indeed. I really want to jump off something very high."

I thank him for his assistance today and ask him to give my love to Isis.

#

Now that Osiris has left, I am finally ready to ask Tonas to share his experience of the concert with me.

"It was as if I were bathing in the sounds," he says. "I could feel the music moving through me like ribbons of light. It uplifted me; it raised me so high. All in presence were brought into ecstasy. You are a genius at playing the instrument."

His lavish praise catches of off-guard. "Thank you. Was your crew able to listen too?"

"Yes, we were all in ecstasy. It was, for us, a once-in-a-life experience."

"Why is that?"

"To be invited to Earth by you gave us the opportunity to come into this dimension that you exist within and to be present for that experience. You are so beautiful; to me you are like a treasured flower."

"What do I look like now?"

"First, let me kiss your fingers. You wear what you always like to wear."

"What is that?"

"It is flowing, it is long and creamy. Mmm, it shows your contour. You always come to me with the barest of feet. Shall I tell you what we do?"

"Yes."

"We go into our room of gazing and I pick two of the small orchids. I leave the stem a little length so that I may place it between two of your toes, and these are your slippers with the beautiful flowers between your toes. This is the vision that I always have of you. Your eyes are violet today."

"Ha, if only you could see me sitting here on my sofa in my front room. I'm wearing two shirts. One is pink and the other is this old sweatshirt that has some holes in it."

"Is this for ventilation?"

Laughing, I explain that it has holes because it's worn out. (No clothes with fake holes or tears for me. All the wear on *my* clothes is legitimate! The strategy I employ with this particular garment is to wear it until I realize it's too disreputable to be seen outside my house. I put it away, and then, after a sufficient amount of time has passed, I convince myself that surely it isn't *that* shabby, dig it out of storage, and wear it some more. I realize some might feel this is a sad commentary on the state of my wardrobe, but the sweatshirt is comfortable and I really like the color that has reached the perfect degree of fadedness.

Clothes are just not that important to me. Orchids, artwork, books, desserts, yes! Clothes, no. My idea of high fashion is wearing a neck scarf with my favorite pants and jacket.) "I need to find another sweatshirt, but I like it so much because it has an emblem on the front that says 'Life is Good.'"

"I like this; that is a focused thought. Life is good, and there is even more goodness that awaits you. You have lived in a time that has been hard; I know this. I know about the 3rd dimension and I understand what the human beings and all of the beings of Earth have undergone. You have had wars, disputes, and struggles to become a society that is evolving. But you have the vision, my dear. You have an incredible vision."

It is interesting to me that Tonas would say this. The idea of having any kind of "vision" has been lacking most of my life. Even now, it feels like I'm just making things up as I go along. But I don't feel that I can really say something like that to Tonas now.

#

A question pops into my mind about his crew. "Are there women on your ship?"

"There are women, yes."

"Good, I'm glad."

"Well, it would be different if there was only the masculine species. After all, the feminine, these are the individuals that have the greater minds."

I am initially skeptical about the validity of this statement, but then find myself hoping it is true. "Perhaps that is true in your dimension. I'd like for it to be true for my dimension as well, but I am not aware of any studies that support it. It seems to me that women just think about different things than men do."

"I wish that I had a mind like yours."

"I can't believe that you would wish that, Tonas! I can't even remember what I said yesterday and you can remember everything you've said through your whole life. That's incredible."

"Ah, but give me your mind in *this* dimension."

"Well, it'll be interesting to experience what my mind will

be like in the 10th dimension. I hope I'm much smarter and really good at math. Maybe I'll even understand second cousins and genealogy!"

"There will be so many exciting things that you will experience."

"Oh, yes, you're going to be busy."

"I have been waiting a lifetime. We will take some time off, as you would say, and I will show you the universes."

"That is an offer I will hold you to. I'm blowing you a kiss."

CHAPTER SIXTEEN

May 5, 2014

Esthra speaks to tell me he is present and accounted for.

"You had some homework," I remind him. "Were you able to come up with anything that would assist me at this time?"

"I believe that there are many opportunities for you. Please use your gate and move your consciousness into the great Hall of Records. This is a journey of heart, for there is a spark of you that is longing to be in the same resonance as the essence of your being."

Instantly, I find myself in a room of many books.

"Within these volumes," Esthra says, "I have handpicked what I would consider to be the pure, sweet imprinting of the many of your lineage who have achieved that spark of awareness that you desire."

I can feel that he has selected hundreds of books—bring them on!

"I have brought into this circle that which is of the greatest of proficiency in the playing of instruments of all kinds. I have art, architecture, horticulture, as well as singing, dancing, and poetry. These volumes are ready to be added as if they were of your story. Are you interested?"

"I definitely am. May I ask an additional question?"

"Of course."

"What about athletic ability and prowess in movement? I know that dancing is part of that, but I'm also interested in just being able to move gracefully on a day-to-day basis."

"This is why I selected dancing," he explains, "because it takes a great deal of strength and also balance as well as timing. There are many kinds of dance, and this takes into consideration the dances that are known on many worlds as well as universes. Do you see?"

"Yes! How exciting!"

"There is a little planet not in this system, not in this universe; it is the planet of Folgor. The dancing is on the fingertips. It is quite beautiful."

"Do you mean that they move their fingers in the air to convey the dance?"

He pauses, as if to consider the best words. "Instead of their legs, they are on their fingers, and it is as if their bodies are of rubber. They are dancing and they are moving. It is quite hypnotic."

"Are they humanoid?"

"Yes, they are humanoid."

At this moment I decide that somehow, sometime, I'm going to see the Folgorians do this impossible dancing. "I love knowing things like that, Esthra. Thank you."

"Now I am of great excitement to bring this opportunity to you. Are you ready?"

"Yes, I am."

Esthra directs me to the center of the room, and once again the books rise off the shelves to "dance" around me; the pages open and the information within them flows into my levels of consciousness in the form of energy.

"As before," he reminds me, "the information will be fully integrated during your sleep tonight."

# # #

I decide I'd better check in with the CEV, so I thank Esthra and release him. Then I gate into presence with the council.

"Greetings. We are most pleased that you are here with us today."

"I am pleased to be with you also."

"We have been preparing."

"May I request that Osiris hears the instructions that you are going to give to me today?"

"Yes, he is most welcome."

After checking with them, Osiris confirms his understanding of their previous instructions for me. When I ask why we can't offer eggs to the 8th and 9th dimensions, the CEV tells me that I can't do that until there is a percentage of physical bodies—as well as energy bodies—in those two dimensions.

They give me the eggs and tell me that we must activate them one at a time in each dimension. We are to begin with the 11th dimension egg, and will activate it aboard Tonas's ship.

"All right, I just love you guys. I really do," I tell them. "Thank you so much and my blessings to all of you."

"We are in great admiration."

# # #

On the ship, Tonas asks, "Beloved at heart, may I assist you? We have a special place for these eggs. Perhaps we should invite Osiris."

"I agree. He listened to the CEV so that he would have an idea of what we're supposed to do, so that I'm not the only one. Osiris, if you will join us?"

Osiris says, "I am present. I was simply waiting for an invitation. There are protocols, as you know."

Osiris waits as Tonas and I activate and stream the energies of the regular orbs to Earth. Then he directs Tonas to bring the ship into the 11th dimension.

Osiris instructs Tonas and me to stand and look at one another, eye to eye and heart to heart. We are to hold the egg between us and charge the energy of it with our hearts. He adds that this energy will reach from our 11th dimension outward into all that exists.

"As the threads open up, the two of you are standing with this treasured egg between you. It is the cosmic element of the vision of the one, and it is transmitting to all dimensions through your joined hearts, touching upon all of the threads of creation, all that exists, all that is, always."

I am grateful that he pauses here—it gives me a chance to absorb his beautiful words. "As this light between you ignites and moves into your hearts, breathe it into yourself and hold the vision as you have before. This vision is of the unity of all that exists coming into focus in all of its timing—and yet, drawn into a dance of its own as it moves each world, each spark of light, every cosmos, every star, every universe. All that is within each of these, whether it is a spark of light, a stream of water, a bird, the sky, it is all one, and linking now to the full timing of Earth itself. It is a reminder to all from this dimension of the 11th that this is the journey home."

We follow this same procedure for dimensions twelve through seventeen. The egg colors were: orange for 11th, red for the 12th, deep-sea green for the 13th, aqua for the 14th, sun yellow for the 15th, gold for the 16th, plum for the 17th, rose pink for the 18th and lime green for the 19th dimension.

# # #

As Tonas and I finish activating the egg for the 19th dimension, Osiris says," I believe your beloved Tonas is ready to stop."

"I also feel a need to stop," I reply. "My body and brain feel too full of this energy to experience any more right now."

"I understand," Osiris replies. "It is as if the two of you are of drunkenness on love and unity and fellowship and the great desires of the heart for unity. Both of you have been instrumental in quickening the greater plan in a way and many ways that are priceless to all of us. We are in gratitude."

After Osiris leaves, I ask Tonas if he's okay.

"I can't describe my feelings," he says. "I'm elated, but my arms and legs are so rubbery that I feel I'm not in control of my own body. And I'm feeling swimmy in the head."

I'd like to offer a sympathetic response, but it's just too much trouble. The inside of my head is swirling.

"My heart is still intact, of course. We were wonderful together. Thank you for bringing these great works into my experience of life."

Too disoriented to say much, I agree. "It was wonderful."

"May we rest together?"

"Of course."

I promise to stay on his ship for a little while.

CHAPTER SEVENTEEN
May 9, 2014

Esthra greets me by saying he is at my disposal, any time.

"Good morning, Esthra. If your memory is not good, you might need a pencil and paper. I've got a long list."

"Let us move through your magical list."

"The last twenty or so years, I've been interested in alchemy and the Kabbalah. The understanding that people have of those modalities or those methods of inquiry are interesting to me. I would like to understand more. Today, it's about knowledge and wisdom."

"I see. You must know that there are many of your lineage who were interested in that knowledge and wisdom as well. They activated those levels of consciousness that inspired within them a greater understanding of what is possible. Through their connection to universal consciousness—the consciousness of all that exists—they were aware of the ability of the mind to create that which is silver into gold, that which is tin into gold."

"Exactly. I have spent quite a bit of time reading about the theories of alchemy."

"Those theories were based on 3rd dimensional beliefs. You will develop the divine version of this skill in the future, because you are advancing your abilities as you move into the higher dimensions," he says. "In the higher dimensions, there is less resistance, so the thought manifests. You'll be able to make a candy wrapper into gold."

I chuckle, thinking of this. "Well, in the meantime, if any of that knowledge would be of benefit to me here, I would like to know more now."

"It is that passion within you that all of us experience in our incarnations," Esthra responds. "In all sentient life there is a passion to know more."

#

"Are there such beings as the jinn?"

"Yes, of course."

"I've always been fascinated by stories about Solomon and how he was able to control the jinn to help him build the temple. Are you aware of Solomon?"

"Of course. Solomon, when he controlled the jinn, was controlling and directing nature itself. He was directing motion, energy, form, function, and all that was part of the greater vision of the creation of what he desired. Solomon was not magical. He was, instead, *inspired.*"

"One of the healers that I worked with in the past told me that, in one of my lives, I was a jinn," I tell him. "Is there any truth to that?"

"Yes, I would say that you have experienced ninety-four lives, as you would call them, of being a genie."

"Maybe that's why I've been so fascinated with them." I muse, and then continue with my list. "Here's some more of my list: people who are mathematicians, scientists, physicists, or biologists. Math has always been challenging for me; numbers have been difficult for me to understand."

My first school trauma happened in second grade when Miss Roland told us we were not to count on our fingers anymore. I still use them—surreptitiously, of course—when counting in the 9s. To be truthful, fingers are also helpful with my 6s, 7s, and 8s. Take *that,* Miss Roland!

"And, of course, with mathematics there is science," he says. "These two go closely together; without the math how could there be the science."

"That's right. If there's part of my brain that can be stimulated to help me understand those kinds of things better, that would be great."

"I see."

"I'm also looking at people who are innovators, explorers, naturalists who have a wide understanding of nature, plants, animals, herbs, and those kinds of things. And wealthy people. I must have had *some* lifetimes when I was wealthy. At one time in my life, when I only had fifty dollars in my checking account, I was struck with this feeling of absolute abundance. There must be a mind-set, an allowing and visualizing and accepting of wealth, that has somewhat eluded me in this lifetime. I know that I will have money."

"Always, my dear."

"Yes, I've been told that by people; however, there is a feeling of being wealthy that I'm not readily able to embrace."

"So you would wish for this?"

"Yes. I want to be able to completely accept abundance in any form and the feeling of being wealthy."

"And?"

"I'm also interested in people who were equestrians who had the ability to bond with horses and ride skillfully."

"And, of course, the ability to speak to the animal."

"Yes. I'm supposedly going to develop that ability."

"Even as we are speaking, you are developing this skill. There are mechanisms already in place that have been applied for many weeks."

"All right. Here's more of my list: artists, authors, singers, mystics, druids, and polyglots. They're called polyglots because they can speak many different languages. Also, is there such a thing as people who are lucky?"

"Those such as yourself, you are speaking about."

"Good. If there's a lucky gene, I'd like that activated."

# # #

On the ship, Tonas says, "Beloved, I must kiss your fingers before we begin."

"Oh good, because I want to have just a moment to say hello and chat before we dive into this work again."

"I wish for you to know what I have been experiencing; it is as if I am a celebrity. Everyone is aware of my affiliation with you and they all wish to know what it must be like to be in your presence. They are most enamored with this project. It is as if my whole life has been waiting for this moment in time! You have given me this gift and I am so grateful!"

"It wouldn't have felt right for me to do this by myself."

"Oh, you must know, I am so committed to Earth. I am so committed to humanity. Every one of my breaths is directed to the focus of bridging the most graceful expansion for each and every element of Gaia."

"I appreciate that."

"It is such a joy to be in your presence and to assist you, as I have been able to in small ways. What we have done in this short period is grander and more expansive than anything that I and others on this ship have been able to accomplish."

Tonas suggests that I invite the others to join us and I request the presence of Osiris, Isis and Thoth on Tonas's lovely Night Sky.

Osiris speaks first, "Oh, if you knew the magnitude of today, my dear. Thank you and my beloved thanks you as well, for it is a gift to her to be in this position to be partaking in the 'great spectacle,' as it was called earlier. I like this word, 'spectacle.' We are in readiness and Thoth is here. He is most enamored with me and, of course, wishes never to talk over me."

"Hello, Thoth. Do you have a partner?"

He tells me Maat is his partner. "If you invite her, she will join us."

Feeling that everyone here should have a partner, I invite her.

When I ask her about their connection, she tells me, "I am the other part of his heart. He is, of course, the other part of myself as well. Shall we begin?"

"Yes."

Maat says that she has the violet egg and that we are starting with the 20th dimension. Isis steps forward and asks Tonas and me to allow our joined hearts to ignite the great spirit of this egg.

As we do so, Isis reminds us that the threads of golden light that stream from it are connecting to everything that exists in this 20th dimension. She then asks us to draw the principles of this higher light into ourselves so that we carry the vision of what is to be. When we are finished, Tonas moves the ship to the 21st dimension.

Thoth directs us in assisting the ruby red egg to ignite and unify all that exists with this 21st dimension of Earth.

Maat directs us in activating a mossy green ovum for the 22nd dimension as well as a sapphire ovum for the 23rd dimension.

Osiris guides us in activating an emerald egg for the 24th dimension. He informs us that, "It is the emerald and the diamond (25th dimension) that birth the new future for Earth, and for all of us in all extremes of that which exists everywhere. This spectacle, as the great councils have coined the phrase, is the deliverance. This is the foundation."

# # #

Isis speaks, "And now, my dears, it is for you, Tonas, with your consciousness...ah, I understand. Tonas wishes for you to, with your mind, direct the ship to the 25th."

I gladly acquiesce.

"He is most greatly excited that you have done so."

After we activate the diamond egg, Isis tells us, "It is the foundational rock that sets the future into its final phase." She explains that, "the true presence of your being exists in this dimension."

"Thank you for your assistance with this."

"We are grateful to be part of this work."

# # #

Tonas finally speaks to say he is high with excitement. "I love that *you* brought the ship into the 25th dimension. Would you like to bring us into the 10th?"

"Absolutely."

Back in the 10th dimension, Tonas says, "I am exhausted. I feel as though someone has drained the essence from me, and yet I also feel as if someone has lit me on fire. You are amazing. You are still in such great form."

"I'm drowsy," I say. "Thank you for your help today."

"I was but a witness, complying with your every desire. No, I was participating. I must, as Isis mentioned, also own acceptance of this tremendous honor that has been offered me."

"Yes!" I'm glad he is finally willing to accept his importance in facilitating our work together.

"It has brought me great celebrity," he reminds me, sounding bashful.

"Yes, movie star status."

"Yes, the stars are in readiness to accept it. (I guess Tonas doesn't know about movie stars.) And the status of them and their great excitement does elevate."

"I'll talk to you soon, dearest."

"As always, we will meet here in our room of viewing, our star window."

"Goodbye for today, Tonas."

"It is never goodbye for my heart; it is always, 'Hello.'"

I smile and say, "Hello."

CHAPTER EIGHTEEN

May 14, 2014

Esthra says, "Ah, this is our time together that we planned. I have been working with my homework."

"What have you done with it?"

"I've been preparing. Of course, your mathematics, your philosophers, all sciences, those that are of great prosperity—the forethought in my mind has been to develop some seedbed foundations so that you can shed that feeling of being in poverty or of wanting and take on the royal robes of prosperity for yourself. It was your desire to feel what it is to be wealthy. I worked with your idea of luckiness. I think that is simply being firmly instilled in an energy flow that allows the positives to come readily to you."

I am impressed with the research dear Esthra has done, and he is eager to tell me more.

"The scientist mind—opening your mind to see that which can be when there is nothing, to continue the inner search for that which could be and can be and seeing beyond the empty screen, so to speak—is something that would benefit you. It would help you to step out of the space of wondering and the needing of yourself to follow certain paths that meet the requirements that you set in your mind most firmly."

"That sounds good."

"The scientist's mind is open to whatever comes forth and then, of course, the direction until the goal is met. It is actually easier than judging that you are not meeting your highest of potentials. It is about what is and what can be rather than what isn't and what you haven't done. Thus, I believe that the greatest of these is the scientist."

"That's the kind of mind I long for."

"Yes, I know that. The singers and mystics—those were easy for me, as well as your authors and your explorers and those who know about the plants of Earth. I have been working to support your understanding of alchemy and wisdoms as well as using the wisdoms that are available to you in your many levels of consciousness. The Kabbalah, for example, is an ancient philosophy."

"I must have had some lives as a Kabbalist."

"Perhaps more than forty thousand lives," he affirms.

This is staggering information to me. No wonder I've been so interested in studying the Kabbalah!

Esthra continues, "There are many of your lineage who are of the ancient world of human through to the present of day, and they have followed these mindsets of the unified force. These support your alchemy as well as the Kabbalah."

# # #

His mention of my staggering number of incarnations has made me wonder something. "Have I ever been someone in history who would be considered famous or someone I would have read about?"

"You would be pleased to know there are many, including your Joan of Arc."

This is quite a surprise to me.

"I spoke to you about her now because I know you are interested in horses, and she had a special knowledge of her horse and all horses. She spoke to horses at a unique level. She had a means of reaching in and uplifting all those around her. She was a great ... we will call her a woman ... and she was young at her death."

"Are you saying that one of my lives was Joan of Arc?"

"She is near you on the matrix. Does this please you?"

"Yes, it does."

Esthra remarks that it pleases him, also.

"And there was an Amazon queen that came up one time. I

forget her name now."

"There is a long line of powerful women in your lineage. You think of yourself as weak in this life. You think that you gave in to men, handed over your presence for men."

"Yes."

"But I know the truth. You are strong, but the passions within you led you to hand over much of your great power. And yet, look what you have done in this moment—and even in the past, leading to this moment. You are and have risen to the position of being one of the powerful women of Earth. Look what you are doing for the world, even today."

While I acknowledge to him that I'm excited about the work we did today, accepting the idea of being one of the powerful women of Earth is difficult for me to own. I decide not to comment, because power isn't really important to me anyway.

Esthra suggests that we postpone this work in order to make sure I have time to complete the work I have planned for today. I agree that's probably best. I still intend to speak with the CEV.

# # #

The CEV announce that they are in presence.

"Good afternoon. Do you have a more personal name than overseer?"

"We are a collective."

"I'll just keep saying Council for Earth Vigilance then."

"This is appropriate. We are a collective."

I'm amused by the council's insistence on identifying as a group.

"I wanted to let you know that I feel that this work is probably the most important work that I can do. I want to make sure that you know that I am willing and, hopefully, able to do whatever you come up with whenever you come up with it. You have my approval to communicate with me at any time, even if I have not directly called upon you. Do you understand what I'm saying?"

"Yes. This meets all guidelines."

"Good. I'm open to your suggestions, but I do have a couple of things that I would like to do in June. I know we have something scheduled for the full moon in June and also for the summer solstice."

"Go on."

"To me, the summer solstice—at least according to the reading I've done—is about the balance of the masculine and feminine. That has been an issue for me personally in this lifetime. I believe there is also an imbalance on Earth at this time concerning the masculine and feminine energies. I would love to have your assistance in balancing those energies, and hopefully that would also assist me."

"Let us understand. You wish assistance with the unified focus of the mind, the unified focus of the heart, the unified focus of the beings all in their joined presence, as well as individuals."

"Yes. Can you assist us with that on the twenty-first of June, as well as anything else you would like to do?"

"This would be interesting for us, as we are in tune with the collective consciousness of Earth. It is the individual part of self that we lack understanding of, though we have witnessed humanity. I will tell you that there would be no wars if what you dream for Earth could be achieved."

"I believe that, because women would not like to send people into war. Most of the women I know abhor that sort of thing. It's not in our nature to want to kill. So ... if you'd like to help me with this masculine/feminine balance issue, that's a little bit of homework for you."

"We are in delight."

I ask the CEV if there is anything additional they would like to assist me with.

"Yes. There is a new star."

"What does that mean?"

"This star, which is just a little spark at this time, will assist the vision of unity you are holding." They tell me the star is to be positioned in the 10th dimension and it has the power to shine through all the dimensions.

"When it is placed within the sky in the specific range that is nearest the Moon, it will take on a greater brightness that will shine. It will most gracefully shine upon the Earth as if it was in its own energy—and yet, many will see this incredible brightness as if it was Saturn."

I ask if the star has a name and they suggest *I* name it. I have no idea what to say, but I'm delighted when they ask if it would be appropriate to suggest, "Joy."

They add, "We would love to see this star named after you."

"I would love it to be named after me!"

"It will shine from the 10th dimension through to your 6th and 7th dimensions, and into the 5th and 4th. This will indeed shine brightly as a mirror onto Saturn."

"This is thrilling for me!"

"It is appropriate for it to be today, for it is the conjunction of Moon and Saturn."

"How do I receive this beautiful spark of star?"

"Move your position to us."

"All right, hold on a minute. I'll use a gate. Okay, here I am."

"Place your hand outward, my dear. It is but the tiniest of a spark. It is *Joy*."

I feel so tender toward this little spark that I say, "I'm going to take it into my heart, too."

"I believe this is appropriate. It is also appropriate for you to move directly into that one's (Tonas's) ship."

"All right, I will be speaking with you soon. Thank you again."

"It is our honor."

#

Tonas comes forward, "Welcome, my beloved."

"Hello, Tonas."

"Let me see what you have in your hand."

"I'm so excited about it! It's a new star!"

"It is small for a star."

"It's going to get bigger and … it's named after me!"

"Ah, this is such a tremendous honor."

"I know it is! And we're going to put it in the sky and it's going to shine onto Saturn and onto all the dimensions of Earth. Ooh!"

"Very exciting. Where will we put it?"

"I asked them to let Osiris know the information also, so I think he'll be able to help us place it. Let me have a hug, please."

I surprise myself with this request, but as soon as I say it I'm glad I asked him to touch me in a different way. I have yet to feel our contact in the dimension of my everyday life; however, this is one thing I have, uncharacteristically, decided to be patient about waiting to experience.

"First, may I kiss—I will kiss the other hand. You may trade hands with this lovely spark of star. Now let us embrace. Mmm, this is a joy for me. Are we inviting Osiris and the human, the Buddha?"

"Yes."

"May I do it this time?"

"Yes, go right ahead."

"If I had trumpets I would play them. I understand there are always trumpets when someone important is being ushered into a sacred space. I will now invite the great Osiris and the great human, Master Buddha."

#

Osiris speaks first. "My dear, this is an electric day. You are unstoppable!"

"I'm excited!"

"I have just returned from the council. I have the full understanding of what is to be applied. Of course, we have Buddha here; he is smiling upon you. I know he has something to say, but let me speak for one more moment so that you are aware."

Osiris always has something to explain, and I am always happy to hear it.

"This is an important time. It is what you would call a 'conjunct.' The Earth's Moon and Saturn appear so close together that the two of them shine as if they are a sun. Indeed, this is May fourteenth, an important day."

"So this is a great time for this star to be born?"

"Indeed. What we can do today is to position your new little 10th dimension star—and indeed it will grow—to radiate onto Saturn. Saturn is taking on the full radiance of the Moon, and Joy will join that radiance, transforming the Moon and Saturn to a brightness that you will be able to see with your eyes this night."

I am overwhelmed by the thought of this.

"It will be at your discretion how you position this star. If it were me, I would move with your beautiful Tonas from the ship out into the expanse and release it like a butterfly."

"I would like that."

"It will find its ideal position in the 10th dimension sky. This sky is always black as ink, as you would say, except for the pinpoints of beautiful stars—and because Earth is right before us, we can see it on this 10th dimension. I will assist where I can. I wish to honor our guest."

# # #

"I am in presence, my dear."

Here is someone, along with many others like Thoth, Osiris, and Isis, that I never imagined I'd be able to say hello to. With a big smile on my face and delight in my heart, I say, "Hello, Buddha. Is there anything we can do to assist the beautiful festival of Wesak?"

"There is a possibility of the rainbow rain of light."

"Yes. Will you explain what that will do?"

"Your kind gentleman here has the ability to magnify the streams of light that are a part of those threads that you have linked to all of the dimensions. You could create rainbow streams of light pouring onto Earth, and then turn them outward to reflect in all directions like a sun. They would move into every space of awareness of each of the dimensions, all leading to the 25th."

I try to picture this amazing sight.

"Following outward on all of those threads—can you imagine what the rainbow rain of light could do to saturate all of those—let us call them 'realms of being'—that are in their deciding moments of experience? It is an elevation that speaks to the heart, which then speaks to the actions of individuals."

"This sounds like a perfect thing to do," I say, thrilled with this grand idea.

"If we are all in agreement, may I be honored by guiding you in the steps?"

After I agree to this, Osiris asks what I would like to do first. I decide that we should put the star in place and then activate the rainbow streams of light. Tonas agrees with me that Osiris can guide us in placing the Joy Star.

Osiris suggests "Let us all move out into the expanse." He sees my hesitation and adds, "You will be fine, Joy. We will all simply step through the outer casing of the ship. Close tightly over your star, my dear. If we can all position ourselves in a circle, we are choosing to be the instrument of the great councils, of the great prince of all that is, that which is our spirit of being.

Each of you, bring your hands inward to the circle. My Joy, please move the star so that it stands on the fingertips of all of us. This is an appropriate time for you to say something."

"I love, I love, I love. I joy, I joy, I joy. I shine, I shine, I shine. And so it is."

"The star is rising upward and positioning directly above this ship. This is most exciting; it is beginning to expand. It is as if pulses of a heartbeat," Osiris continues. "I wish to offer you advice, if you are interested in hearing some wisdom from me."

"Yes, please."

"This star—would it be more helpful with a sentient essence of being within it?"

"It would, indeed."

"Hmm, I was thinking of someone from your lineage who is waiting and hoping to be of great service. There is an essence of being that is present and desiring to enter that place of incarnation. To incarnate as this star would be a most grateful opportunity for any essence of being."

"How can we make this happen?"

"You can petition a council." Osiris offers to assist me. When I accept, he steps with me into the presence of this unnamed council whose function is to define which essence of being enters which presence of being.

Following Osiris's suggestion, I speak to this council. "We just placed a star in the 10th dimension above Earth. The star is named 'Joy' after me, and this is a great honor that I am delighted and blessed to have. I would like for a sentient essence of my soul lineage who would be interested in being part of this joyful star to be able to incarnate into it."

The council says, "It is granted."

"Thank you."

Osiris interjects, "I think we should leave. We are all in gratitude; let us move back to the ship."

As we move, Osiris says, "This is something that you will be doing yourself with your physical presence, your thoughts bringing you exactly where you wish. Tonas can turn the ship so that we can see the star. Joy, do you have something that you wish to transmit to this new, incarnated being that is about to change the history of Earth?"

"I'd like to thank them and hope that they enjoy being joyful and shining. Would they like to speak?"

"This one seems to be speaking directly to your heart. It is new; we will let it grow. The star knows what it is meant to do. This essence of being has entered and it is integrating its placement. She likes her name, I am sure, for joy is a vibration in itself of great sweetness. I think we should hand the next stage to Buddha."

# # #

Buddha speaks, "I am in awe of what is occurring. I was aware of the exploits of you and this one, and we are all excited about the vision that you have. You will be quite excited about the vision that is coming, for as you continue to expand your awareness, you will have even more visions that will draw the curtain on the oldest stories and open to a new pleasurable dream of bliss."

Buddha's energy is delicious. I can see why people revered him as a teacher and holy man because his words are powerful yet gentle. I could listen to him all day.

"Your heart is pure; you may not see it as pure, my dear. I see your heart as it is; you see your heart as it was. Draw now into the present moment with your dear Tonas. He has the ability to turn the fractals of the crystalline outer casing of his ship into a pinpoint director, much like a laser beam."

I do my best to be fully present for this astonishing experience.

"There are many colors within all of the dimensions of those threads that came from your eggs. Those can become rainbow streams unto Earth first. And so, Tonas, I ask that you affect your ship in some way to bring this reality into being. Very good, the essence of the colors of the threads is being amplified. And now, as if the rain of the most beautiful light beams of radiance, you can cause these energies to rain the streams onto the Earth. You have this in your heart. I ask that you cause this to be."

I decide to tell them what some part of me is witnessing. "I see the light beams of radiance flowing. They intertwine, they split, they blend and they flow, flow, flow around the Earth as they touch all the grids and every molecule of Earth. They flow down through the Earth, into the center of the Earth, and then flow back out again to the surface and into the atmosphere and into the grids—pulsing and beaming and flowing with beautiful divine light, twinkling and sparkling while the star shines down on it all."

Buddha continues, "Your star is becoming quite bright. It is dedicating its energy beams to Saturn and the Earth's Moon. There are places on Earth that are in darkness already and the Moon is, in this moment, becoming ever brighter. And of course, the beauty of this exquisite planet, the planet of Saturn, is caught on the energy streams of the Moon as well as its own brightness—and now Joy shines upon it."

"And so it is. Joy shines upon us all!" I say with great delight.

"Joy does shine upon us all through this dimension. It is important for you to know that the corona of the Moon is brought into the greatest of radiance from this Joy that becomes brighter and brighter," the Buddha tells me.

"Will the people and astronomers in this dimension be able to see this star?" I ask.

"They will in this 10th dimension, certainly, and perhaps even in the 6th and 7th. It would be somewhat difficult in its positioning right at this moment, because it is positioned specifically like a spotlight onto the planet Saturn."

"Do you think it will be moving?"

"I believe we should ask."

"Whom do we ask?"

Joy, the star, makes herself known. "You would ask me. I am Joy."

"Hello, hello, hello. I'm so glad to hear you speak!"

"I am so glad to meet you. You have given me purpose."

"I feel like crying."

"Instead, my dear, bathe in the radiance of my beauty. I am crystal clear and transmitting all of the colors."

"I am excited to know what you are doing and to have you named Joy. Will you be moving, or have you planned that out yet?"

"I believe that my purpose is to be in position wherever I may be of service, and so I will migrate."

"That sounds like a plan. And you will be joyful as you do it?"

"Oh yes! I believe I will dance across the skies."

"It's a new dance."

"It is a dance of joy. Thank you for my life."

# # #

Tonas reminds me that we should say something to Buddha.

"You can thank him, because I am already thanking him."

"It is our supreme pleasure and honor to have you on my ship and supporting my dear beloved and her world—which has now become my world."

Buddha replies, "It is my desire to hold a vision of you in my heart all this day and of all you have offered through this bright and shiny Joy Star. I will hold this throughout the whole day of celebration. Like a candle shining upon the Sun and the moonlit Earth, you are Joy."

Tonas tells me Buddha is gone.

"What a day!"

"It was quite amazing, and we are all aware of this Buddha."

"I've never worked with him in this manner. It was a privilege to meet him."

"I thought he was lovely. His clothing was understated."

I find this statement humorous. "You always wear black," I tease. "That is understated."

"That is untrue. I also wear jewelry, which I design and create. And my hair parts on different sides, where it will. I coiffed it so that it is extra fluffy today."

No man on this dimension would ever say anything like that—well, most men would not, anyway.

"I coiffed it so that it is more fluffy," he repeats, "and long, as you like it."

Long, beautiful hair is one of the most sensual things I can imagine for a man to have. If only I could feel the silkiness of his hair.

"Mine is beautiful. It is of the darkest, like the night sky," he explains.

My compulsion to attempt to feel the texture of his hair overpowers me. I can no longer resist asking him if I may touch it.

"Please do. You make take some with you."

"Oh, really?"

"Of course, put it under your pillow."

"You can grow it back, right?"

"With a thought," he assures me.

#

It occurs to me that Tonas never has much of an opportunity to tell me about anything that is happening in his personal life. I am always asking him questions. In an attempt to be more courteous, I ask, "Tonas, is there anything you want to ask me?"

"Yes. I am somewhat reticent to bring this to your attention. My mother and father wish some day in the future to come into your acquaintance. They are interested in my passion for you. They are very much *parents*."

"That's how parents are. I told my parents today that I was going to be traveling tomorrow and they were immediately worried about my safety."

"Do they know about me?"

"No … they wouldn't understand. I've only told two close friends about you. People would think that I was crazy if I started talking about what I'm doing, especially if I mentioned you. Everything I've been experiencing is so beyond the possibility of most people in this reality, they would think I was making this all up—or that there really was something wrong with me mentally."

"The days for this prejudice and close-mindedness are soon coming to an end, I am sure."

"I hope so. What I do with you is really wonderful."

"You must know that it is awesome, even for us, that such things should be occurring from this point in space."

"I would love to consciously meet your parents. I'm sure your mother could tell me some interesting things about you. Do they know about our work?"

"They're excited about what we are doing," Tonas replies. "For them to be in your presence is perhaps a feather in their hat, you see."

"When you say things like that, I always have to remind myself you're talking about me. My mind just says, 'What? What is he talking about?'"

"My parents are aware of what we are doing and it is such an excitement for them."

"It's exciting for me, too—but I just feel like a regular person, Tonas. We are doing wonderful things together, I know.

However, I'm sitting here in my blue sweat pants and my old blue sweater that, I see, has a stain on the front of it. I'm just Joy."

"You are wearing a beautiful golden gown with a pearl belt that is so beautiful and delicate. Your hair is flowing to your hips and it is also golden today."

Giggling, I remind Tonas that I'm still just trying to get to the 8th dimension so that I can see him.

"You will see me before then, I hope. Whether it be today or tomorrow or any day, is not determined on your 8th dimension as much as it is on your development, which is coming beautifully along. Look how you were directing today! It was as if the great Isis herself was leading. You were amazing! You must know this, of course."

"There were wonderful people helping me," I say. "The star was so special."

"It is, even in this moment, shining so beautifully. Am I meant to continue the radiance to Earth through the whole day of Wesak?"

"I think that would be a good idea."

"Then it will be so."

CHAPTER NINETEEN

May 19, 2014

Melchizedek speaks, "Ah, at last, my dear."

"Sorry to keep you waiting."

"It is not about being late," he says. "I am excited that at last I may speak with you about our project. I need your permission to extend, for we are nearing our time of completing our work together."

"I've been traveling and I missed a few nights, and last night I felt just like sitting and not moving around."

"There is no way for you to apply this incorrectly, as long as your mind is in action," he reminds me. "As long as your mind is visioning what is possible, that is what we are focusing on."

Melchizedek continues with a description of some minor changes he wants to implement during our sessions together. Knowing of my love of music, he asks me to pretend, for one minute, that he has an orchestra director's baton.

"As my wand directs you, it is as if you are becoming fluid in the energies of that transmission from my mind, my heart, and my inner energies of muse. Now, imagine a song that you would wish for me to direct and that your hands are gracefully holding your violin and bow."

I lift my hands into position, but Melchizedek says that is not necessary at this time—it might be useful later, though. He continues his explanation with, "It is as if the wand in my hand is directing your heart, for it is the heart that feels the deepest of movement within the movement. That is where you become fluid; that is where you become fully immersed in the music. Know that you are the music and you are the instrument, for the music is coming from your heart."

Melchizedek says that, since we are moving into a higher range of energy, we can shorten our practice time together to a period of nine or eleven minutes.

"This is agreeable to me."

"If you wish to go longer, just indicate that telepathically to me. Remember, you have individuals that you revere who are the players of such instruments. These individuals hear the music not in their head— they feel it first and hear it first in their heart, and that is what transmits the energy to all points of the body through the vibrations. You are made of water; imagine that radiance of water carrying the beauty of that sound."

# # #

"May I ask you a question about my third eye?"

"Yes, of course."

"What is the status of it currently? Does it work? Is it open? How is it supposed to work?"

"The third eye," he says, "directs energy as well as thought and form. It is instrumental in manifestation, creating and forming energies, as well as drawing energies to you. It is one of the chakras, and as you know, these chakras are part of the energy of forming in all of your realities. Yet the third eye also is linked to your pineal gland. It is as if one hand holds the bow while the other hand positions on the strings to make the notes. The physical and energetic work together."

"Have you been working on that also?"

"I have been working more with the energy in your physical structure, as well as on your heart itself. Perhaps it is time for me to add your third eye."

"Thank you. I would like that."

Melchizedek agrees to assist me with energy from my third eye as well as the energy associated with my pineal. "Most of the other chakras make connection to that point, you know."

"I didn't know that, but anything that you can help me with, I appreciate."

"Very well. Thank you for letting me know of your desire. I

will ponder this. I will become creative."

I remember that he is not the only being guiding my development. "Esthra is going to do some work with me with some of the traits and abilities of my soul lineage that I admire, like artists and explorers," I tell Melchizedek.

"May I witness?"

"Yes, I'd love that."

# # #

Esthra speaks. "My dear, it is quite exciting for us to begin and, of course, I am aware of your collaboration with Melchizedek. He is quite someone that I admire."

"Me too. As usual, I do have a few questions."

"I am at your disposal."

"You mentioned a while ago that I've had maybe forty thousand lives as a Kabbalist. How many lives have I actually lived?"

"The question might be, 'How many more are associating with this incarnation?'"

Esthra and I have a rather long discussion, during which he confirms that forty-seven goddesses created this universe and that all universes experience forty-seven soul lineages. Three of those lineages are referred to as the masculine, feminine, and neutral lineages. My soul is of the feminine (mother) line, and every thirtieth or fortieth person I might meet in a large mall would be from this line. He also tells me that, although I shall always be of the goddess line, I will begin experiencing more neutrality as masculine and neutral energies blend with me.

"Think of the matrix that the forty-seven lineages form as a colorful kaleidoscope. The fractals move and shift to create new pictures."

I loved looking into a kaleidoscope when I was little, but this analogy does not help me understand what Esthra is describing. It does help me see that the matrix is completely unlike the multi-level marketing plan picture I've been imagining.

Esthra adds, "You are not meant to grasp this fully. If you were to take all experiences and the connections of the matrix of all you have at your disposal at this present moment, it would create madness. The smaller framework of connection within the matrix is more important, for this helps you to stay in the present. Also, some of these incarnations are interesting experiences, but they are less important for you to bring into this incarnation. Please know that many of your lineage are in other universes and other worlds and dimensions."

# # #

This new information is shaking up my previously held ideas about my own incarnations.

"I've had past life regressions in which I experienced some of my incarnations," I tell Esthra.

"Those are in the pod of the smaller number of individuals that are within the shorter length of the matrix," he explains. "There is no linear progression that is matched within the matrix. There is no way that you can say, this person, and then they had this person; it is not like your genetic lineage. It is random in that you are existing now and Isis herself was/is as old as time."

"I guess I'd better just let this go."

"If you ponder this at your sleeping time, your mind will work it out."

And now I decide to find out more about something that happened to me in the 1990s.

"What about the walk-in experience that I had? I have a different soul now than I had when I first came into this life."

"This has not been a detriment, my dear."

"Yes, I know that it wasn't. But I've only had one walk-in, correct?"

"Indeed. Let us call it that you *stepped* in—you, Great One, stepped into that body. You are not a walk-in. The body experienced your essence taking presence within it."

"That feels nice."

"It is an honor to that body that you and your essence are within it."

This description feels so good that I am content to find out no more about the experience.

# # #

"I'm ready to do the work that we were going to do the other day."

"I have many volumes for you. I have interwoven many of the different worldly advanced experiences that will be transmitting. Some worlds have a completely different flavor of art than Earth. If you are dabbling a bit in the non-dual and you can imagine the forever of experiencing that which is of great beauty, imagine how your heart will expand taking within yourself those means of expression!"

"That's an exciting prospect."

"So, of course, I have expanded on the visions. I broke down what is possible with art, with the fortunate, with the essence of philosophies and adventure, and all the topics that you defined for me. I broke them into the bigger visions of what would be possible to understand from the non-dual perspective."

"That sounds fantastic! Excellent work, Esthra."

He guides me to move into a circular chamber in the Hall of Records. "I am now using something more than books. Instead, there are vessels of the full experiences of all those in your soul lineage. Expand into all of your levels of consciousness, breathe from all of your chakras and, draw into you that which is within each of these vessels. As you breathe them, they will begin to turn into particles."

I can hear the happiness in his voice at all he has set up for me. "I have thousands of vessels in this room; they go to the ceiling and are all around you. Imagine there is a vacuum in each of your chakras drawing in. Yes, I am watching this happen. These are great knowledges and, more than that, they are something that will be excited by your academy training. Every part of your being is drawing in the sparkly essence of this awareness. Ah, you are becoming the jinn! Imagine all of the lineages of jinn that exist."

"I'd like to speak with one of them."

"That will be possible. I will suggest Liponie. He is quite jolly and one who I consider to be of the highest of ethics."

"Is he blue?"

Esthra chuckles. "Yes, he is quite blue. We are almost finished. The top of the row is empty and many of the positions around the room have been fully addressed. There is nothing for me to activate, for you are using your academy training, and that will support what you and I are doing. And ... now we are complete."

I feel different, but not in a way I can describe. "Esthra, thank you for your assistance today and the information you shared with me. I will remember to speak with Liponie. Bye for now."

#

I intend to speak with Tonas, but I forget to use a gate to do so.

I hear him say, "Ah, you are here! You have made your connection; come to me, my dear."

"Gladly."

"I love that I can hear you before you arrive. You are there and I can feel you in front of me before I actually view you."

"I certainly would like to see you."

"Well, I can imagine kissing your fingers, but it is easier when you are in front of me. I wondered once what it would be like for me if I were in your position. I think it would be heart-sickening."

"Yes. It's exceptionally frustrating."

"It is the desire of everyone to have such a joy in their life; to have someone like you to be so much enamored with, in love, in heart. Others on the ship witness me and they know what I am experiencing. They are not jealous of me. They are happy for me that I have found such a great beauty to be in my life. The beauty of my heart and the way it feels for you. I believe that your heart has longed for someone like me."

I can't reply to that directly. "Tonas, I'm still finding out a lot of things about myself."

"Yes, indeed. And yet, imagine what it would be to have my strong arms around you dancing the tango—for us to tango across space and time, to feel my eyes upon you always with such admiration. And it would always be so pleasing to your eyes to witness me."

I am becoming almost desperate to confirm his vision of our dancing across space and time. But as much as I want to do that, I have an even greater desire to spare his feelings, in case this relationship doesn't work for me.

Tonas now informs me that there is a red, blinking light around me. Figuring that Osiris would know what this is about, we ask him to join us.

He tells us that this is the CEV signaling their wish to speak with me again. I decide to take him as well as Tonas with me to visit them, saying, "I can visualize one of you on each of my arms."

"This is a welcoming to my world; all that I desire is there for me and I would only desire that which is honoring of all." Osiris is talking about the reality of a non-dual world.

"Thank you, Tonas, for mentioning the red blinking light."

# # #

The CEV speaks. "We are greeting you. We have an idea."

"What would you like to tell me?"

"Our idea is this: The link between you and your beloved—which you hold as a constant—is the imprint of each ova within each of you. Through that constant, there is the opportunity for a continuous energy stream fueling the higher realms of presence. It is possible for you to introduce into all of these regions simultaneously the imprint of expansion that is possible. Do you remember as each of the eggs made connection?"

"Yes."

"Those reconnections can be made if you choose. Periodically, we can offer new eggs to you that are designed for one burst through all positions, through your joined hearts. That is a means that would be less cumbersome and consuming of your time."

Tonas and I like this idea and the CEV offers us the first of these eggs. They inform me that the egg is golden with pearlescence within and that it may be applied from any dimension beginning with the 10th and upward. I gate both my "guys" back to the ship.

# # #

I ask Osiris what dimension we should begin with. He checks with the CEV again and says that, since we are going to be doing many of these eggs, it might be interesting to pick a new dimension each time we activate one. I suggest that we start with the 13th.

"This is a magnificent endeavor," Osiris says. "Since the two of you hold all of the positions that you connected before, and they individually connected to all of the other dimensions, you now have the conduits to connect—everywhere."

Tonas and I make a heart connection and assist the egg to disburse through the conduits to all dimensions. At Osiris's suggestion, we draw all that has been sent outward into our hearts.

Osiris tells us, "Everywhere that a thread touches is now released from many burdens, simply because of this installation, this infusion of greater promise you have offered."

"Thank you for your assistance today."

"It was most pleasurous for me."

# # #

Before I can leave, Tonas requests a moment with me. We stand at the window of the stars.

"It is the same, looking out onto the night sky from this Night Sky—and yet, it is different because you are consciously here with me. I know that you are choosing when you visit in the evening, as you would say. And yet, when I am speaking to you and you hear that reference of my voice and you know that my arm is around your arm with both of us looking out onto the sky—with all that you are touching, all that you are making possible for everything through your great works—it is somehow more. This is why I know that when you can see me, when you can truly feel me, it will be the answer to, perhaps, your prayers. I am thinking positively."

This man is the ultimate romantic. But romance and thoughts of romance have been so little a part of my life for so long that all I can say is, "Me, too."

"It will happen, my dear."

# # #

Thoughts of romance bring to mind the city of Paris, so I ask if there is a Paris on the 10th dimension of Earth.

"Paris? Are you meaning the village of Paris?"

"The city of Paris."

"It is a city. Pardon me. The city of Paris exists, yes. There is no reason for a city to be evacuated from reality."

"I'm thinking about visiting Paris in the fall. I just wondered if it was still hanging around where you are."

"Paris is a city of art and it is a city of pleasures for the eye. It is quite a wonderful place. When you are on the 8th dimension and you are in Paris, I will be able to transition into Paris to be with you—and you will see me."

A first meeting on Earth in Paris sounds like such a delicious experience that I enthusiastically agree to this rendezvous.

"Yes, Paris still exists on the 10th. You can see the same city as you move forward in time into the higher dimensions. There simply is no one there at the present time. You look into the time when there is civilization integrated into them, and, of course, they exist."

"That was confusing."

"Let me explain this to you. When you ask, 'Does Paris exist in the 10th dimension?' I look at the time when you are in the 10th dimension, and I see that all over Earth, as individuals move their consciousness into the 10th dimension, there it is. Yes, the land is there, everything is in presence. But your big tower of the Eiffel is not yet there. It is brought into that realm by the consciousness of those moving into that realm, and as it comes in with a higher awareness, everything comes in sparkly. And so, I simply move into the framework of time where you are in the 10th dimension, and then I project myself into Paris, and there we are. And, of course, everything around is shiny and beautiful, and it is a place of art, music, and great happiness."

"Is it that way now? I've never been there, but it's a famous city of art and it's called the *City of Light*."

"It is sparkly on the 10th dimension in the future of time,

when you are there, as well as the 8th and 9th. As you are in those dimensions, it will be possible for us to be together there. Of course, I must say this so that you remember it. It will only be possible when I am invited by you."

"Oh! Well, I already invite you!"

"I will hold that invitation in my heart."

CHAPTER TWENTY

May 23, 2014

The CEV inform me that they have prepared an emerald jewel for me. It holds the code for ascension and supports the release of 3rd dimension energies. (It seems that even though that dimension is no longer connected to Earth, some people are holding the energy of it in place with their thoughts and beliefs.) I am told that it will take six or seven weeks for the energies of the emerald to transmit into collective consciousness.

"Can you guide me through this?" I ask.

"We are prepared, if you will take the emerald," they reply. "Our focus is upon you."

"I have it."

"Now transition to the center of the Earth, where Gaia still remembers the 3rd dimension. If you will join our collective, your thoughts will become the focus and link to our thoughts. Then our thoughts will move with you as you gate to the center of the Earth and position the emerald in the heart of Gaia."

"And then … I just leave it there."

"Indeed. But first, you must activate its birth unto the world."

"Do I just think that and it happens?"

"Touch the emerald. Bring your hands upon it. Draw in from the presence of your consciousness that which is the 'on' switch, as you might call it, activating in all directions the energy of your baby."

Before I begin speaking Language of Light to facilitate the activation, I center myself and enjoy the energies of the large crystalline room in which I manifested my energy body.

"This has activated in all directions, moving through all of the energy points of Earth," the overseer says. "It is now active. You may release your connection to our collective. In gratitude we are."

"Thank you so much. Love and blessings."

# # #

Esthra comes forward. "Indeed I am in presence, my dear."

"Did you get to watch the big deal that we just did?"

"I am agog."

"Me, too. I'm dizzy."

"It made me dizzy to watch."

"I want to add one more item to the list of attributes I gave you that I wish to embody. It's feeling magical. I want to lead a magical life. Do you think Liponie would be able to help me?"

"He is quite magical, indeed."

"Since I've had those lifetimes as a jinn, I thought maybe he and I could work together. Do you feel he is trustworthy?"

"Indeed he is. He is an individual of Andromeda."

"Will you add magical abilities to your homework for me?"

"Yes, I can add that easily. Magic, to me, is the instant development of what you desire."

"That feels like a great definition. Please tell me ... have I been any of the beings I think of as magical, like a fairy, an elf or a dwarf?"

"You have experienced many forms and many species," Esthra says. "I am thinking now that these might feel as though they are magical—and yet they are simply the life of that species, you see, as with Liponie. I selected well with him."

"May I speak with him for a little bit?"

"I will step aside for you to speak with him. I have my homework assignment."

"Thank you, Esthra."

# # #

This genie is on the ball, because as soon as I finish speaking with Esthra, I hear the words, "I am Liponie."

"Hello, Liponie."

"Are you delighted to meet me?"

"Yes, I am. Do you mind if I call you a jinn, or do you prefer just to be called Liponie?"

"You are Joy. I am Liponie."

"Okay. Esthra, my guide who recommended you, told me a while back that I'd had several lives as a jinn or a genie. My desire is to feel more magical in this lifetime."

"You must know that I am of your lineage, and so my life is your life."

"Yes, well ... I still don't quite understand all of that."

"I am, of course, in beautiful color. "

"Blue, right?"

"I am a beautiful blue, a deep, almost violet-purplish blue as you would call me, and I have been a jinn on Earth."

"You are not currently a jinn?"

"I am of Andromeda; it is less effective now to be on Earth as a jinn. In the more ancient of days, it was more accepted. I appeared to have many kinds of magic, both because of my abilities and because those who lived in those times lacked a recognition of my abilities."

"Supposedly, Solomon had jinn who assisted him to build a huge temple."

"We did, indeed."

"I'm impressed. Can you assist me with magic or with some of those fun things that you could do when you were here?"

"In the times of my Earth residence, I was capable—as everyone in my realm is capable—of appearing as though all is magic. For us, it was simply our presence of being. The color of us drew much attention, and we are less of height, you see. We are perhaps your height (5' 6") which was uncommon for those individuals of Earth species of human. Many of the individuals we assisted were much taller than us. We could make ourselves taller if we wished."

"Were you ever captured or stored in bottles?"

He laughs as he says, "That is such a myth!"

"Oh, darn. I'll have to get rid of my Aladdin's lamp, then."

"Oh, never do that, for it does make a beautiful light."

"I thought it would be interesting to talk to you because I've been fascinated by stories of jinn. They are supposedly beings of fire. Is that true?"

"There is much that we projected to bring the attention to our great powers—which, of course, were the same as their powers. We simply experienced less resistance. We can, with our mind, just as you with your mind, create the greatest of palaces, the treasure of your Solomon. This is what I believe you require of me, for it is in your potential to create just as I do."

Liponie makes it all sound so simple, but in my experience, it has not been. "I've had difficulty holding that vision of being able to do those kinds of things," I try to explain. "They tell me that I'm doing wonderful work with some galactic councils, but I still feel just like an ordinary Earth human being."

"Have you ever thought of how magnificent the ordinary human being is?"

"No, I haven't."

"Perhaps it is time for you to begin seeing the extra-ordinary within the ordinary."

"Yes, I guess. I've never thought about humans that way. It just seems like people have so many challenges and problems and health issues. They're just caught in this *quagmire* of stuff."

Liponie exclaims, "I love this word! I love it!"

"Yes, well, it's not so much fun when you're stuck in the mud. It's exhausting."

"I am learning my English. *Quagmire* will become one of my special words. Thank you. I am most grateful."

He seems to sense my frustration with his cheerfulness, since I am learning nothing. His voice takes on a more somber tone.

"Now let us talk seriously between one another. I, and those of us, performed what could be considered the great magic. You have the same abilities as I—it is simply that you lack confidence, you see. And also, it is somewhat difficult when you are connected to others who are impinged from being fully aware and accepting of the energies that transmit into form that which is thought. And so, you have the desire—but you also have the belief that it is impossible."

"Right."

"How can anything be created in this atmosphere?"

"I know. It's impossible!"

"So this is your task. This is the focus that you must bring to your presence of conscious: If there is a belief that something is impossible, it is truly impossible. And so, as you begin to believe more in yourself and your ability to create, you will be developing your jinn. I will work with you to develop your jinn. Your first task is to release from your heart all that believes in what could be considered impossible."

This sounds like such a tall order that I'm feeling a little dour even thinking about it—but of course, Liponie is laughing as he says, "This is so wonderful; we can do this together. You will start small. You will make your list of all that you believe to be impossible. Oh, it will be a small list, I am sure. And then I will immerse within you. That which is within me believes and *knows* these things to be possible. We will have this immersion; we will bring your Esthra, who is my acquaintance. I know him from the life when he was experiencing it."

I am not yet convinced. "Here's the thing, Liponie. Everyone tells me, 'Oh, it will come. It's just challenging in this current dimension.' Supposedly, the 8th dimension is when I will be able to see Tonas, this man I've been doing work with."

"Why should we wait until then?"

"I don't want to wait until then!"

"This is not impossible at all! So we must move beyond

those beliefs that tell you these things are impossible. You have what I would consider *positive* energies, and so it should be easy for you to release all that is in suppression of your positives. You will make your list and contact me again."

"Okay. It will be a few days, but I will be in touch with you again."

"I will make this time open for you whenever you wish, my dear. I am in the midst of a great celebration here on Andromeda. I am in charge of decoration."

"Oh, what is the celebration about?"

"The celebration is of the beginning of the new regime of light that is linked to all dimensions as the framework comes together. It is known that there is now a link from all dimensions to Earth, and this allows for the beginning of a new regime where all frames of time are moving—in their own space of grace, ease, and motion—to come into the same pinnacle moment."

"When do we reach this pinnacle?"

"There might be some that are forty million years away and there might be some that are two weeks or months from now. Yet they all will configure around the Earth's rise to that higher pinnacle. It is an inter-connection with your Earth dimensions. It is a great celebration, my dear. Please do come to it."

It has taken me a little bit to figure out what he is talking about,

"Is this celebration about the work that Tonas and I did?"

"You are the one," he replies. "You are the one. I am speaking to the one. You are the Joy. Oh! I will be famous after today. I will be most famous. This is delightful, and I can help you. It will be my great honor to assist you."

"Have fun with your celebration!"

CHAPTER TWENTY-ONE
May 26, 2014

Esthra says, "I am at your disposal."

"Hello, Esthra. I hope you don't get tired of questions, because it seems like I'm always going to have some for you."

"I am prepared to try to answer for as long as you wish to ask."

"Thank you. I need to know something personal. Will I ever get to see the animals I've owned that have died? When I was little, I had a pet rooster and my dog, Queenie, and our cow, Glory. Are they still around—or do they get absorbed back into the group essence of cow or chicken?"

"Animals are part of the collective of energy of Gaia," he replies. "Because they are of the collective energies of her, their essence is reconstituted into the Earth when they die. But your heart holds the energy of the spirit of the chicken. So it is easy for you to bring into your presence the essence of that exact ... it is certainly poultry."

"It was a rooster," I remind him. "I carried him around when I was little."

"It will be easy for you to recreate all of these energies. That is the beauty of your 8th dimension. That is the magical golden carrot that is floating outward to beckon you forward."

Oh, boy. More carrots, I think to myself.

#

"Tell me, do I visit you at night? Is there a place to visit you?"

"There is no bungalow with my name on it," Esthra says. "I exist as energy."

"I thought it would be helpful if I had a chance to visit you somewhere."

"There is an energy field where we exist. It is easy for you to make the connection with your SVH. You can simply gate into our energy field. It is the stream of energy that we exist within, and we are bright of consciousness. You can bathe in us almost as if you are in a pool of light. This would be a positive experience. If you are ever feeling put upon, make your way into our energy realm. We will uplift you. We will bathe you in the wonder of us."

"Thank you. I'll try to remember to do that. What can you tell me about the anger? Have I been able to do enough to clear that, finally?"

"I believe that you are making marked advancements. You must notice this yourself. Look upon your present mindset compared to the tenor of your energies even seven or eight years in the past. Some of your angers have become less and less, especially over the last year and a half."

"You're saying I still have issues with anger?"

"Very few. And you will work through this easily—you must know this."

"To me, it seems like I just keep shoveling the shit."

"Put down the shovel, my dear."

# # #

"Several years ago, I was working with some Native Americans," I tell Esthra. "It was vivid to me that I was there in their presence and talking with them and encouraging them. Did that really happen?"

"Indeed, it did. You would wake up exhausted."

"Yes. I think that was why I stopped being open to receiving information all night long. It was making me so tired."

"If you began again, within five days or more you would be back in the stream of that experience."

"Are you saying I can reopen that kind of deep connection with the Native Americans?"

"It is impossible to separate you from those in your matrix who are Native American, simply because you have a deep desire to assist the tribes. These individuals call to your heart, and there is no framework of time that separates them for you. As you know, all is occurring simultaneously."

"Yes, I'm trying to wrap my brain around that. Is there a tribe I work with more than any other tribe?"

"I think that it is as if there is only one tribe, and they are all connected as individuals. These individuals are of tribes connected to their roaming patterns, and yet they are deeply rooted to the Earth itself, and so it is as if they are of one tribe of Earth. You can feel that pointedly, because of your deep commitment."

"Are there any who would be able to connect with me and assist me?"

"You are assisting them, my dear. You are as the great star in the heavens that they pray to."

Esthra continues to explain, but I don't register what he's saying. I am assisting *them*? They pray to *me*? I know he's gotten something really mixed up.

"I don't understand," I say.

Esthra tries again to explain. "You bring them inspiration. You must recognize your bigger vision of self. You are incarnated onto Earth with your higher dimensional awareness and connection from the origin. From your higher consciousness, you have been assisting as if there were telephone wires leading thousands of years, even into the past. They connect with you and they receive that information spoken directly to their hearts."

So ... what I'm starting to understand is that he's talking about the part of me that is considered my Higher Self assisting the Native Americans—not me, Joy, walking around on Earth in my sixty-eight-year-old body. Still, this information is really daunting and I tell him, "Other than that little window of time a few years ago, I'm not aware that I'm doing this kind of work."

"That was a vision into the role you have been playing for these tribes of beings throughout your whole incarnation. It will be easy for you this evening, as you go into your sleep cycle, to find that frequency where you are timelessly connecting to each of these individuals who desire to connect with you."

He tries another tactic. "Imagine the stars. They are above this Earth every evening and night for every cycle of being of Earth. When the Sun goes down, the stars are present. It is easy for those of the tribes to see the spark of the sky and to feel their connection to you."

"Are you talking about the Joy Star now?"

"No. You are not seeing the big picture. The Native Americans say, 'Oh, Great Spirit, we call to you this day to give to us of your wisdom. What can we do for the hunt on this day? How can we bring about the rains when there is a drought? What is your wisdom, Great Spirit?'"

"Yes, I can picture them doing that."

"To you, you are Joy; but to them, you are a timeless spark in the sky that they look upon. They have many that they pray to, and you are one of them. You are the spark of light that gives them the wisdom spoken to their heart for the ways of survival and the moving of the herds. There are so many things that you have not yet discovered about yourself."

"I know. I wish I could talk to you for hours and hours."

Esthra adds, "I know where your energy goes when you are asleep. I know that, as a child, you felt close to the animals and to the land. You became one with the trees as you climbed into them."

"That is true. In all kinds of weather I spent most of my days outdoors."

"Now imagine that beside that little girl was the grand goddess, the essence of great consciousness incarnated onto this world. The goddess is the same as that little girl—and yet, you are the essence of that being that shines hope onto these indigenous beings of North and South America."

I'm struggling to understand and embrace the things Esthra has been telling me. I had no idea that I was assisting the tribes in the manner he has described, but this information does help me make sense of many events I've experienced in the past.

"Now, you are more than that little girl grown up," he assures me. "You have been a spiritual connection to the Earth itself and to the stars from which the tribes know they come. As well as a connection to the important elements that make up life for those individuals, such as the rain, the wind, the snow, the trees and how the seasons move. Everything is spiritual to them, even the foods they consume.

"You have been the instrument of unity for all of these things as well as supporting awareness brought to light, and giving counsel to these individuals. They feel your message within their hearts. Yes, you are born into this line of time, and yet time cannot hold you, for you were connected from the moment of your awareness of birth on this world. With your first breath in this life, you became the timeless thread connecting those that you speak to. This is a small piece of what you are applying here on Earth; that is one small thread."

"Thank you for all this information," I say, unable to take in any additional revelations for the moment. "I'm having a hard time thinking of anything more magical than what you just told me, but I know you were going to prepare something for me."

"Ah yes," Esthra says. "I took great pleasure in preparing for you the works of all magic on Earth. There is the magic of nature; there is the magic that exists within all that grows and lives, all that takes the light that is the spark within itself and ignites to become part of the story of what is blossomed into being. Do you like my poetry?"

"I do."

"There is more magic than simply that which has been brought to the attention of an individual, where wands and spells are used. These are simply means to focus energy. Once the energy is focused, there is no implement outside of self that is required. I wish to take you to the heart of magic; the heart of magic that exists within all of Earth. You know that to be the center, the beating heart of Gaia herself. You know how to make your presence there."

"Yes. I'll gate to the core of Earth."

"Stand there in the light that is the spark of creation, which can be focused to create anything," he instructs. "Open your mind to the geometries that make up the forming of every idea. Take those ideas into your heart and send them outward into the Earth. Feel yourself become the Earth. Feel also your connection to all the lines of time and to all those for whom you have been the spark of wisdom. Feel the magic, my dear. Feel yourself a part of Earth and the greater spirit of that spark of essence of the magic that exists."

I silently focus on feeling this communion with the Earth herself.

"Feel the buffalo running upon the Earth, upon the core of your outer shell," he advises. "Feel what it is to have the pounding of the hooves as they thunder onward. Feel the beaver chewing through the wood to make its home and to build its dams, feel the birds in the trees, and feel the heart of Gaia beating within all of these. Feel the running of the horses and how their freedom drives them. This is the magic."

"I understand."

Esthra is caught up in his instructions, and in the poetry of his own words. "Feel the great magic that beats within the heart of each of these horses as they run, these great herds of horses. One leads and all follow, as if in oneness. Feel all the beautiful fish in their little schools, darting. Feel the presence of this all-knowingness. It guides you in your deliverance of valuable intelligence directed to those who are in prayer to you. Hear the drums. Hear them beating in your heart."

This connection feels delicious. I intuit that it is resembles the closeness I felt to nature when I was little.

"Feel those in leadership calling to you, 'Great Spirit.' Feel the smoke from their fires rising up to the sky as if to reach you, and feel yourself ever-present sparkling down, ever sparkling. Feel the transition of information from your consciousness through the timelessness reaching into their hearts. They can hear you through their hearts. Even the animals can."

"The animals?"

"Yes. Feel the bear awakening in spring, hungry, ready to move outward from its cave to find its food and to continue the cycle of life. Feel the connection, the presence of the bear with that of its prey and know that it is a cycle of magic. Everything is a part of the great oneness flow. Do you feel the magic?"

Before I can answer, he continues. "Now in this magic, feel what it is to have riches beyond that of Midas and the great Solomon. The riches that you have in you are the same as for them, for the gold and the jewels are of importance only because they show them that they have the power to amass such greatness of spirit—for wealth is the greatness of spirit manifested into form. Feel what it is to be of that richness. Everything is at your disposal. All that you desire to create is capable for you to complete. That feeling of ever-presence contains everything you need or desire. It is at your presence with simply a thought."

"Is this what it will be like to live in a higher dimension?"

"You will develop this skill more and more as you move closer to your 8th dimension—simply because once you are in the 8th dimension, it will no longer be a quest for you. The thought is instantly manifested. It is your development of this skill, in this framework of time, which supports your enhancement of that clarity that you will surely find."

"Are you telling me all these things fall under the category of magic?"

"Indeed. The magic of love, the magic of passion for what you desire, the magic of music—it is all included. Feel your consciousness entering the music and feel the magic in the music, feel the magic in the poetry, in the dance, feel the beat of your heart that is the beat of the heart of Gaia. Feel the future blending with your present and know that all these things shall come. They all shall come to pass, just as your gift to all of the lines of time, when you have been the voice of Great Spirit. There are many voices of Great Spirit; yours has been the voice guiding the spirits of those of the land. It has been through you that the sound of the thundering herds and their direction of Earth and their positions can be felt within the hearts of these braves."

"How long can I remain in this incredible energy?"

"You may remain in this exercise or return at any point in your existence," Esthra replies. "To me, it is a worthy exercise."

"It was dreamy…"

# # #

I am feeling drowsy, so I ask Esthra to tell Liponie I'm sorry I didn't feel up to speaking with him today, but I will soon. Before I can completely release my connection, I hear Liponie say, "I cannot believe that you would disengage without our connection. I longed for this excitement and, of course, there are many that believe me to be in extra-specialness, for I have told everyone that there will be a report of our conversation today."

"I was just feeling so swimmy and dreamy after Esthra worked with me. I did want to speak with you and say hello— and I have to know about the celebration. What are the decorations that you are creating?"

Liponie seems to cheer up at my question. "Imagine streams of sparkling stardust as if swirled like ribbons throughout the sky, and I have light shining upon with many colors. Of course, there are many colors here on Andromeda that are impossible on Earth. This beauty," he adds, laughing, "is quite impressive. You are familiar with bright silvers and golds; imagine these streams moving in all directions and the colors as if they are the aurora borealis. It is quite magical and exciting for me to have thought of this. I was inspired by Earth."

"Fireworks?"

"You call them the northern lights. What you call fireworks could be considered occurring within the streams. Imagine these ribbons of stardust sparkling with all the colors and imagine that one should begin leaking as if a fountain and dripping downward and being caught on the wind and carried throughout the whole arena of the space of the great celebration."

"That sounds amazing! Are you talking about one planet in Andromeda?"

"What I am speaking of is the main city; you would call it a capital. This is on Andromeda and it is the capital of this great region. The excitement is presided over by Isis and Osiris."

"When we think of Andromeda, we just think of a galaxy."

"I know. There is a position that we are naming Andromeda simply because you have called it that as well."

"That was kind of you."

"We are taking your words and designations and playing along with the names of them. We are certainly not calling this place Andromeda."

"Do you have a name for it?"

"It is *She on ih* … ." This is followed by a long bunch of guttural sounds.

"That's a little bit of a challenge for humans to say. How long does the celebration last?"

"It could move onward for as many as another twenty-one days. This is a great celebration. You must be aware of the importance that you have brought this to my attention. You are the Great One. You must certainly be excited about the experience. There are dramas and plays, as you would call them, where the experience is being played out."

At first, I am so amazed by what he just said that I don't have any questions to ask. Then I start thinking I should find out more about the celebration.

Liponie continues, "Imagine that there are many performances of theatrics of your incarnation, your many accolades of experience leading to this great moment. There are, as yet, even more that are being developed. Of course, I've seen all of the dramas; they have been quite enlightening. We are most excited. Please be not of embarrassment of your life. Enjoy the celebration, as we do."

"How can I not be embarrassed? There has been quite a bit of drama and some large ups and downs in my life." I shudder to think of some of those moments displayed in a theater.

"This brings great interest to all of us," Liponie says. "It broadens your story, giving it character and excitement. It gives us the vision of how much you have evolved, you see, as a species, and also as an individual. Of course, there is the greater part of you that is applying much more, and this is in another theatrical production. The production of your existence is one that is running for many days."

Hoping I won't be too horrified, I say, "I should come and see it. I guess I can come to Andromeda."

"I will leave open a place beside me, my dear. I do not wish to say that I am one of the individuals that would wish to pat myself on my own back—but I was deeply disappointed, for I have told everyone that I would have a report of our communion today."

"We can go ahead and do what we were going to do, because I have my list of impossible things."

"Indeed, this would be of great excitement to me."

"Do you know what's on my list?"

"You would perhaps give me this information, and then I would be able to move forward with it."

"Okay. I'll just read it to you then."

"Speak to me, you have my every attention."

# # #

I begin to recite to him from the list he requested, the abilities that I believe are impossible.

"Things that are impossible to be, to do, or to have in this reality at this time:

- I can walk on water and through walls.
- I can levitate, bi-locate, and teleport.
- I play the violin as well as or better than Heifetz.
- I am a genius.
- I easily access all my levels of consciousness and am able to utilize the information there.
- I talk to/see/hear God/Goddess
- I have perfectly aligned, beautiful white teeth, with no fillings.
- I have 20/20 vision.
- I appear to be twenty-five to twenty-seven years of age, but can change my appearance at will.
- All the systems of my body work perfectly, especially my digestive system.
- I have an athlete's/dancer's body.
- All my 'clair' abilities are fully activated.
- I love myself and my current appearance, including my hair.
- I feel and am wealthy.
- I feel and am magical.
- I understand, write, and speak fluently Spanish, French, Greek, and Russian.

- I have dancing shoes that feel great on my feet and I dance divinely.
- I manifest what I choose and my choices are divine. I have no fear of making a mistake.
- I experience balanced, unified masculine, feminine, and neutral energies within myself.
- I focus only on that which I desire to manifest.
- For those things that I wish to change, I am able to maintain a vision of the desired result.
- I have released all anger, fear, resentment, bitterness, regret, shame, guilt, envy, judgments, doubt, mistrust, all the lower emotions.
- I remain neutral about the actions and words of others."

Liponie waits to be sure I have finished reading. "And these are things that you believe are impossible?"

"Right now, yes."

"Mmm."

"Or *nearly* impossible."

"Well then, leave this list with me. This is, to me, another story that will become part of the theater. This is a bit different than the list I thought I would be receiving. This had so much depth that I would wish to offer you the greatest of opportunities to reach beyond these impossiblenesses."

"I will greatly appreciate whatever you can do."

"We will create what you call a 'think tank' on this. This will be quite an endeavor. Leave this with me, and I will rejoin the celebration and wait for you to join me."

"I will come this evening."

CHAPTER TWENTY-TWO
May 29, 2014

Esthra greets me, as usual, by saying he is at my disposal.

"Hello, Esthra," I say. "I want to ask about the time in June of 2001 when I spoke for several days with many Native Americans. At the end of those meetings, I was talking with three individuals and I gave them each a ring. I remember that they were Hiawatha, Gray Wolf, and another whose name I did not know.

"As I was conversing with them, I had a feeling someone was coaching me about what to say. I remember pausing and waiting to know what to say and then saying it."

"That was your heart-mind," Esthra explains, "your inner awareness, which is linked to your essence of being. It is a transmission that comes from that part of the mind associated with the intellect of your own consciousness, receiving from the higher part of self."

"I would like to be able to do that more."

Esthra tells me that, during that time, I expected to hear the guidance and was patient to receive it. He adds that I am considered a "heavy hitter." When I ask what that means, he says, "You are able to connect with the hearts and minds of a great mass of individuals throughout time. Even as a child, you were making the deepest of connections with them in different frameworks of time."

"I really did this work as a child?"

"Yes. You are a great healer who is linked to the heart of the Earth itself, and you have always been so. Your love for animals was something that could be felt by those Indians; they associate with the animals the same way you did when you were a child."

"When I was working with them in 2001, they wanted to touch me, so a part of me must have been there physically."

"When you manifested before them, they could see you. Let

me tell you how they could see you: They smoked certain plants which opened up their awareness to be able to see you in form."

"They actually *did* touch me, Esthra, because they asked permission to do that. I don't think they believed I was there."

"And, indeed, you were. Now, of course, you are capable with your SVH gate. And you could begin again, more consciously."

"I would like to talk to them again—but I told them things would happen that haven't yet occurred. And I don't know that I could communicate like I was able to back then. I guess I've got some work to do on myself."

"And you are doing that work. I believe that is part of a different kind of communication and connection, and I also know to be true that they will recognize you. They will recognize the timeless nature of you. You are in the collective of the consciousness of the Indian that has existed as a forever moment over many thousands of years."

# # #

"You said recently that I am 'being prepared to be the carrier of the vision of what is considered to be the perfection vision and you are the perfection vision.' Can you explain what that means in a way I can understand?"

"What that means, my dear, is that as you move into that higher realm—the first steps of the 8th dimension and then beyond—you will be one of those who are the earliest to make that transference. Through that, you will become perfection itself. Why would anything exist in a non-dual reality that would be less than perfection? Through that and through your preparation to reach that dimension, you will have the ability to radiate this to all those who are still in their 6th and 7th dimension, and those that are in the 5th, and those that are still lagging behind even in the 4th dimension, if that should still be considered a possibility."

"It's just hard to picture."

"Those who met your great Buddha considered him to be nearly perfect because his mind was so focused. He even smelled of the Earth itself, and the sweetness of the breeze. Imagine having that ability to smell as a beautiful rose, and then these individuals of Earth witness you in your perfected body. They witness the before and the after, you see."

Esthra's description of this future me is wonderful and magical. He reminds me my appearance will inspire others, and that what he has described will be a truth for my existence. I am totally ready for this—except for one thing.

"I'm a little nervous about instant manifestation," I confide.

"You need not worry. With SVH, you have many things in place to prevent disasters."

I thank Esthra for his assistance and the information he gave me today. I decide I'm ready to speak with Liponie.

# # #

The genie greets me enthusiastically, "Ah, gay celebration, it is you!"

"Hi, Liponie. So tell me, what did you think my list would be like? You seemed surprised by what I had included on it."

"I thought that things you would consider to be impossible would be perhaps the walking on water, bi-location, and perhaps some of these other things. The feeling of being wealthy does not seem at all impossible to me, you see."

"There's one thing that I wanted to add, and that is being successful in business."

"Ah, this would go along with being wealthy," he says, "and, as you mentioned, the dancing, the athlete body. I considered all of these to be quite possible in your existence; to find a shoe that fits your feet does not seem impossible to me."

"Well, you think it would be easy, but I've looked a lot. I

have skinny feet with a high arch. Plus, I think there's something symbolic about shoes fitting my feet that would have to do with feeling comfortable on my path and able to stride forward confidently. I'm much happier than I used to be about the direction I'm going—and what's even better is that I *have* a direction to go. I'm sixty-eight years old, which is youthful in your realm, but here, that is past middle age."

"My goodness!"

"My body is still relatively fit for my age. And I hate that expression 'for my age.'"

"Oh, and the other term that you used was quite shocking to me, to say that you are sixty-eight years old." Laughing, Liponie repeats, "It was quite shocking for my hearing."

"Aging has been a part of our reality, and I'm ready to quit doing it. Help me to change those things, Liponie. Were you planning on doing anything with my list today?"

"I have a better understanding of your list at this time. I do not believe that you see many of these things as impossible; I believe that you see them as a *challenge*."

After a period of discussion, I agree to downgrade some of the things on my list from impossible to difficult. Liponie still insists that even my "impossibles" are merely challenging—which is, I suppose, a more positive description.

"Things are much easier on the higher dimensional frames," he reminds me. "You are already connected to those times and those energies. You are already in the future—you are simply living your moments leading up to it. I wish for you to know that it will be a short time. Yes, I will help you. I will move back into this adventurous list of yours."

"You have a different concept of time than we do here on Earth," I say. "I am approaching old age. A short time for you guys could be a thousand years, but for me a short time is maybe a week."

"May I tell you a truth?"

"Yes."

"You are not approaching old age, and you are nevermore sixty-eight years old. You are destined to exist in the flesh of the body for hundreds of years, so these beliefs are reaching their time of release."

"I think so, too."

"At our next connection of conversation, I will assure you of assistance. But I will return to the merry-making now."

I remember the big party in my honor that I promised I would try to attend. "Was I able to show up at the celebration?"

"Most certainly you did. You created quite a stir when you appeared next to me—for, of course, the drama of your life was being played out, and then there you were. You were dressed humbly, as if in rags. It was not a comely dressing gown."

I laugh in surprise. "Why? What did it look like?"

"It appeared as if you were wearing baggy things that were not shapely to your beauty and nature. All in presence were simply in awe. I am a fashionable dresser and quite ostentatious, so I immediately made some magic for you so that you would be dressed in robes of gold."

I'm relieved to hear this. "I do frequently wear baggy old things around my home. Fashionable clothes have never been of much interest to me. Perhaps I need to start thinking more about what I wear. Thank you for your help with my wardrobe."

"It was my pleasure, of course. I gave you a little bit of a Greek flair."

"That sounds like fun."

"It was quite an elegant party, so I felt it was important for you to look the part."

"Well, thank you again."

"It was my pleasure."

#

I request to speak with the CEV.

"We are in presence; greetings to you."

"Greetings to you, also. What would you like for me to do today?"

"I would like to receive your insight."

My heart drops at this statement. They want an insight from *me*? Then I have an idea and ask them if they will tell me their ideas first.

"Certainly, our idea would be to blanket Earth's atmosphere with spheres similar to the emerald, each holding the same codes that are supporting the elevation of the Earth to the higher dimensions. Each of these spheres could be connected with each of the threads of the higher dimensions that you have applied. The emerald spheres you place will be assisting individuals to find their footing to rise to the higher dimensions. It is in our consideration that this process might encompass at least six or seven months."

I tell them that timeframe is acceptable, since at least we're moving.

"If you choose to do this, we will guide you in placing the emeralds in the atmosphere and then connecting them to the great emerald in the center of the Earth. That emerald will act as a battery, continuously charging, and progressive encodements will join it."

#

I am to first activate the emerald in the Earth, and then from my current 6th and 7th dimension, to reach into the upper atmosphere.

"I'm going to the center of the Earth," I tell them. "Let me do that now. Hold on a minute. All right, I'm with the emerald there. I just love looking at it. What do I do when I reach into the upper atmosphere?"

"We will guide you."

I focus on Earth's atmosphere and report, "I'm reaching out in all directions evenly."

"Now, from your position, draw from the stars the emeralds that will come to each point of the threads of your energy in the upper atmosphere. Do you see how each of the points now contains an emerald? Now connect each of them to one another, as a grid. You allow yourself to become fluid within the grid itself in the upper atmosphere."

"All right."

"And now that the grid is fully formed, from your position within the upper atmosphere, follow each of the emeralds to the center of the Earth to the great emerald there. As the connection is made, you are the *ignitress*. Find your position within the great emerald and feel yourself ignite the energy."

"This part is complete."

# # #

The CEV asks me to draw energy from the threads linked to the 10th dimension and above to each of the new emeralds in Earth's atmosphere. This is like lighting a flame in each of them.

"How many emeralds are there?"

"Seven billion," they reply.

Next, I am guided to draw the final ascension energies from the 25th dimension to the 24th, then to the 23rd and so on down to the 10th dimension. This ascension energy is then imprinted into the emeralds in the atmosphere.

The final step is to move that energy from the emeralds down through the threads to connect with every point of the essence of Earth's being. This imprints the energies of ascension into Earth. The CEV tells me that now the grand emerald in the center of the Earth has been truly activated.

"It feels beautiful."

"It is glistening, and it is as if the emerald is beating in synchronicity with the heart of Gaia. You have done great works today. Now the vision is of Earth meeting that goal of the evolution. You will hold these good thoughts with you."

"I will. Are we through for the day?"

"We are complete with this function."

"I would like to speak with my friend Tonas briefly today. I will be speaking with you again soon. Thank you, thank you, thank you."

"We are in gratitude."

# # #

Tonas's voice welcomes me, "Ah, my beloved, you have come to me. This is a great delight for me. We have many eggs."

"I just did this wonderful activation with the CEV with the emerald and with the threads. I wonder if you can see what we did."

Tonas seems to be able to perceive the emeralds. "I am seeing bright orbs in the atmosphere; they are creating a spectrum of light. It seems as though it is pulsating."

"They are beating with the heartbeat of Gaia. We have the ascension vision now with all the upper dimensions linked to Earth. And right now, I'm swimming my way to you."

"It will be soon, I am sure, with such magic."

At the mention of magic, I share with Tonas that I'm going to be working with a genie from Andromeda.

He tells me, "You are as though a genie that is awakening the heart of me every day."

I mentioned to Tonas recently that I had a brief period of loneliness. He seemed stricken.

"I am in sadness that you have felt alone," he says. "I promise that, if you choose, one day you will never be alone or feel alone again."

"Thank you, Tonas, for saying that. You are ever constant. My life has been one where I've been afraid to depend on anyone completely. People in this dimension will, the expression is, 'let you down.' I want to feel strong and confident by myself. Perhaps then I will be a worthy partner for you. Thanks for being patient with me."

Before we activate our "regular" orbs, Tonas tells me that he can now juggle twenty objects. This is another way, he thinks, to impress me. I wish he would stop trying to do that; I'm already in awe of the abilities he has. Maybe this is just a universal attribute for guys?

"When Liponie told me that they were doing enactments of my life in theaters on Andromeda, I thought, 'Oh, no!' because there's been some…"

"It is impressive, my dear."

"Impressive is one way to describe it—but to me, it's really just some dark, depressing stuff that I've been working years to rewrite. My life has not been fine and dandy."

"That is the most impressive of all. For if it was sugar-coated, imagine how boring it would be as a story."

"I definitely agree. It's not boring!"

"No, it is not boring. I have learned things about you that have made me so much more in appreciation of you. The journey of you is beyond description, is it not?"

"Perhaps. I've rewritten a large part of my life with SVH. At least, now I feel good most of the time. I just hope that there wasn't much portrayed about my relationships with men, because those have not been good."

"I did not notice this at all in any of the enactments."

"That's good."

"But now you have my curiosity."

I reveal to him that, as a little girl, I had some sexual experiences that I did not remember until I was an adult. Consequently, as a young adult, I did not have pleasant sexual experiences with men.

He assures me that there is nothing I ever experienced or ever could experience that would cause him to cease admiring me, and tells me, "You are such a treasure, that you even have these concerns. Never have them again. Never, never, my dear."

"You know I can't promise that. I never know what new thing I'm going to learn that will turn my world upside down. In the past, I've always dreaded surprises. There have been many in my life that were not pleasant. I'm not really afraid of the future surprises *you* may provide for me, though. I have a feeling they are all going to be wonderful. With that note of anticipation, dear Tonas, I must be going. I will talk to you next week."

"I am living for the moment of that."

CHAPTER TWENTY-THREE
June 2, 2014

Hoping to get the maximum amount of assistance for the days ahead, I visit all the appropriate galactic councils of light. They give me nine orbs that will help prepare the Earth for the work we will do on June 21. These orbs will help us disconnect the old paradigm energy of the need to manipulate in order to have intimate relationships. This shift will facilitate stepping into the power of the Goddess, realigning the energy body, and laying foundational grids in preparation for the summer solstice.

The CEV announce, "We are in presence."

"Hello, I have some orbs for you," I say. "I don't know exactly what they contain, other than work to be introduced to the planet."

"These are integrative elements that can be used to bring forth a higher vibration within the balance of the human species," they reply. "This is an introduction to the pleasure of the blended feminine and masculine. This pleases you?"

"Yes, very much."

After a period of discussion, I learn that these nine orbs will affect only the 4th through the 7th dimensions. Tonas and I will be moving backward and then forward in time to place them in the Earth.

The CEV comments that the Earth is now a sexual planet, but that in the 8th dimension and higher, there will be a more balanced energy of whole beings. "The Earth will no longer be a sexual planet," they explain. "It will be a heart planet. The heart will lead rather than the sexual organs."

They inform me that they have nine cubes for me, one for each of the orbs. Each cube holds a full grid matrix (threads) that will connect the emerald orbs in the atmosphere to locations about six meters below the surface of the Earth. After all the orbs and cubes are activated, they will create a system of grids that encompass the Earth. Then the grids will move to the upper atmosphere. The CEV agree to tell Osiris what we will be doing, since I'd like for him to assist us.

Osiris speaks, "My dear…"

"Hello, hello."

"You are once again bringing forth a great wonder. I have the full complement of understandings of this great endeavor. You have in your presence something important. You must bring this to your Tonas. I am in presence there now."

I gate to the ship and Osiris compliments me by saying I look exquisite today in beautiful robes of blue. He is ready to begin, but Tonas is not going to be rushed in greeting me. Osiris capitulates by saying, "Oh, my goodness, I will wait, of course. Your dear Tonas is quite fetched by you."

"Hello, Tonas!"

"My dear, it is my greatest honor to be of assistance once again. If we can put the great piles of these many things from your hands and allow me to kiss your fingertips, please?"

"Yes, thank you."

He kisses my fingers and then sighs before saying, "And so, my dear, shall I collect a cube and you an orb?"

"That would be fine."

As Tonas and I hold the cube and orb between us, Osiris asks us to use our hearts and minds to send the energy of the cube to the Earth. It opens to become a beautiful grid. Then we release the orb and our hearts send it to the grids of the 4th through the 7th dimensions of Earth. The orb activates points on the grids which then send golden threads to penetrate points just below the surface of the Earth.

Osiris tells us that the grid has been activated but is waiting for us to transmit to it the "design of harmony" that I received from the nine galactic councils at the beginning of this session. After we do this, Tonas moves the ship forward in time thirty-two hours.

We are able to release the cube and orb simultaneously because of the grid we just positioned. Osiris directs us forward in time to different positions where Tonas and I release all but the final set of cube and orb.

For the final activation, on June 20, Isis steps forward and speaks. "My dear, I am most delighted. You are bringing the beautiful energy of the Goddess into the greatest and brightest of light. This does not in any way diminish the God energy, as you would say. The masculine and the feminine are to be in the greatest of balance."

"Won't one energy always try to overpower the other?" I ask.

"When one is in heart, there is no possibility for the masculine to be overshadowed by the Goddess. The Goddess is the energy that brings the elevation to all that is masculine and bonds the energy between the two, allowing them to be braided in a fashion that it is most delicious. They will be most deliciously unified, for it is the goddess energy, the feminine, that allows the braid to come together to bring the greatest of heart, the sweetest of unity. It is our hope, our desire, and our vision joined with yours that this shall be—that this which you bring forth will assist to support that reality."

As the orb and grid activate and unfold, Isis tells us that we now have a grid of the flower of life circumnavigating the globe of Earth. "The energies that stream to Earth also hold the most delicious light and the focus of the heart, the hope of the spirit of humanity," she says, "for the animals already understand this unity. The plants understand it too, and so the water, and those that fly. It is in the rocks and sand, this fellowship, my dear. If you will send your words, I will join you in them, for I am the energy of sister to your blessed Gaia. I will speak to her as well."

Isis and I then speak the Language of Light together to smooth and complete the work. This is a delightful experience for me. I have felt and enjoyed her goddess presence within me, but only two or three times in the past.

"I enjoyed that our words were joined, my dear," she says.

"I did, too."

"We are the spark today of the spirit of that vision that you have for Earth."

Osiris adds, "My beloved is most taken with you. Both of you as a team are quite efficient and dedicated. Do you have further requirements of us?"

I'm not sure what they are allowed to tell me, but now seems like a good time to try to find out if there is something I need to know. "What can you tell me at this time that would be helpful for me?"

Osiris replies, "You are choosing to restore your body, and yet I believe this is faulty thinking. It is not necessary to restore. It is important to move beyond the archetype of the body as it was and become something that is even more pleasurable to the vision and the senses, you see."

"That's exciting. I really like that idea."

"Why should we restore anything? Why wouldn't we design a new vision, instead of bringing back to us that which was part of a story in the past? You are already reforming that story, for aging and death are part of someone else's story and not your own."

"I wish I could restore the health of my parents," I say, knowing that would be impossible for them to accept even if it was allowed.

"We are all aware that you are experiencing the final stages in the existence of the physical presence of your parents," Osiris says, his voice reassuring. "It has been quite challenging for you and for many who have experienced the same or similar. Of course, this is not something that *we* have ever experienced, and this will become a thing of the past for those who live beyond the 7th dimension. And yet, there will be many who will choose to remain in the old story of existence where you are born and then you die."

"I'm not one of them," I say.

"It is not of interest to you or to me. I will help you in the tutorials you are studying."

"All right, thank you both for your help today."

"It has been our great pleasure, my dear."

# # #

Tonas returns and says, "I make you laugh. Together, we laugh a lot. I expend great efforts to make you laugh."

"That's a side of you I would like to be more aware of," I say. "When we are together doing this work, you always seem so serious and dedicated. Laughter is becoming a large part of my life here, so maybe your efforts do have some carry-over into this reality. Interesting, isn't it?"

Then I add, "Here is another Earth expression to add to your vocabulary. I'm going to sign off for today."

"What will you sign, my dear?"

"That's an expression to announce the end of something. It is my way of saying goodbye till next time."

"Farewell. I have discovered this word; it is magnificent. If you think of it as may you fare well, is it not wonderful?"

"Oh, yes, it is."

"So I bid you, farewell."

CHAPTER TWENTY-FOUR
June 4, 2014

Tonas speaks. "It is I, my dear."

"Hi, Tonas! I have something exciting to propose to you."

"Ah, a proposal!"

There is a subtle tone in his voice that immediately leads my mind to think of the word marriage. I decide to resist making a witty comeback, as that is definitely not a topic I want to venture into right now.

"Have you ever had a party on your ship?"

"We did for the inauguration of the ship."

"Well, how about having another party?"

"Whenever you desire."

"Okay, you know June 21 is the big day."

"The cumulative day for much of our work, yes."

"Right, with the Goddess and God blending and unifying. I think we ought to have a party with couples, the instructors of the academy, your parents, any of your friends, and my friend, Jill Marie. How about that? Is there a room big enough for that?"

"This ship will expand as we desire."

"Could you get enthusiastic about that? Would that be something you would enjoy?"

"Any opportunity to dance with you makes me enthusiastic, my dear. May we have the cupcakes?"

"Oh yes! Anything! Any desserts you would like and anything you think I would like. Wear something svelte so we can dance. Here's my other thought. Jill Marie is single and she works all the time, She keeps saying, 'Oh, that Tonas, I wonder if he's got a brother?' I told her you have millions of brothers; they're all Ashtar Commanders and I bet they're handsome, too. Do you have any friends who would be a good match for her? Are you any good at matchmaking, Tonas?"

"I have never taken on that role. I do have thirty-six

biological brothers. Of them, all but three are partnered."

"Yes, she wants to be sure the men she would meet are single. But when she's speaking about your brothers, she means someone handsome like you and who is just as gentle and nice as you are. Surely there must be someone in this dimension who would fit those parameters. She could mingle at the party and maybe find someone she likes as a friend or a possible partner."

"I can help. We will invite all of the eligible males. Should we alert them that she is actively searching for a mate?"

"She's considering it, and I think she'll come to the party— but I just want to introduce her to some men who might be a match for her; someone whose company she would enjoy. I don't know how she would feel about being labeled as 'searching.'"

"I think *you* are the matchmaker."

"Well, yes, but I don't know all these people you know."

"Yes, of course. We are nearing the time when there will be no cross barriers, so it will be easy to carry on a relationship. It could be quite physical. There is something to be said about having your beloved in your arms and looking out to the sea of stars and having both you and your partner in physical presence. It is delicious enough as it is; I am not complaining."

"You know I do want to see you, Tonas—and the sooner the better."

"Ah, it will be worth the wait."

I pause as I consider what he said. I've seen a few of my guides, and recently I even saw Liponie—a compact-looking, blue man with short, wavy brown hair, a big smile on his face, and one golden earring, of course. But I still have not seen Tonas. It's interesting that the person I most want to see I have yet to even catch a glimpse of. I take in a deep breath and let that puzzle go. There's a party to plan, after all.

# # #

Tonas asks me what kind of physical body would be attractive to Jill Marie. I have no idea, but I am not concerned because everyone on this dimension must be exceptionally attractive. They all can change their appearance with a thought, anyway.

We decide to have all the eligible males wear a certain color, maybe green. The party will be right after we do the solstice work on June 21. Tonas asks if he can invite his parents; I say yes and that I'd like to invite all the academy instructors as well. I mention Osiris, Isis, Buddha, and Melchizedek. Tonas says he can find out about the others. I let him know I'm going to invite my guides, and I ask if I can invite Liponie.

Tonas agrees; I was sure he would. I also suggest inviting Hathor, Sekhmet, Sananda, Metatron, Archangel Michael, Thoth, and Khnum.

Tonas remarks, "This will be a delightful honor for us to have individuals of such magnitude. It would not be in my capacity to invite such dignitaries; and yet, because of your stature, it will be easy—if you are open to the invitation coming from both of us."

"Yes, I would like that."

"It is you that is the heavy hat, you see."

He must mean "heavy hitter." I find it endearing when something like this pops out of his mouth. You can only do so much research into a culture, after all. I'm never going to correct him when he comes up with these interpretations of Earth expressions. Heavy hat, indeed.

Tonas and I discuss ideas for party decorations. I have always hated doing this kind of thing. I even dreaded planning birthday parties for my children, especially trying to come up with ideas to keep a bunch of kids entertained. But when Tonas tells me he can extend the ship to make a room with a clear, crystalline dome and then project a swirling cosmos above it, I discover an excitement about party planning that I never thought possible. I tell him I absolutely love that idea and then suggest one of my all-time favorite things, fireworks. There is a slight planning hiccup here while I explain that he does not have to work any fire. Fireworks are part of celebrating my favorite holiday, the Fourth of July. He gets that right away and we're working in synch again. This is so fun!

I remind him to invite all nine hundred people on his ship; he's delighted to do so. Then we discuss who to invite as possible matches for Jill Marie. I've been thinking of all the Asthar Commanders Tonas must know and picturing them as dashing, cavalier types in their space uniforms. I'm quite dismayed when he tells me some of them are quite "stodgy." After taking a moment to absorb this disappointing information, I inform him that Jill Marie will absolutely not be interested in anyone like that. She works a lot, but when it's time to party, she has fun.

Tonas replies, "All right. By the way, this is another of my favorite sayings, 'All right.'"

"I say that a lot, don't I?"

"I love it. You are teaching me so much of the English. I bid you farewell."

"Farewell."

Esthra teasingly greets me with, "Well, it is about time! The two of you are mooning together."

"Esthra, we're going to throw a party on the ship."

"Oh, yes, I am not deaf."

"I wanted to make sure you were paying attention. Even though you're always right by my side, I still want to invite you and all my guides to it."

"This is an excellent opportunity for me to express to you how I exist," Esthra says. "I exist in thought and focus and in action; I exist not in particles, and yet I will be there with you. I am always offered the pleasure of being present in everywhere that you go. I am a little dimensional field away, and yet I am with you energetically. I am reading your energy. Today, your energy was so loud and clear that even the words came through with clarity. You are excited about this party, and you are a fixer."

"I've never thought of myself that way, but I'm definitely interested in seeing if I can assist Jill Marie to find a partner—or at least some men friends. All she does is work."

"Are you ready for a round of questions?" I ask.

"Let us get into this then."

"I'm thinking about the 8th dimension and wondering if you have witnessed a dual planet going from the 7th to the 8th?"

"Yes, I know of this. Earth itself has not experienced moving into that dimension yet. I sense that it will be your contingent moving into the 8th dimension and then waiting for the Earth to meet that."

"I'm unsure about the transition itself," I say. "When I move into the 8th dimension, I'm wondering—do I go to bed with wrinkles and cavities one night and then wake up the next morning without them? How does it happen? Is it a gradual thing, or does one become different all of a sudden? Do you know what I mean?"

"Yes, I do know. I know a great deal about this from my incarnation. I had great interest in worlds of duality, knowing that when the time came, it would be my great honor to be of assistance to you. I have studied other worlds that evolved. One of the things I noticed was that individuals moved from their dual to the lesser dual, and then farther into lesser dual, right to the point where the dividing is clearly either dual or non-dual, as with your 8th dimension. These numbers are made for you; they are named so that they will work for the linear mind.

"As I have witnessed other civilizations make their leaps, I've noticed that great changes began happening maybe as much as two or three years before the major shift into the higher, where there is now none of the old dimension and it is solely in the presence of the higher."

"You have seen this process happen on Earth?" I ask.

"When you began moving from your 3rd dimension into your 4th dimension, those two dimensions gradually merged. They both existed together and then 3rd left. It became no longer attached to the world that you existed within. The same will happen for you on your 8th dimension, and yet there will still exist the 6th and 7th dimensions and, perhaps, even the 4th and 5th. It is your great works that will make the difference; it will be possible for only the 6th and the 7th dimension to exist and the 4th and 5th to completely release."

"So I can look forward to a couple of years of transition before I move into a higher dimension?"

"Yes. I believe that, within that two or three years, when the dimensions are merging—before your motion into the 8th dimension— you will notice many shifts and changes. Then when you move into the 8th dimension, you will be, from this point of your interest, a little bit disappointed. But you will not be disappointed in life in the 8th dimension at all!"

"Disappointed? I don't understand."

"If I were to show you right now, you would be quite disappointed, because you won't care. You won't say, 'Oh, give me my good teeth and hair.' Instead, you will already be evolving into those perfected states. It won't even be in your mind; it just will happen. It sounds fun to make your plans and to have your lists of what must be; however, you simply won't care, because all that you desire will be made manifest."

"It sounds like you are saying I'll start to manifest things I desire, like wavy instead of frizzy hair, a little *before* I reach the 8th dimension."

Instead of a direct confirmation, Esthra describes, "You will see someone with hair that you like or some shoes, or color of eyes and you will think, 'That would look lovely on me,' and without even having to look in a mirror, you will see that you have these things. It will be like trying on clothes. 'Today I will wear this face.'"

"Let me try to get a little more timing on this. I know everything is still evolving, so it changes moment by moment. I know you can't say on this day, such and such will happen. But I want your best guess about when I could move into the 8th dimension."

"I knew that you were going to ask me that."

"Uh-huh." I don't feel embarrassed about trying to pin Esthra down. I want him to "spill the beans."

"Before I answer, I must celebrate you; I truly must, my dear," he says. "You are evolving so smoothly and gracefully. You are truly rising in your evolution in a graceful manner. It is a joy for me to witness."

"Thank you, Esthra."

"Now, to your question. Without giving away the important pieces in the puzzle, I can tell you that you will know it is close, and that in my estimation, it will be less than ten years of your experience. I am giving you simply my estimation. It might be three or ten; it might be more. I do not believe the last, because what you are doing is quite advanced. The thoughts, the focus of these things—they are making a difference."

"Good!"

"And ten years would go by fast."

"It's just that eighty years old seems *old*," I say. "Eighty! I know I'm going to laugh about it one day, Esthra."

"You will very much laugh, because when you are two hundred and eighty, you will likely desire another two hundred and eighty years—because you will be in such great joy. There will be a time when you will retire me as your advisor. I look forward to being, instead, your dear friend. I will have the option to re-embody."

"Oh, Esthra, that could be interesting. You have become such a good friend to me. I hope that we can stay in close connection."

#

I remember something I have wanted to ask him about. "One area I'm still struggling with is the whole concept of business."

"Would you be interested in picking up the pen?"

"I did a lot of poems and poetry and jotting things down in the past, but I haven't done any of that for a long time. Sometimes, I start a story and get a little dribble of something, and then the words don't come. I guess that's the writer's block thing."

"It is my thought that you will put this aside for a bit, and simply wait. Perhaps you could begin to prepare for when your ageless body attracts many to be mentored by you."

"Yes, that's my thought. Once that happens, I *know* people will be interested in hearing about my journey."

"I leave you with the thought that your greatest desires will come to you when they are of little interest."

"Thank you for your counsel today. I'm going to say farewell, and then I'd like to speak with Melchizedek."

"Indeed, my dear. There is no farewell for us, simply stepping aside, as I would."

#

I check in with Melchizedek about my violin playing and he tells me I am an apt pupil. Reassured by that information, I happen to casually ask him, "If you ever have any ideas about anything beneficial I could do for the planet, please tell me."

His quick response surprises me. "I do have an idea. Thank you for asking. My idea is that there is a core within Earth that reaches outward in all directions from its center point, as you are aware. If you were to imagine from that point that there were coordinates linking to each point from the center outward, it would be possible to create a new phase of energy points that could reach out into space.

"I realize that you have many energies coming in to the planet, and yet there are none so far that are a part of Earth that are created to move outward. This is a piece that is waiting, I believe. And you are the one who would, perhaps, be able to make this happen."

"All right. I'm going to talk with the CEV next. Thank you for your assistance with my musical abilities."

# # #

The CEV speaks, "We are in presence."

"Hello, I just asked Melchizedek if he had any suggestions for me; he said he did, since I asked. He mentioned that everything is coming into the Earth, but nothing is going out from Earth into 'the all and the everything.' He was speaking about a new phase of energy points that reach out into space."

I hear a lot of "Hmming" from the CEV as they consider this information. "We have arranged for much to enter and move outward from that space. He is most correct. There is no part of Earth that is designed to move outward beyond its own dimensional frame—except, of course, through the matrix of all that are connected. There is nothing similar to what we have applied."

"Would it be beneficial to do something like that?"

"It is our belief that there is an important wisdom to what is spoken."

"Could we do something on June 13, or is there a better time?"

"We are committed to assist. There are others who must

bring pieces to the arrangement before we can act."

"I'll go to the councils to get that information."

"If you bring us what you have from the councils, we can make something of it. We are greatly excited, greatly excited, greatly excited."

"You know, I just love working with you so much!"

"It is our greatest pleasure to be in partnership with you."

"I feel the same way. I will work on it right away and, hopefully, I will come back to you today."

"This will be a great joy." They exclaim, "A great joy! Oh, we are excitable. We know something big is about to be offered. Our hearts are all in the greatest excitement."

# # #

Since the CEV needs pieces from other councils, I gate into several hundred positions in different universes through individual doorways to retrieve additional pieces that will assist what we're going to do on the solstice.

These pieces, as well as what the CEV is putting together, are going to create another matrix that will link out to all the universes. The work Tonas and I have been doing with the eggs needed a framework to sit in, and this is it. This framework makes it so that everything connects. I realize that it needs to be done before the solstice.

I take what I got from the councils and gate back to the CEV. After I hand the information to them, they tell me it is more than adequate.

"On June 13, we will give you the piece we have created," they say. "It will be an egg of the greatest magnitude to be planted in the Earth."

# # #

"I'd like to speak with Liponie, please."

"Ah, it is most exciting. I am most honored to be speaking to you."

"I was going to speak with you earlier but, as they say, work kept coming up to do. I want to invite you to a party on Tonas's ship on June 21."

Liponie asks if I'm talking about the "galactic" Tonas. I confirm he is correct and suggest he can bring a partner to the party if he wishes.

"I am currently between partners, but I will attend and wear my bells!"

That certainly adds new meaning to the expression about being somewhere with "bells on."

When I tell him I caught a glimpse of him the other day, and he was wearing an earring in his ear, he says, "You did, of course." Then he springs a surprise on me. "I will tell you something else, my dear. This shall be our beginning, for I will be your jinn."

"Oh my."

"If you will have me, of course."

I know I'm going to agree to this proposal, but I do hesitate for just a moment. I remember some stories about jinn who were not so nice. But Esthra did recommend Liponie, and so I say, as I knew I would, "I will."

"It will not be the same as those of Earth who preceded me," Liponie says, sensing my hesitation.

"How will we work together? What will we do?"

"I will grace your presence whenever possible. I am thinking of this as an idea for helping you with these 'impossible' things. We can think of this and talk of it later. I wish not to tire you, and yet I have already told a few people that perhaps you might take me as your jinn."

"I am delighted to, Liponie," I say. "It sounds like a lot of fun. I'm moving into a new phase here of having fun. Lately, I can't stop laughing."

Liponie, sensing I have another request, waits for me to continue.

"Here's something else for you to think about," I tell him. "I want a new, magical body that is above and beyond what it used to be. I think you'd be the perfect one to help me with that."

"I believe that you would be a beautiful maiden in the brightest of orange."

"That's an interesting choice, because with my complexion, orange is not a color that looks good on me," I say. "I've never really worn orange, but I'm willing to try."

"I'm talking about your skin being orange, my dear."

I'm thinking 'ugh,' but I diplomatically say, "Oh, I don't know."

"We could mix a golden tone with the orange."

"Liponie, I think of pumpkins when I see orange."

"Or we could try some blues. You could try *my* color as well. I change it periodically."

Planning a new color for my body is just not something I want to do now—actually, maybe never. So I change the subject.

"Remember, you are invited to the solstice party."

"It would be unfortunate if I were not invited, being your dear jinn. Others would have wondered why I was not in presence. It would have been interesting to explain, for I have a new status, you see."

"Tonas says the ship is part mine, so I can invite whomever I would like."

"May I be on the decorating committee?"

"I didn't suggest that, but I would like for you to. Next time I speak with him, I'll ask him if you can be included in the decorating, because I know you're good at that."

"Ah, I'm expert. Oh, it is so delightful."

"I'm going to have to say goodbye. But I want you to know, you're special to me. I do love you, Liponie."

This is easy for me to say, because I know I really do love him. He is so light-hearted, and I feel that way too when I am with him. I haven't been able to feel this free with Tonas. Maybe because I have so much fear of making a commitment I won't be able to keep.

Liponie says, "This is such a delight for me. Of course this will be in the next play. There is going to be a chapter of us."

"That sounds good to me. I'll say farewell for now."

CHAPTER TWENTY-FIVE

June 11, 2014

Liponie's lovely greeting is, "I am in delight, my dear."

"Hello, Liponie."

"I am, of course, delighted every time that I am brought into your link of consciousness with mine."

"Has Melchizedek spoken with you lately?"

"He has brought to my attention that there is a wanting within you, a great desire within you, to feel the fluidity of what he considers to be playfulness and joyfulness. This feeling is brought forth from the essence of your cells of being and out into the world through a conscious connection with the heart—and the essence of your physical being—which makes the music. It is a bit of a dance, you must know."

"Liponie, these words describe exactly what I am longing to do. Is there any way you can help me with that?"

"I would wish to bring to your heart the greater gladness that I believe is the answer to uplifting all that you believe is impossible, and that which you have desires in your heart to bring into presence," he says. "It is through an inner acceptance, as well as moving beyond the vision of the 3rd dimension, which has crowded into your mind the vision of what is impossible. I believe that much of this came from early indoctrination, my dear. And, of course, there is between us the vision of no limits."

"I'd like to embrace that vision more fully."

"It is nearing that time. A day is coming when you will create and I will be in the fullest of readiness to assist you."

"You know, I hear a tinkling noise sometimes when you are talking."

"Ah, I wear a necklace of crystal bells. They are always ringing when I am in joyfulness and laughter."

More questions about his bells reveal that they are nine, clear crystals he wears around his neck. The bell-like sound they make is actually a resonance of sparkling light. I love the thought of a sound like that, and I am especially intrigued when he tells me the crystals are mined from the deepest heart of a special place on Andromeda. Maybe someday I can visit that place and have some of those crystals to wear myself.

Liponie lets me know the celebrations on Andromeda are winding down and checks to make sure he is an invited guest for our solstice party. I ask if he's still interested in doing the decorations, and he tells me he would be pleased to do so. Then he adds that, if I wish, he will find a thousand or even one hundred thousand crystals from that special mine and "string them as little stars in the atmosphere of the upper part of the ship." He adds, "When the stars themselves shine through that crystalline dome that is in presence, it will make the most delicious of sounds, for these are singing crystals."

As I visualize what this genie plans to create, I'm thinking it was a lucky day for me when Esthra suggested I become acquainted with Liponie. How can I possibly go wrong with a genie like this on the decorating committee? Nevertheless, I tell him that I'm going to check with Tonas.

"I see," Liponie responds. "It would be a stepping on foots for me to simply step in and say that I would wish to do so."

"How will I let you know if it's okay?"

"This ship captain, as you would say, he would send the request to me."

"I will ask him; I am sure he will be agreeable."

"I believe this one has a desire to please you always."

"Yes, I think you are right."

"You could ask him for the Moon and he would find a way to get it for you."

"I love talking to you, Liponie. I'm so glad to know about your beautiful bells."

#

Intending to speak with Tonas, I hear him say, "Oh, I am in gratitude. You have come to me!"

"I can't be here for long."

"Even if it is for just a moment, it is wonderful to be in communication. Will you come to me for this conversation?"

Realizing I forgot to gate to the ship, I immediately join him there.

"You are so delightful."

"I have a little request."

"Any request is small; I will do anything for you."

"I started thinking the other night about the emotions you experience. I'm not used to being with someone who is never angry. *Are* you ever angry?"

"Why would I be?"

"This is the reality that I've grown up in," I tell him. "People can be angry and jealous and even spiteful sometimes. It's different talking to you because you do not react to the things I say or do the way that people, especially men, in this reality have. I've never been in a relationship where a man was always interested in doing what I suggested. I usually found myself participating in activities that interested my partner and they were not interested in reciprocating.

"Disapproval was the most difficult thing for me to experience. And even when it wasn't verbal, I could sense the unspoken: 'Why in God's name would she want to do that/wear that/investigate that?' I'm not used to relating to a man like you. It's a whole new way of being for me. If I can get used to not being nervous about possible unpleasant reactions to my words or actions, it will be extremely refreshing."

Then I remember my primary aim in this conversation.

"Tonas, do you remember Liponie, my genie friend on Andromeda?"

"Yes, he is the colored fellow, a pretty color."

"I asked if he would contribute to the decorations for the party, but I need your approval." I describe the singing crystals Liponie wears and how he intends to decorate the ship with them. Tonas agrees to open the ship and work directly with Liponie so that he and his crew are in harmony with Liponie's desires, adding that they are an "extension of my desires." I love the way that this guy thinks.

"Are your parents going to be on the ship on the thirteenth?" I ask.

"They are most dedicated to be in presence at the party, so they are planning to be in presence on that day."

"I will make sure I save some time to talk with them."

"Indeed. My mother adores the color of turquoise; I am mentioning this to you in advance. She will love you no matter what, and yet, if you were to wear this turquoise, she would be most excited. It would be an honor to her."

"I don't know what I'll wear when I come," I remind him. "When I visit you, I have no idea what I'm wearing."

"You are unaware? You are not planning this?"

"No, I just show up and I don't know what I've got on. It's kind of interesting when you say I'm wearing a golden robe or whatever, because I'm sitting here and wearing a purple t-shirt and gray shorts."

"My dear, today you are—from top to bottom—wearing the most beautiful streaming energies of greens. Your robes are diaphanous, flowing materials. And, of course, your feet are bare."

I'm sure 10th dimension Joy looks lovely, but for me the most appealing part of that description is having bare feet.

"You see, I had no idea what I was wearing. I can intend to wear turquoise, but I don't know if that will happen."

"Let us try this," Tonas suggests. "I will whisper to you that you are wearing the beautiful color. I think she will see it as a great honor. She will love you, in any stead."

"Tell me their names again."

"My mother is Firona, and my father is Emmon. They would love it if you would call them Mother and Father."

I think, *Yikes!* But I calmly reply, "I will consider that."

"Yes, of course. It is also that one day you will feel this in your heart as well."

"All right, I'm sending you hugs and kisses and love today as I say farewell."

"Farewell, my dear."

CHAPTER TWENTY-SIX

June 13, 2014

Tonas says, "Ah, my dear one, much has transpired since we last spoke. There is much excitement aboard my ship. Everyone is in great hurriedness to make sure that all is ideal. We have expanded the size of the ship by three-fourths to accommodate our many guests comfortably. We are in readiness."

"That is so wonderful, Tonas! I appreciate all your efforts. Please invite these people: Horus, Gaia, Joy Star, Jesus, Magdalene, Mother Mary, St. Germain, Kuthumi, your friends and siblings, and any other Ashtar Commanders you would like to be in presence. This is a party for you as well, not just me—so please feel free to invite all those you would like to attend."

"Some of these have already been invited. It was simple for me to make the invitation for all of those of your academy."

"Will we have music?"

"Of course, there will be your music."

Tonas says that they have recorded my past concerts and that music will be played throughout the entire party. I'm not sure this is a good choice. "But the classical music I've played is not the kind of music people can dance to," I explain.

Tonas assures me that all he has to do—and he says it will be easy—is enter into the archives of the history of music, snap up some tunes (not his words, but he makes it sound that easy) and we will have dance music to play.

"And can there be live music as well?"

"Oh yes," he says. "I'm going to create a ballroom and then invite, oh, perhaps fifty or a hundred different players of orchestral music from different worlds."

I'm reminding myself all through his casual description of party additions that this is reality for people in the higher dimensions. *We* will be able to do things like this in Earth's 8th dimension!

Coming back to Earth, figuratively speaking, I say, "Maybe we can talk more about it again on Monday. I have a limited time today, and I want to make sure I say hello to your parents. I will gate to you."

"This would be most efficient."

"Please let me know when I am there."

"You mean, now that I can kiss your fingers, I may begin?"

I say, "Yes," and giggle.

"Mmm, you are beautiful in your exquisite clothings."

I know he would say that no matter what I wore, but I do ask, "Did I manage to wear any turquoise?"

"You have the turquoise. You also have hints of a beautiful green which is liked by my mother as well as my father."

"Before I meet them, I want to give you a gift. Do you know about the Nazca lines in Peru?"

"I know of them, but I would need to move my ship to witness them."

"I flew over them in a little twelve-seat plane, and when I was in the city of Nazca, I purchased some of the jewelry that has pictures of the geoglyphs. The one I'm holding has been designated as the hummingbird. I don't know how much you know about the Native American peoples, but in their traditions, the hummingbird stands for joy."

"Ah! It is named for you!"

"Yes, so I'm going to give you this little medallion."

"I will treasure it, my dear."

"You can change the color in the background; I want you to make it into…"

"I will change nothing."

I knew he would say that, but I persist and say, "I would like for you to make it into a piece of jewelry that would suit you. My thinking is it's more feminine because I wear it on a silver band around my neck, but you can make it into a pin."

"Ah, you have worn this piece?"

"Yes."

"It has touched your skin?"

He sounds intense as he asks me this, and I'm thinking, "Oh, boy…"

"Yes, I'm holding it right now."

"I know, but it has been up against your chest?"

"I wear it around my neck."

"Then it must be the same for me."

"Well, no, not really."

"Do you believe that it is not appropriate?"

"I want you to wear it the way you would like to display it. And you could, of course, make another copy and wear it as a pin, or a bracelet or a ring, however you want. This is a gift to please you. I know it pleases you that it's from me, but I really would like you to use your inventiveness and skill to make it into something that fits you personally. Do you know what I'm saying?"

"What fits me perfectly is to wear it against me as you have worn it against you."

I knew this would be how the conversation ended, so I gracefully capitulate, "Okay, then, however you would like."

"It will be considered one of my greatest treasures."

"I'm glad you like it. It's one of my favorite elegant pieces. I also brought some gifts for your parents. Are they around?"

"I will summon them when you are ready."

"Let me meet them now," I say, explaining that I have more preparatory work for the solstice to do today and my time is limited. "It's okay with me if they want to watch the work."

He's delighted with that idea. "It would be magnificent for them."

# # #

Tonas presents his mother, Firona, and his father, Emmon, to me.

"I am delighted to meet you," I say. "Since my time is limited today, I would like to complete my work with Tonas first, and then we can chat. Perhaps you have interesting tales to tell me about your son."

Emmon graciously replies, "Most assuredly, my dear. You may call me Father, if you would wish. Our dear Tonas is much taken by the beauty of you and your inner radiance of purity. This, of course, we can easily witness."

I smile to acknowledge this compliment and Emmon continues. "We don't want to be in the way. We will simply be available if you wish to converse more. Can you explain please what it is that you are about to do?"

"Certainly. I'm going to go to a collective group of beings who call themselves the Council for Earth Vigilance to get some energy work they've put together. I have additional work from some of the galactic councils and even from councils in other universes that will assist us on the summer solstice. This is one of my favorite days of the year, but it's also a little bit sad for me, because the daylight begins to lessen every day."

I briefly explain my goal of facilitating a balance for the masculine and feminine energies of the planet on the solstice. "I'm going to gate to the CEV to get the work they have prepared for me and then bring it back to the ship."

Tonas assures me they will be waiting and asks if I would like for anyone else to join us. I ask for Osiris, as usual.

# # #

The CEV speaks, "Greetings."

"Greetings, here I am."

"Mmm, indeed. We are in great excitement. There is much that will be brought through today, although more is possible. It is our considered opinion, as a collective, that the balance of energies within humanity has been contrary to that of Gaia herself."

"I agree."

"The vision of the masculine and feminine is, in her, perfectly balanced. It is possible for this first seed to be planted in the past in the 3rd dimension." The CEV add that this needs to be done in a specific framework of time, prior to the development of humanity.

"I need to travel back in time?"

"Yes. Tonas can take you there in his ship."

I'm excited to learn that we are going to be planting several "seeds" within the Earth. The 4th dimension seed will be in 1999; the 5th dimension seed will be planted on the summer solstice of 2009; the 6th dimension date is the summer solstice of 2010. And for the 7th dimension, we will need to move forward to the solstice of the present year.

"What do these seeds look like?" I ask.

"They are glowing, golden seed pods of radiance."

# # #

I return to the ship and, of course, Tonas wants to know what we will do with these seeds. I relay the information about timing and placement to him, and he asks if I would like to speak with Osiris.

With my acceptance, Osiris tells me, "I am most inspired by you. You are developing quite an amazing story."

"What I really want is for this work to help bring about a new story for the Earth."

"Yes," Osiris says, "there is a great story that is playing within the theaters in all dimensions, the realms of everything. I understand that you must take one of these seeds. They are specific, and so you must be sure that you are planting the correct seed."

"Oh, no pressure!" I joke, and I hope he is joking, too.

"There is no pressure at all," he replies humorously. "And yet it is important for this 3rd dimension seed to provide a foundation for the birth of that species from which you developed. This is unprecedented, as you would say."

This information is quite startling, but also inspiring for me. Providing a foundation for humanity of balanced masculine and feminine energy seems a magnificent idea. Osiris states that he will only be an observer of our work since Earth is not his world, but he does suggest it would be important to involve the people of Agartha, a city in the inner Earth. "Since the Earth is their home, they have the power to support your work more than I do."

It's interesting for me to learn that Shiva and many of our academy instructors live in Agartha.

I ask Osiris how to coordinate all of this work.

"I believe that you could initiate the first planting from the position of Agartha," he replies. "I think it would be lovely for all on this ship to be part of this experience. Do you agree?"

"Yes."

We ask Tonas to bring his ship to the appropriate position in the 3rd dimension.

Osiris gives me the details of his plan, and, as he does, I put it into action. "From this viewing screen on the ship, we will be able to view all that is applied. Leave all but one of the seeds with Tonas. Take the appropriate one and move into the space of Agartha, where all are in presence waiting. From that position, plant this seed of balance within the 3rd dimension. It is already expanding; it is already almost as bright as a sun. Burst through all positions as if you yourself were expanding to the full measure of Earth, so that your energy is carrying this bright sun outward through all parts of Earth, into the upper atmosphere, taking in all regions of the expanse of the aura of Earth itself. That seed is planted, my dear."

"It feels nice in this position."

"The seed is indoctrinating itself," Osiris says. "It will have many eons of time to find its balance. Now move your presence back to us on the ship."

# # #

Tonas moves the ship to the 4th dimension on July 4, 1999. Again, I plant the seed in Agartha.

Osiris comments, "All in presence are envisioning with you the masculine/feminine balance catching on the wave from the 3rd dimension and moving forward from this placement. This radiance continues to expand outward, as it did before. Feel it becoming brighter and brighter."

Next, we move to the 5th dimension to the summer solstice of 2009. Osiris mentions that the ship has special cloaking, so there will be no witnesses to our work. I again place the seed in Agartha.

I remind Tonas that the 6th dimension seed is to be placed in Agartha during the summer solstice in the year 2010. When we return from placing this seed, Osiris asks us to notice that the wave we created when we planted the seed in 3rd dimension is still moving forward.

Tonas moves the ship forward to the solstice of this year so that we can plant the 7th dimensional seed in Agartha.

I explain to our group that I am smoothing, blending, and visioning the beauty of the Goddess and the God in love with each other and balanced perfectly. "I send that love, that vibration, and that blessing to the Earth and to all of the universes, through the threads, outward into all that is, the blessings of Gaia and the love of the Earth."

"What is the vision you wish to project as a result of completing all you are bringing forth?" Osiris asks.

"We are moving toward the androgynous," I reply, "the blending of the masculine and feminine in divine harmony and an appreciation and love of the gifts of each of those energies of the masculine, feminine, and neutral."

Then I send forth a prayerful intention. "I ask for the divine blending of these energies and their gifts to unfold smoothly and easily for all of us on this planet, especially for those who are ready to accept the awareness and guidance of their Higher Self, their divine nature, their love of the Earth, and for each other."

Osiris says, "There is much wisdom in your words. I wish to speak to you of the divine balance within, where the feminine continues to be the radiance of that presence of the divine feminine, and the masculine sees itself as an accompaniment, like I see my beloved Isis. I see myself as a part of my journey. That part of my journey is in partnership with her and it is the richest of all my parts. She shines the radiance of the divine upon me, inspiring me to become the greatest Osiris."

He seems to speak to all of us as he continues. "The feminine is the greatest part of the seed. The feminine is the leap that allows all to follow as they cross the bridge into their own worth and the greatest productivity of life experience. It is important for all beings to feel the balance of these two within themselves, so that all male and female beings of Earth feel that thread of competition between the two falling apart—for there is no competition, only joy and bliss and excitement for the race itself as it is run."

"Yes, I agree," I say.

"This is most exciting," Osiris says. "You have completed this glorious part of your work. I know that your Tonas is eager to be of assistance. Obviously, it is important for him to be of the greatest service to you."

I have wondered, so now I ask, "Can Tonas hear me as I talk with you?"

"We now make it so."

"Tonas, if we invite the people in Agartha to the party, would that be all right? Osiris, if he decides it would be possible, could you assist him with who would be coming?"

"It will be my great pleasure," he says. "It will be transmitted through Shiva himself, for he is your emissary from that realm."

Tonas speaks out. "My dear, whatever is your desire is my greatest pleasure. You, perhaps one day, will understand that such a request from you brings me even more delight. We will increase the size of the ship to accompany the full measure of all those of Agartha. Ah, this will be what you would call the party of this century—although I have a feeling that you will move beyond the magnitude of this one quickly."

# # #

"Tonas, I want to give your parents the gifts that I brought for them."

"Oh, they are most excited. I believe they are in awareness that there is something that is coming to them, for Osiris himself let the cats out of the bag. Let me call my parents into the room."

"My dear, I am Firona. It is my great pleasure to speak with you."

"Thank you for coming today. I have a gift for you."

"I see it. May I take it from you?"

"Yes, of course. This is one of my favorite necklaces. The star is made of turquoise; I like the way it fits between the points of the crescent Moon. We always think of the Moon as feminine, so I'm giving you the Moon and the star."

"Oh, I will treasure it, my dear, of course," she says. "We already treasure you. We have heard so much about you, and I'm sure you would like to hear something about my beloved son."

"I certainly would. He has not shared anything about when he was little, that I am aware of."

"I will give you a nugget of information," she says. "He sucked his largest finger until he was ten years. He was greatly enamored with this finger. Of course, we saw this as charming."

"I'm glad to know he did that, because I sucked my thumb for probably longer than that," I say. "Thank you for that information. I'm eager to talk with you again."

"I'm looking forward to our coming to know each other as women, as well as ones who are dedicated to my beloved son. I know you are dedicated, my dear. He is certainly dedicated to you."

"I know he is. A lot of this work, believe it or not, began just because I wanted to see him."

"It is unfortunate that you are unable to see the beauty of him," his mother says. "I know there will be a time when it is possible."

"I'm afraid that I might swoon the first time I see him."

"I am sure that you will," she says, chuckling. "He is quite beautiful."

I intended that comment to be a bit of a joke, but when I think about it, from the way several people have described him, "swooning" might indeed be a possibility.

"I also have a gift for Emmon."

"My dear, I always enjoy gifts," he says.

"I've done much work over my lifetime that I was not aware of until recently. One of my guides tells me that I've been helping the Native Americans through all timelines. I have a little leather pouch; here, I'll hand it to you."

"Are these the indigenous of the continent that you exist on?"

"Yes."

"Ah, we are aware of that history."

"This would be considered a modern day version of a medicine bag. They probably would have worn it around their waist, not around their neck. They would have put things that were precious to them inside, like a feather or some kind of totem. The other present I'm going to give you is a pretty pebble called a sunstone. I want you to use it however you would like, but if you would want to make it into a ring or some piece of jewelry that you would enjoy, I would love that. So your wife has the Moon and the star and you have the Sun."

(In case you're wondering if the gifts I'm giving miraculously disappear from my hands when I hand them over—they don't. How wonderful is that to be able to give a gift and also to keep it?)

"You are poetic, my dear, very poetic indeed—and quite comely I might add."

"Thank you. I'm sorry not to be able to visit with you longer. I really did want to talk more."

"What we witnessed today has been most enlightening," he says. "We are honored to have been able to be in the presence of this."

"Please know that Tonas has done magnificent work assisting me with things that we have done previously. I'm hoping that he tells you about it if he chooses. It's been wonderful working with him. I appreciate his help so much and his gentleness and courtesy."

"I know that he is greatly dedicated to you, and, as all of us, greatly dedicated to Earth."

"Tonas," I call, "I'm blowing you a kiss. Farewell."

"Farewell, my dear. Will you come tonight?"

"I will."

"We will be waiting."

CHAPTER TWENTY-SEVEN

June 16, 2014

We are close to the solstice, and I still have a long list of areas for which I would like to receive assistance. After I gate to councils on non-dual worlds to retrieve templates, grids, and sacred symbols that will assist Earth, I receive ideal versions of the following systems and principles: Sri Yantra, free energy, teleportation, string magic, divine plan, leadership, alchemical grids, commerce, Christ consciousness, anti-gravity, teleportation, education, government, prosperity consciousness, divine version of religion—that one is particularly exciting for me—and the Golden Rule. I also receive ninety-four activations from four galactic councils.

Today, my intention is to first speak with Isis about her view on the union of masculine and feminine energies. After we greet each other, I request her version of the relationship she has with Osiris.

"I am most aware of his impressions of the balance of the masculine and feminine and, of course, my impressions are much the same—except that when I hold my beautiful beloved in my arms, when I gaze into his eyes, I see a reflection of myself in his eyes and I feel his great joy and love. And so, when he looks upon me, he sees the same."

"That is beautiful," I say.

"I believe the balance of the masculine and the feminine is truly the vision of that harmony. It is the unity of both in perfect blossoming, like the lotus. One side of the lotus does not say it is different than the other; it simply knows itself as perfect and whole. Does this help you, my dear?"

"Yes, it does. Do you have anything you feel would be important for us to add with the work we will be doing on the twenty-first to facilitate this balancing?"

"Oh, indeed, and I am most pleased that you would ask me

of such things. Yes, the vision of the figure eight demonstrates the balanced masculine and feminine. It is the unity; it is the harmony. And so, you could request—from some worthy councils—the blending of the masculine and feminine energies that make up the whole of that perfect, blossoming lotus. There are those who have the ability to provide you with such grids. This is simply a unified grid of harmony."

"The CEV could do that, I believe."

"I would never presume—yet I believe that you know that this would be a likely source."

"I'm going to speak with them next. I will see you at the party."

"I am designing a specific gown that I believe will be most pleasurous to you."

"I look forward to seeing it! Thank you."

# # #

I visit the appropriate galactic councils to ask for the unified grid of harmony and I am given all unified grids that are associated with the evolution of Earth rising up to the 8th dimension and beyond, as well as additional grids for the balanced masculine and feminine. I put what I receive into an orb and I take it to the CEV.

The CEV speaks, "You are welcome."

This is an interesting greeting, but I roll with it and say, "Thank you. I have a present for you. Here it is."

"We are pleased."

"I am, too. It has some wonderful new grids in it."

"This is most relevant. We are bringing our collective mind into focus of this gift. We are most excited."

"Good, I love it when you are excited!"

"There are a multitude of opportunities associated with this important gift. We will have something most magnificent ready for you. We are deliberating. We have many orbs for you; these will be precursors. These will be best taken directly to the ship of that one. We have much to deliberate, my dear."

On the ship, Tonas greets me with, "My dear, you are here."

"I'm here and I've got more orbs."

"Oh, let me help you! You are burdened by so many. Come, all of you, help us please. How did you manage this? This is amazing that you should manage such large amounts."

When I ask how many I have, he tells me there are perhaps two hundred. I'm eager to begin, but he asks if he may, as usual, kiss my fingers first. Then he concludes our greeting ritual by placing violet-colored flowers between my toes. My comment that I love violets reveals that he does not know of that flower. He's always placed orchid blossoms between my toes, since he knows I love those flowers.

#

"Do you have everything under control for the party? Are we going to have dance music, so we can … dance?"

"We have a ballroom set beautifully. There will be many orchestras. It is exciting."

"I just want to make sure we're on the same page, since we have such different backgrounds. I'm eager to experience the music you know and the dancing that you like to do."

"I do wish to show you how I enjoy dancing. And also, I wish to learn all of your dances. Perhaps I can send out a request that everyone who comes to this party learn of the dances you have experienced in your lifetime."

I agree to this plan, but request that Tonas make dance lessons optional. I also suggest that we might limit the types of dance we do to the more classical ones like waltz and fox trot. I can't imagine the attendees wanting to dance the Mashed Potato—*I* don't even know how to do that one—or the Monkey.

On second thought, I do request the Twist.

"You have no idea the excitement you have stirred within the ranks of all of the highest, as well as those individuals of my ranking," Tonas says. "Simply to be included is of great excitement to everyone. And there is a long line of suitors for your friend."

"How is she going to know?"

"I think that whatever she decides is what we will do."

"I'll ask her to come to you."

Tonas tells me his ship is now fifty times bigger than it originally was, and that it is almost as big as Commander Ashtar's. I can't believe he asks me if he should invite the commander. I gently advise him we certainly can't leave that man out. He really must be invited. Tonas shares some good news: no one has refused an invitation.

I realize that Tonas and I haven't done a lot of planning about entertaining the guests. I'm wondering if maybe people will be content to listen to the music, and/or dance and just talk with one another other. Tonas tells me they will want to talk with *me*.

I hadn't planned on being any kind of center of attention, but he assures me the guests will like to be in my presence and to celebrate. He adds that tasty fruits are being harvested throughout practically every universe, and that since this is going to be a three day party, he has created greater lodging.

I ask him if he knows about the planet Folgor, where people dance on their fingers.

"My goodness! They dance on their fingers?" Tonas sounds as astounded as I was when Esthra told me about these dancers. "That would be incredible to witness. Would you like to have these dancers in presence?"

"I think it would be mesmerizing to see them dance, if they would like to come."

We decide to invite dancers from different cultures

throughout all universes, and I suggest he ask Esthra about the Folgor dancers.

"And they really dance on their fingers?"

"That is what Esthra told me," I say. "But I still find it hard to imagine."

# # #

Tonas and I have to stand farther apart to activate the orbs, since I brought so many—but other than that, we follow our standard procedure. As usual, I feel euphoric at the end of our work.

"That felt wonderful," I say.

He matter-of-factly replies, "It is what we do."

"I'm looking forward to talking with your mother again. Did you hear what she told me?"

"I was in presence."

"I sucked my thumb until I was eleven or twelve," I tell him. "As you grow up here, thumb-sucking is something to be embarrassed about. I was grateful to learn that about you, because it makes you seem like maybe you're not as completely perfect as you are."

"Ah, but it was so perfect for me to suck my finger."

"Yes, I can see that."

"It was perfect for you to suck your finger!"

"It was my thumb that I sucked."

"The perception that it was wrong or imperfect is incorrect, my dear."

"I was really embarrassed by it, though. If I went to a friend's house for a party and stayed all night, I didn't want people to know that I sucked my thumb, because it was a childish thing to do."

"We are more alike than you can imagine."

"Learning that about you made you seem more human. I

know you're not, really, but it just made you seem more so."

"I am delightful, and so are you," he says, adding in a whisper, "And we are delightful together."

"We are. I'm going to be coming to the party. Let's hope I wear something nice so we can also appear delightful together."

# # #

I have a sudden desire to share more of my past with this intriguing man. "I want to show you some pictures. Let me gate back to my home and then come back with my picture book." I'm gone for just a moment.

"What is this?" he asks.

"These are pictures. Do you know what pictures are? Do you have pictures?"

"Visions?"

"Not exactly. We take pictures with a camera. We can't remember things like you do, so we take pictures. These are pictures of me. Let me hand you the two that I'm holding right now. One is me when I'm two years old, and I'm holding my pet rooster. Can you see that?"

"It is an animal, my dear."

"It's a chicken. He was my pet rooster."

"Did he have a name?"

"I was too little to name him, but he was my buddy. I carried him around everywhere. Can you see the pictures?"

"I can see the energy of them. Were there no children to play with? I am so delighted that you loved animals."

"I lived out in the country, so there really weren't any children around. Here's one of me and my brother with my favorite cow, Glory."

"It is a glory that you have such a connection to animals."

"Yes. Here's one last picture, taken about four years ago. It's me and my youngest son standing in front of an apple orchard that we go to almost every year. The flowers all around us are chrysanthemums. When I was married we used to take our boys there every fall, when the apples were ripe. They have delicious apple cider and apple cider doughnuts."

"Should we have these at the party?"

"We could have apple cider doughnuts!"

"And the apple cider?"

"Yes, it's a good drink."

"Oh, it is a drink. Something to consume as a food as well as a drink is perfect. What could be better? A delightful human delicacy."

"Yes, agreed."

"It has been my great pleasure for you to be here with me today. It is hard to say farewell, but I know it must be so. You will be back soon, I know."

"If I leave this book with you, could we look through it together at night? That way I could explain the pictures."

"That would be such a delight," he says. "It is what we will do tonight."

#

I intend to speak with Esthra, and I hear his voice now.

"How are you, Joy?"

"I'm fine," I assure him. Then I ask him a question that has proved useful in the past. "Is there anything you want to tell me or that I should know about?"

"I hope you are comfortable with fame," he says.

"I guess I'll deal with that if and when it happens, because I don't feel famous now."

"The time will come when you will."

"I think I'll be all right. Anyway, the possibility of fame seems so far in the future, there's no sense in thinking about it now."

"You are evolving, and you will meet that, of course."

"I wish I knew what Osiris was referring to when he recently mentioned that the next eighteen months will be significant. Can you give me the scoop on that, Esthra?"

"Ah, you know that I am a talker."

Laughing, I tell him, "Spill everything you know, or I will twist your arm."

"Good luck with that. I will tell you that, in eighteen of the Earth months, there is a pinnacle shift that is possible. At that time, your 7th dimension will have an elevation point that will supersede anything ever experienced on Earth. It will not be the 8th dimension fully, but it will be easy to step across into the eighth from that point."

"Will I be able to progress more rapidly then?"

"You will manage that 7th dimensional elevation point with such exquisite understanding," he says. "You will come to understand in that framework what it is to be in a non-dual plane of existence. Of course, that is something that you will not want to rush through, because it is like learning to dance. It is a wonderful thing to watch the intricate steps and to imagine what it would be like to glide across the floor moving in such gyrations. And yet, until you are able to master the steps, it might be disappointing to have all eyes on you on the dance floor as you, perhaps, experience a wiggly heel on your shoe. This will be an exciting time."

"So this is something that gradually happens over the next eighteen months?"

"It will be most progressive. Guiding my mind through the vision of what you are performing, I have no way of imagining how much quicker things could be, simply through what you are applying. You are unquenchable in your desire."

"Yes, I know."

This information is so exciting to me! I think about asking him more, but I'm sure that's all I'm going to get for now.

Instead, I thank him and let him know I appreciate the tidbit he shared with me.

"You bent my arm very firmly," he jokes.

"I know. You can tell them that, 'She made me tell her.'"

"I am in a position to speak, where maybe others are not."

"Yes, thank you, Esthra."

CHAPTER TWENTY-EIGHT

June 18, 2014

I decide I would like to offer gifts to all the people on my list of 30,544 names. This list is composed of people who have died who had skills or abilities I admired. Through SVH and with Sananda's assistance, I have been able to integrate the divine version of their genetics in order to enhance my own abilities.

Sananda and I go to the Fifth Realm at the near completion, and I ask all of those on my list of names for gifts to give to their progeny and to every aspect of their genetic lineage for the whole history of Earth. Sananda hands me the gifts he received, I compress them—along with the ones I received—into an orb. Then I step into one of the places we use in SVH to implement our work, call everyone forward, and hand them their gifts.

Liponie is standing beside one of the individuals on my list who turns out to be George Frederick Handel. I wonder out loud why Liponie would be a genie to that man, and if Handel knew he had a genie.

Liponie speaks up and says, "My dear, of course Handel knew I was his genie."

This is fascinating information—I had no idea genies did things like that—and I ask Liponie why he decided to be Handel's muse.

"It was my desire to assist," he replies. "His family had no interest in music, you see. It was as if he was a prodigy born to a family of idiots! They could not imagine the beauty that he could create. I was his inspiration."

I like Handel's music, so I think it's awesome that Liponie helped him create it. What's even more awesome is that Liponie is helping *me*!

# # #

I'd hoped to invite some of the people on my list of names to our party, but Sananda informs me that those in the Fifth Realm wouldn't be able to come; however, he does remind me that if they were on my list, I had already brought them gifts from their future selves. Then he asks me if I realize what I did.

For a moment, I don't understand why he sounds so excited. Then I realize what the gifts I brought from their future selves to the people on my list of names—the best, the brightest or, at least, the most interesting in their fields—could have meant in the way of assisting them to develop their abilities.

"*I* could be the reason why Heifetz was such a fabulous violinist!" I exclaim.

"That is possible," Sananda says. "You don't know *what* you gave them from their future selves!"

"But it had to be something awesome, didn't it?"

Even though I only transported their gifts, at least I played *some* part in assisting the many individuals on my list to experience extraordinary lives. That is something I plan to savor.

# # #

I decide to talk with Esthra to see if we can do anything else for the people on my list or if there's some additional way that they can assist Earth's evolution.

He muses for a moment and then says, "Hmm, yes, indeed, the angel realm can inspire those to enhance, to elevate, to spirit the instilled areas of self that have been sponsored through the gifts that you brought through. This would ripple forward and touch upon many. Imagine their progeny! Of course, not all would have such a gift of progeny, but many will have."

"So you're saying the gift that they gave themselves would have assisted their progeny."

"Yes, it would. So if we in the angel realm addressed each of these individuals, as well as their progeny, we could perhaps radiate outward to the social network of all these individuals, who span throughout the world through the different lines of time. It is a large number of individuals; it would be quite exponentially expanding."

"So guardian angels would be working and watching over these individuals?"

"It would be their position to assist, in any case. We would ask them to enhance and amplify these attributes that were offered. Does this sound like what you would wish?"

"Yes, it does."

"I believe this would be expansive." A few seconds later he says, "I am complete. This has been done and continues to be done."

"Oh! Angel speed is extremely speedy."

"Oh, well, it takes us one thought, my dear. I had to put the thought into some kind of system that could be replicated. And now, it is done."

"Is there any additional way that you or Melchizedek could assist me with the gifts that might be rolling to me from what we did today?"

"That is part of all of us," Esthra replies. "We are amplifying this in full measure already. You are not of the progeny; instead, you are like a treasure chest filled with the sparkles of your delicious presence amplified."

# # #

I ask Esthra to suggest one of my guides who might be able to accelerate my success in my business endeavors. He recommends Teressa.

Teressa announces, "I am in your presence. I believe it is important for you to know that you are already prosperous. Good things attract to you; you are like a magnet to lovely experiences. It is time for you to allow those to come into your life. I wish for you to know that a new world exists for you in the next years, and it is important for you to prepare yourself to be surrounded by the luxuries of life. Know that you will always have shoes that fit."

I agree that sounds good, because I'm tired of wearing ones that don't feel exactly right.

"Yes, it is important to believe these things now and to see yourself as extremely prosperous. If you are extremely prosperous in your mind, of course, it is easy for it to magnetize prosperity to you. Those who want to be prosperous will feel this in you. Do you understand?"

"Yes."

"If you consider your life, you *are* prosperous. You are not living in a castle, but your castle is your home. You have your needs met nicely. There are many who struggle and you have no such experiences beyond struggling with the human condition, which is, of course, soon to transition away. You must be prepared for that which exists already and shall come."

"I think I still need to do some work on being prosperous in my mind."

"Yes, it is important. I, of course, have never incarnated. I have always been an angel, and yet I have witnessed a great deal. I know energy, and I know that like energy attracts like energy. I know that when you see yourself as less than you are choosing to be, it is a deterrent, my dear. As you release, I will do some intending to amplify that which you project as prosperity."

I am touched by Teressa's helpfulness. "Thank you, all of you, for your assistance," I say. "I'll see you at the party."

"I first wish to tell you that there is a human tradition about angels, and so I am specifically honoring that tradition at your party. I will have wings and, of course, a golden halo."

"Oh, thank you."

"Yes, it is in your honor, of course."

# # #

Tonas speaks, "Yes, my dear, I am at your disposal. Before you begin, may I say that it was such a great honor and such a treasure for me and my parents to view the story of your life in a pictorial."

"Oh, that is wonderful, Tonas! I am honored that all of you looked at the pictures. I have about six more books."

"We must have them all, of course."

"Were the presents for your mom and dad acceptable?"

"You are, of course, in your joking. Listen, you must know something. Had you given them a feather, they would have been in the greatest of excitement and honored. These implements meant something to you and they were thoughtfully chosen. And because of that, the gifts were even more enriching for them."

"I'm glad they enjoy them. I did spend quite some time trying to think of things I had that were unique and that I really liked."

Tonas reveals that they have been studying many Earth traditions, foods, cultures, and all that is part of the human existence. He's planning on having milk shakes, complete with a soda jerk, apple or cherry pie, French fries, mustard and ketchup, Coca-Cola, Sugar-free Bubble Up, and a juke box. They have been viewing TV commercials to get food ideas. He sounds excited about all the foods they have "discovered" so far. I'm a little bit nervous about such a random collection of things to eat, but maybe on this dimension, all foods will taste good.

# # #

As soon as I ask to speak with Liponie, he says, "Yes, my dear. You know I am right here beside him. I have been working now for several days; there is much to do still. I am inspiring. You will be pleased."

"Are you going to be okay with designing some gowns for Jill Marie and me to wear?"

"That is an interesting challenge, for I must design something that sets you apart from the rest. When you enter, it must be that you are as a bright sun—and the color you have chosen will be easy to work with, because I think others will not have thought to wear that color."

"Fuchsia is one of Tonas's favorite colors."

"Oh, so this would be extra important. I am now designing a gown that somewhat resembles clothing a sea maiden might wear. The bodice is as if made of shells of the clam, and the waist tapering small, as you are. And if you can imagine, the materials flowing over your hips and long for the back. Of course, you will have no trouble with people stepping on it. They will be most vigilant, because everyone will have all eyes on you. No one will take their eyes off of you with this gown that I design for you, believe me."

The idea of clamshells on my dress does not sound appealing, but I swallow my apprehension and tell him that I appreciate his efforts.

"As soon as I am finished here, I will be collecting some of the most beautiful shells for you and they will decorate the bodice in a sweep as if of stardust across the front, and then as if a belt of it—although it will not be a belt—at the waist and flowing full length through the front and then sweeping to the back and to the tip of…it is not a tail…it is more of a draping that falls perhaps as long as your elbow to your middle finger of a distance, flowing behind you."

I am confused trying to picture what he describes, but I'm just going to trust him and so I say, "Okay."

"I am, of course, thinking of something for your hair. There is much to be designed here. Are there other colors for the other days? I wish for you to have a costume for each day."

"Yes, I love the blues, purples, pinks, silvers, greens—so

I'm leaving the choice up to you."

"Well, whatever I design, it will be magnificent!"

I feel like crossing my fingers but I take the plunge and say, "I am sure you are correct. I'm looking forward to wearing your designs."

"Indeed."

CHAPTER TWENTY-NINE

June 19, 2014

Tonas says, "This is a surprise, my dear, and a glorious one."

"I came to bring you a present."

"A gift?"

"Yes, I didn't want to be rushed on the solstice because there's so much to do. I wanted to make sure that I had time to give this properly. What I have is actually from Gaia, for your service to her over these thousands of years. I'm hoping you can make a bigger stone that is the same composition as the one I have on my ring. I don't think a stone the size of mine would be appropriate on your finger; do you understand what I'm saying?"

"Yes."

"This stone is actually fused from rock gathered after Mount Saint Helens erupted and it comes from ten to twenty miles below the surface of Earth. I've had my ring for years, and I like to think of it as coming from Gaia's heart. I think it would look really good on you with the green pendant that I gave you. You can make it whatever shape you would like it to be, but I think maybe the emerald cut would be nice."

"And you wish for me not to have the same?"

"I think a square or rectangular stone might be best on your finger, but if you want to have a large, circular one, that's okay. I just wanted you to make something yourself that would fit your beautiful personage."

"You delight me."

"Oh, Tonas, you're so dear to me. I want to see you so much."

"Ah. I think you are falling for me."

Laughing, I admit, "I think so … pretty hard."

"I am patient."

"I am not able to be that patient."

"I am very patient, my dear."

"I know you are, incredibly so. I don't know if what I've suggested is possible to do, but I think a ring like mine would be perfect for you. You've done so much wonderful work for the Earth. Thank you from my heart and Gaia's heart to yours."

"From her heart ..."

"Yes, from her heart."

"Yes, I accept this gift with my heart. I will have this prepared; you will see me wearing this beauty."

"I love the deep green color."

"It is quite engaging. I've never seen one like it. It is unique."

"Yes, just like you."

"I am unique?"

"Yes, you are."

"Just as you."

#

"Did you invite Commander Ashtar?"

"I believe that it would be difficult for him if I did not invite him. I hesitated, of course. I did not wish to create a feeling as though I was pressuring him to be a part of something that ... after all, he is the leader of our coalition, you see."

"Yes."

"I am not the least of the coalition, but I am, perhaps, the youngest. And so, I was pondering the best way to engage this invitation." He pauses for a few seconds. "Yes, he has accepted."

"I'd like to greet him when I'm at the party."

"He is genuine. He is like Osiris with that volume of presence that enters the room before he arrives. You know, it is exciting, this experience."

"I think so, too. I am curious about the guys you invited for Jill Marie, but I know she'll tell me all about it."

Tonas assures me that the men he has lined up are quite

handsome and that none are stodgy. I comment that it's hard to believe there is an Ashtar Commander who is stodgy.

He says, "Believe me, it is true."

I ask to speak with Osiris. He immediately responds and asks how he may be of assistance.

I question him as to whether we should do the work on Saturday in private or in front of everyone. "As you wish," he says. "But I believe it would be the event of the millennium if you allowed people to witness your work. They could also assist you by holding the vision of success for your work."

"I have another idea," I tell him. "I would somehow like to invite people to give me ideas about ways to continue assisting Earth."

His asks me to leave this with him and I'm glad to do so. I know he gets things done.

# # #

When I ask to say goodbye to Tonas, I hear him say he is pleased for all that is happening. "It has brought to me something that I have never experienced, and that is the opportunity to be in the presence of so many of the great beings of all universes. It is, of course, most exciting that they are coming to my ship. You must understand what you created. You have great notoriety. My parents, of course, are greatly excited."

"Me too!" I tell him. "My mind keeps going over the details at night before I go to sleep, trying to think of things that would make the party even better. Are the people from Folgor able to come?"

"The dancers? Yes, it is arranged. I have witnessed them and still I cannot imagine how they do it."

"Is there some way you can record this so that, when I actually can see in this dimension, I'll be able to view what happened?"

"Of course. We will make a chronicle, my dear."

"Thank you, Tonas. I'll see you in just a couple of days. Farewell."

"Farewell."

CHAPTER THIRTY

"Greetings to you—and you have my gratitude, my dear."

"Greetings, Tonas. I have no questions, but a request, please. I would like everyone at the party tomorrow to have a gift that they could wear as a pin, bracelet, or necklace. I want something that would be divine for each one of them, as a gift from us—if that's possible."

Tonas says Gaia could provide gems from Earth for people to choose and I think that's a perfect idea. I like the idea of having the stones placed in settings, which causes a little bit of a quandary for us, since somebody will have to create the settings. Liponie's name pops into my mind and Tonas is agreeable to asking him to join us.

As soon as Liponie's name leaves my lips, I hear him say, "I am in presence, of course. I hear my name and instantly, I am beside you."

"We have a large task for you," I say. "We've asked Gaia if she would provide some kind of a gift for everyone who's going to be at the party tomorrow. She said she can provide all of the raw materials, the stones and the crystals, but we're searching for someone to design jewelry in which to place the stones."

"Ah! Oh, you have come to the right person."

"Oh good! I didn't know if it would be too much for you."

"You have come to the right jinn. I will masterfully create a showcase with designs that will sponsor a great deal of excitement in all present. And then, of course, you may individually present to each of the recipients or you can allow them to make their own selection."

"I think it would be best to let them select what they like."

Liponie advises that we should have a room specifically for these gifts and I agree. He continues by saying he has another idea for the room. "It will be quite a large room of showcase, and as individuals make their selections from the room, the casings will become smaller and smaller, so that it does not appear as if … well, my dear, how would you feel if you walked into a room and there were only seven pieces left? You would feel as though you had not witnessed the full measure of it, correct? So we will allow the display to shrink."

"That is genius!"

"I think of everything."

"And something for yourself, too."

"Ah, I will keep the best piece for myself, of course," he says, laughing.

"Please make sure that Tonas's parents, Emmon and Firona, select their gifts early."

"Ah, I am acquainted with the parents now as well," he says.

"I don't know if Tonas invited any of his siblings, but it might be nice for his whole family to have something."

"I will find the whole guest list and determine who will be there from Tonas's family. Firona has been much help for me with the decorations."

"Commander Ashtar is coming, too," I remind him.

"I understand. There is much hustling and bustling."

# # #

I show Liponie an orchid I have that's blooming; it's white and yellow with a little bit of fuchsia. "Should I gate to where you are so you can see it?"

"No need," he says. "I can feel the energy of it."

I wish I could understand exactly what that means. It must involve more advanced knowledge of the geometries, since that's what everything is made of. He asks me if I would like for him to recreate the flower. I tell him I would like that—and also ask him to please create flowers I can wear every day.

Now, Liponie mentions that there has been great

consideration as to whether or not I will wear shoes. "Ah, this Tonas of yours, he is a little difficult with this. He is insistent that you will be of the bare feet."

"I don't mind wearing shoes," I say. "Just tell him I can wear shoes."

Liponie sounds exasperated as he says, "This is what I *have* told him. You are the greatest of delicate creatures! You must have your beautiful shoes. Everyone will see your feet. But when I mention them, it draws him into the greatest excitement. He says, 'Yes, now you understand. I wish for them to see her feet.' We have gone around and around the table on this, my dear."

"Tell him I can be barefoot part of the time and I can wear shoes part of the time—how's that?"

"I believe that you will need to intervene."

"No problem, I will."

# # #

"I would like to talk with Chamuel, please."

Chamuel says, "I am in your presence."

"Thank you for appearing," I say. "I have a request for tomorrow."

"I am at your disposal."

"My friend Liponie was the muse for Handel. Handel wrote a beautiful oratorio, which I love, called *Messiah*. I play many portions of this work at Christmas, and I was playing some of them again today. Could we have an angel choir sing some of them?"

"You have only to ask, my dear. "

"Here are the ones I like: 'Comfort Ye,' 'Every Valley shall be Exalted,' and the last is called 'And the Glory of the Lord.' Could the choir sing those sometime during the party?"

"It will be our pleasure."

"One of the most glorious songs is called the 'Hallelujah

Chorus,' and if they could sing that sometime on the last day, that would be nice. Oh, and one more, 'Joy to the World.'"

"Ah, in your honor, of course."

"Yes, I love that song."

Chamuel hesitates. "There is a price to pay for this favor," he says softly.

"What is the price?" I ask while I wonder what an angel could possibly want.

"That we will dance."

"Yes! And it doesn't even have to be on the head of a pin ... That's just a little joke."

"Thank you, my dear, although we *could* do that. And so the price will be paid."

"I hope you're taking part in the party."

"I am where you are. I'm always nearby."

"All the angels are invited, you know."

"All of us that are part of your entourage are *always* in your presence."

"Thank you for reminding me of that. Can you invite others who would like to sing also?"

"There will be a choir, my dear."

"Once again, my thanks, Chamuel."

# # #

Tonas says, "Yes, my treasure."

"What a lovely greeting. Hold on a minute, I'm going to gate there. I have a chocolate chip cookie for you to taste"

"Ah! Oh, glory!" He sounds notably excited to sample this treat, which I had mentioned I'd like to have for the party.

Once I am with him, I tell him, "It's okay for me to wear shoes a little bit at the party, Tonas."

"Oh, he is difficult." I hear his exasperation as he speaks of Liponie.

"He's saying *you're* difficult," I inform him with a laugh. "I would like to have some pretty shoes that might be fun to dance in. I haven't been able to find any in this reality, as you know. I'm fine with going barefoot part of the time. Can we just kind of compromise and do shoes some of the time and barefoot some of the time?"

"If you saw the shoes he is creating for you, my dear, you would wonder if he thought you were from the fairy kingdom," Tonas says. "They are most exquisite and," he pauses diplomatically "I do believe they will accompany your beautiful clothing nicely."

I love it that Tonas can switch to tactful in mid-thought.

"How about I come in barefoot and then when we dance I can wear some shoes?"

"Certainly, my dear. Whatever you desire."

"This is your party as well."

"Yes, I am taking into my heart that it is truly our party, our first. We have great works to do tomorrow," Tonas says. "How do you wish to manage this?"

"Well, we're just going to kind of play it by ear—but everybody's going to watch so ... "

The fact that this party will be happening in just a few hours suddenly unnerves me. Wondering how Tonas is feeling, I ask, "Are you nervous?"

"Only a little."

I believe he is more than a little nervous, but it won't help either of us for me to admit I'm nervous, too. I casually say, "I'm just hoping I don't forget anybody."

I can almost feel him shudder as he informs me that many great ones are here, "and more keep arriving."

If I had ever attempted any party with a scope this grand, I would have simply hired someone else to take care of the details. Now, I am amazed that I'm having such a great time directing all this. I wish this side of me had been around when I was planning birthday parties for my kids.

I remember that I'd like everyone to have an orchid from Earth and I offer mine. Since I never did get around to bringing them to his ship, Tonas suggests that I just intend to bring them with me through the gate when I come back in the evening. That is workable.

"And I have two musical requests," I add. "I'd like to have *Serenade to Music* by Ralph Vaughan Williams played sometime during the party, and I'd like to be present when the angels sing 'Joy to the World.'"

"Joy to my world happened the day you entered my life," he says.

"Tonas, I believe you are a dream of mine that's been waiting to come true. Farewell until tonight."

"Farewell."

CHAPTER THIRTY-ONE

June 21, 2014 - Summer Solstice

The CEV announces, "We are ready, my dear."

"Greetings and Happy Solstice."

"Greetings. There are many pieces to this intricate formula that we have collectively prepared for you. There is much that you have already laid out as a foundation. What we have for you now is a grand ovum. There are over ninety-four million pieces that are part of this procedure. You will need to memorize each of these pieces before moving forward."

Laughing, I comment that I hope that was an example of their sense of humor.

"Indeed. We will apply this immersion for you. It will be as automatic."

"Let me ask you, before you do that—is there any way at all that you can come to the party we're having?"

"We are aware of your party. We will allow ourselves to be further aware."

"Oh, good. You've been so wonderful with the work, and I'd like for you to be able to enjoy it. I'm going to conscript the assistance of all the people there for the further work we do. Some of them may be getting in touch with you to say, 'Make this suggestion to Joy.'"

"What is a conscription?"

"It's like saying, 'You're part of the team now and you're going to assist me.'"

"Hmm, this was inspired. We will instill much of our focus into these steps. And now, it is time for you to engage the immersion."

"How do I do that?"

"We are selecting three of your many consciousness levels to be the receiving of each of the ninety-four million steps."

"All right, I'm opening them up."

After a couple of breaths in and out, I hear, "This transmission is complete. I have a small seed, the smallest of all that we have offered you. It is quite small, and yet it is a seed that will grow to become the foundation of many greater bridges that will open up the causeways of future expansion."

The CEV go on to tell me that the collective focus of all those at the party will amplify our work. They instruct me to begin by bringing the seed into the 6th dimension and then move through all the higher dimensions with it.

I repeat what I think I am to do.

"Don't worry," they advise. "Tonas can guide you in the implanting within the dimensions."

They give me the seed—which they call "fields of unity"— in a small capsule and wish me good providence.

# # #

Tonas greets me with, "My dear, I have been waiting. I am in great excitement, of course."

"First of all, am I wearing something that's nice?"

"You look exquisite. We are, of course, in a separate room. They are waiting in the next room."

"Am I barefooted?"

"You have no shoes on your feet."

"I wanted to make sure you were happy about that."

"Indeed, I was silly. We have your flowers; they are in the same space. Liponie is somewhat difficult; he has decided to take over our party. He has many good ideas, and so I have allowed it, of course. I am a little out of my element. He has the flowers in the space and, as each individual selects their jewel, he will present them also with a choice for one of your beautiful flowers. Since there were not nearly enough, we have made more."

"I was worried about that."

"Never be concerned. He was adamant about it, this

Liponie."

"Today, I'm not going to be the one who is doing all the talking. We've got to greet these people and say 'Hello' and then …"

Tonas again admits that he is a little nervous—because everyone is waiting behind the door in front of us. I finally admit that I am nervous, too.

"It's going to be all right. I have this one little thing from the CEV, and they say you'll know what to do to guide me."

"Oh my goodness! I have no means to make this connection. I think perhaps we must defer to Osiris."

"What is your plan?"

"The moment we enter, there will be the choral. They will wish to announce with the trumpets and then they will make the song of 'Joy to the World.' That will be my opportunity to announce that Joy has entered."

"How do you want to involve Osiris in this, if we need a little guidance?"

"I am concerned that I am unaware of what you wish me to know how to do."

This admission leaves me somewhat panicked. Dismayed, I ask Tonas," Would you know what to do if you held the seed?"

"I am not sure what the CEV intends," he replies.

That's when I send out a call to Osiris for "Help!"

Osiris speaks immediately. "My dear, you know this delicious Tonas of yours—he fully understands. He has missed one of the integral pieces of the directions."

"Can you help both of us understand?"

"Let me give you some insight. In the cultures of many, such as my own, the thought is held between two that are in union, and between their hearts they create a nest of light which is required for a gestation. I believe that when you place this seed, which you are holding so carefully, between your two hearts, you will be able to gestate and send the energy forward to immerse the full measure of each of the dimensions."

As I digest this concept, Osiris continues. "I am most surprised that these of the council have offered you this opportunity. Of course, each of them has their input; you notice that there are ninety-four million pieces, and that is because there are ninety-four of them. Each has been very much involved in the direction of this project."

"Will this gestation happen instantly, or slowly?" I ask.

"I believe that, in each of those dimensions, the gestation will take several minutes. Then you will leave the energy of yourselves for the full amount of time necessary to complete the gestation. The full measure of the birth of this must be completed as if it were an actual child being gestated. The higher dimensions will be much swifter in manifesting that connection. Once you have cleared the 11th dimension, there will be a great ease, for those of Earth who made their earlier transition to the higher dimensions are on the 10th dimension. (He is speaking of the Atlanteans.) So you will have their assistance."

It seems complicated to me, so I ask, "Tonas, do you have any other questions? Will you be able to guide me through this?"

"I am understanding now," he replies. "Shall the three of us enter together and allow the spectacle to begin?"

"Tonas, can we hold hands?"

"Yes, of course. Perhaps we could implore Osiris to guide the others, as well as us, through each of the steps. Would that be acceptable?"

"Indeed," Osiris agrees.

# # #

Tonas begins to guide me. "The announcement is ready; the horns are playing. The angels have begun their song. Let us enter now. I am of concern that you are feeling but you are not yet hearing them, and so I will let you know when the song is complete."

"Thank you."

"Yes, my dear. Your shoes are lovely."

"Oh, I was going to be barefoot."

"Oh, no, your shoes appeared ... the moment you crossed. It was a, what you call, a deal. I made a deal with Liponie."

"Thank you."

"And now, I wish to announce to all of you the great presence of Joy."

With my heart in my throat, I graciously greet everyone, "Hello, hello, hello. Joy to the world, and joy to you. Thank you all so much for coming. Thank you for being here on this magnificent ship with my beautiful partner. Tonas, would you like to say a few words?"

"I am in so much excitement to have all of you here," he says. "It is our great honor to have you present. You are invited by my beloved and me to participate, if you wish, in a grand spectacle that will assist in Earth's transition. My beloved will tell you more."

I hadn't prepared an explanation, but now that I've moved into the spirit of this endeavor, I begin my speech. "I want to share with you that you will be able to assist with the balancing of the divine masculine and the divine feminine for humanity," I say. "That has been one of the major challenges of my life, and it's wonderful to be able to help myself, as well as others on Earth, to be able to experience the balance that Gaia already knows."

Even though the crowd is quiet, I can feel their presence and energy.

"Those of us on Earth have had quite a struggle with this balance, with competition and with issues of control," I tell them. "So again, thank you for helping me not just to hold the vision of the non-dual balance of masculine and feminine, but to expand on that vision. Help me to allow, know, and feel the complete joy of the blending, the union, the love of myself and the masculine and feminine within me, as well as the neutral."

Now that it's time for the work to begin, I dive in by requesting, "Osiris, please guide us in the steps that we will be taking to assist the 6th through the 25th dimensions—and thank you for your help."

Osiris announces, "Indeed, my dear. If you wish, turn toward your beloved and place the seed between your hearts. There is a field of energy from the two of you, through your collective unity, that will hold that seed in presence. Tonas, if you will move this vessel, cloaked, into the 5th and 6th merged dimensions."

I feel the subtle movement of the ship as Osiris continues. "I call now forward all of the guests from Agartha to surround these two in a circle, so they are fully encased as if they are the ovum itself. Then all others join me as the two of these, joined in heart, vision into the 5th as well as the 6th dimension.

"Tonas, move the ship directly into the 6th dimension," Osiris says. "We all are immersing our focus to support what you are creating, everything you are choosing actively focusing between you. Transmit as if it were your only desire to commit to this union of spirit between the two of you. Let the levels of your consciousness that are known to hold the steps to be applied engage in each of the dimensions of the 6th through the 25th now, and allow the streaming of that which you know to activate."

Tonas informs me, "The seed is becoming so bright, and it is stretching outward beyond our vessel, out onto Earth, immersing Earth itself. It is as if our love child has created a new existence for itself in this dimension, emerging and fully immersing."

I am awed by the vision I have of what is occurring.

"Please take your hands and cup them upward, reaching beneath the seed to my fingertips that are also cupped," Tonas instructs. "It is the seed of love that we transmit onto this dimension, to this world. All of the grids that we have created and linked with our preparatory work are now catching onto this energy. Feel the streams and threads of light carried upon it."

Osiris asks us to move the ship into the 7th dimension and tells everyone with a partner, even if it is not their life partner, to turn toward each other and envision the same seed between them.

In the 7th dimension, Tonas says that it is as if the spaces between our joined fingers are sending streams of light to the Earth similar to when the Sun shines through the clouds. I can feel that the energy is streaming powerfully, yet gracefully.

He begins whispering to me, "Everyone is..." Tonas trails off as he observes the crowd and then leans into me and asks, "Can you hear me?"

I whisper back, "Yes."

"Everyone is mimicking us. They are all attending the same experience. It is real for them, I know; there are, of course, many rules."

"But I asked for their help."

"Yes, you did. I have, of course, set firm boundaries with Ashtar, who wished to move into my position."

"Oh, good, thank you."

"Yes, indeed. It would be inappropriate for him to do so, of course."

# # #

Osiris says, "Now, my dears, all of you, feel the presence of Earth in this dimension, and in the feeling of it, immerse in it."

"It feels better; it feels nice," I remark to him in a dreamy voice.

"Let us call it 'silky smooth.'"

"Yes, like the milkshakes Tonas is going to provide," I joke.

"I have never shaken milk, so I have no idea how lovely this will be," Osiris declares. "I must say that, for all to hear, you are a vision today. You are bright and sparkly."

"Thanks to Liponie. I'll talk more about that later."

"I know my beloved will be calling upon him for certain after seeing your gown."

I guess the clamshells worked, after all.

#

Tonas and I move to the 8th dimension, and Osiris suggests that we send our energy from the 6th and 7th dimensions to this dimension, to create a bridge. Tonas remarks that he can still sense himself in the two previous dimensions as well as this one. He adds that he feels as though we are gestating a child of light between us and that this 8th dimension is the most important of all, because "it is possible that you might give me your heart. And, of course, I will give you mine. It is in this dimension that, no matter what, you will see me."

"I'm waiting for that time, Tonas."

"And you'll have your arms around me and you'll know of it. The Earth is responding to this seed. It is responding as if Earth itself is beating like a heart to match that of our beautiful seed between us. Ah, I am somewhat whelming. It is as if my heart wishes to laugh and cry. I feel almost giddy."

I admit that I'm feeling dazed as well.

"I know we must move on—but I am in such a link with the Earth. So long we have held the vision of this harmony, and now I can feel it to be true in this dimension."

Osiris says, "Indeed it is true. This energy matches most readily. Now if you will move this vessel into the 9th dimension."

Tonas remarks that it is as if we are, between us, holding

another Earth.

"Oh, Tonas!"

"This is how it feels, as perceived by me. Osiris, is this true?"

"Well, I would not have uttered these words—yet, now that you have, all in presence are in joyfulness of this. It is not something that will be uttered to others, of course."

Osiris has more details about the end of this work, and his voice is quite serious now. "After six hours, there will be another essence of Earth radiating, beating within the parameters of that of the world, the physical and the energy world," he says. "As that orb of presence which radiates the fields of unity begins to meld into the physical Earth, you will know of the transition."

Tonas whispers to me, "I must have spoken out of turn. Yet it was there for me to feel and to know—and within the six-hour parameter, naturally, we would have seen it."

"Yes," I respond. "I felt it as well."

"It is my great honor to be the one to guide you. It is not as though you have the white stick tapping, my dear. You are aware."

"You are so funny."

"I am?"

"Yes, you are; I love it."

He reminds me he is not stodgy.

"Nor am I."

"I am never stodgy. This is almost complete. I can feel it as if the echo back and forth, Earth to seed, seed to Earth, is completing its heartbeat. It is amazing."

# # #

As we move into the 10th dimension, Osiris reports that all in presence are holding their hands and envisioning that they also hold a seed between them. He asks me to call forth the

Atlanteans, who ascended from Earth ages ago into this dimension. "They will feel the rain of this energy to Earth and they will assist to hold the vision of unity backward as well as forward in time."

As Osiris transmits our gratitude to them, one of them, an Atlantean woman, speaks to us using Language of Light. I ask what her name is and Osiris tells me it is Nosheeah. I can feel her loving energy and gratitude.

The activations in the 11th through the 24th dimensions go swiftly. When we reach the 25th dimension, Osiris guides us once more. "And now, for all to see, hold the seed between you. Vision that seed opening, and rising from it the spark of light that reaches outward in all directions of Earth, to birth and create a higher dimensional vibration—a piece of heaven within Earth."

We pause to enjoy the beauty of these words and vision this reality.

"This is an evolution, for truly even Gaia must live up to it," he says. "You will show her, and all that are a part of her, the way to this. There were many pieces of work to be done today. Somehow, you compiled all of these into one glorious task that all here have enjoyed participating in."

Osiris asks me what I wish to do at this time. I reply that I have homework for everyone. He says all are listening carefully.

"In the future, I would ask for any and all of you who have ideas, suggestions, news, exciting or wonderful things to share with me about ways to continue assisting Earth's evolution—and, of course, my own evolution—to somehow please get in touch with me, Tonas, Osiris, or the CEV. I know that you can't just tell me things, because this has to be a process of discovery, but I'm really good at asking questions."

I can feel their receptivity and affection.

"My main goal always is to assist Gaia—but an important goal, in case you haven't gathered it from our conversations, is that when I get to the 8th dimension, I'm going to be able to see this beautiful man standing next to me. If you can be of assistance, please let one of us know. That's your homework. Tonas, would you like to say anything before I do some acknowledgements?"

Tonas says, "Indeed, it is our joined hearts that are truly the instrument of this grand spectacle today. It is through the joined hearts of all of us that the vision continues. My Joy has gladly allowed me to participate in this endeavor, and I am grateful. I know that you, too, are grateful to be a part of this journey. She is, of course, one of the leaders of Earth, and it is our great honor and our great pleasure to welcome her and also …"

He whispers, "I will step aside from you for a moment, my dear." Then he continues to address the gathering.

" … to give her the accolades that she is due for that which she has created, for all of Earth has a stepping stone leading them into that new world we saw just now being birthed unto Gaia. I congratulate this blessed one and I give you all this opportunity to send transmission of your greatest accolade as well."

Again, he lowers his voice to say, "All you have to do is receive, just receive. And now, my beloved has more that she wishes to share with you."

I clear my throat and begin, "I first wish to acknowledge my partner, Tonas, a wonderful man who has been so helpful, kind, and patient. He's known me for a long time. I've only known him for, well, fifty years, but only consciously for the last four months."

After I move through my list of people to thank, I mention the gifts of crystals and orchids furnished by Gaia and myself. I wrap up my speech with, "I hope you all enjoy your gifts as well as the Earth foods and the entertainment we have provided. Again, I give you my gratitude for your assistance today and your continued assistance and support in the future. Tonas, do you have anything you would like to say before I say, let's eat, drink and be merry?"

Tonas speaks, "I would like to give thanks to each of you for accepting our invitation to join us here today and, of course, for the days of festivity. We have three days planned; it may evolve to be even more.

"When you enter the room with the beautiful gems that have been created into crowns as well as jewelries for each of you to select, please know that this Great One, Liponie, has allowed his genius to develop what he knows will be the most exquisite gift from my beloved to you. Liponie made it so that when you walk into the room of jewelry, even if it is on the last moment of the last day of the party, your beautiful gem will be waiting for you."

Tonas concludes by saying, "And now, I wish to thank and to bring the greatest light to shine upon Joy, for she has not only brought joy to my life for more years than her life exists, she has inspired me to be the commander, to be the partner, to be the being which I have become. And so I congratulate you, my Joy, for it is through you that I am the commander of this ship."

Deeply touched, all I can do is thank him for his beautiful words.

#

Tonas informs everyone that there are attendants who will guide them through all the spectacles that await them. "Spectacle" seems to be a favorite word for the people working with me. Also, I have learned several versions of "overwhelmed"—whelmed, whelming and even "over the whelm."

Tonas lets everyone know that, throughout the vessel, they will find opportunities to taste foods from many different Earth cultures. He mentions to those who consume foods that the foods here are physical, (Can you imagine the need to say that to anyone?) and says, "These foods are as if you are on your home world, consuming something in celebration."

Tonas surprises me by extending an invitation to our guests to visit Earth and try more of our … "delish" is the term he uses. He also cautions them to manifest in a body that looks like people of Earth. There is even research available so guests will know where on Earth they can find the different foods we are offering.

He adds, "It is our hope—and I believe my Joy will give her acceptance of this idea as well—that you will spend a great deal of time on Earth consuming these delicious treats so that the energy of your presence will help to elevate all of Earth. It will be a means for you to continue to assist Earth. Do you agree, my dear?"

"I agree wholeheartedly. There are so many different foods and cultures on Earth. I've visited other countries, but I'm more familiar with the foods in America. Since I have quite a sweet tooth, there are many desserts here, but there are also wonderful vegetables and juices. Cupcakes, cookies, ice cream, and pie are all delicious sweet foods, though they are not considered healthy foods. On Earth, much of the food that *is* healthy is not sweet. So I recommend you try a balance of all foods. Please, please enjoy, with Joy."

"That was clever," Tonas whispers to me. Then he announces that the merriment may commence. "Please find your way upon the ship. Know that this vessel is your home."

# # #

I ask to speak with Commander Ashtar, and when he announces his presence, I greet him.

"It is my greeting to you, my dear. I am honored to be in your presence."

"It's nice to meet you. I want to thank you personally for all the things that you've done to assist the Earth. I know you're part of our team now, so if you have any thoughts or ideas about ways that we can assist you and the Earth, I would like for you to share them with me or with Tonas, whoever is most appropriate for you to speak with. I don't know if you can speak directly with the CEV. I'm not sure of the parameters of what is allowed and what is not—but, of course, you are."

"We will learn these things together," he says, his tone gracious. "We have several on Earth that we communicate directly with through transmissions, as they are open to receiving. It is not in our normal procedure to be communicating as you and I are today. This is a beginning for us—and, of course, Commander Tonas is a capable individual. He will, I am sure, be one who will bring information to me now."

"I am sure that he will be glad to. There must be many of your ships. How many are there?"

Asthar informs me there are eighty-six million ships existing in graduated levels of dimensional planes above Earth, and that they are always just a little bit off of a dimension. This makes it easier for them to work without interference and to avoid being seen.

I share with him that I would love to be able to see all of Tonas's ship and that surely I will do so one of these days. Asthar is kind enough to tell me he senses that I will. "Tonas is quite taken with you, my dear," he says.

"Thank you so much for coming today."

"It is my pleasure. I was afraid my invitation was lost in the mail."

I laugh and reply, "Tonas was a little hesitant. I'm not sure why. I think he's finally stepping into the idea that he's important to me and important to the work that we are doing. He tells me that, at twenty-five million years of age, he is the youngest of your commanders, which I find absolutely incredible."

"I must say that Tonas comes from a long lineage of great commanders, and his own father is a commander of our fleet. So he has been trained from birth to have such abilities. He is quite accomplished. We are bringing our attention to him more, of course."

"I hope one day to be able to travel with him and visit all these wonderful universes and places that he's told me about. It's a possibility that I greatly look forward to."

"Anything is possible, my dear."

"I hope you enjoy the party."

# # #

"Tonas, I'm wondering if I could speak with your parents a little bit."

"Certainly, let us move into a more private space."

Firona greets me by saying, "Dear one, I am touched by you and your commitment. This was one of the most amazing spectacles."

"Tonas said he could chronicle it for me. I'm not sure what that means, but I asked him if he could record it. On Earth we take pictures of things and then we can review them. I don't know if you do things that way."

"Our technology is a little different," she replies, "and yet I imagine that it would be the same concept. As you can see, I am wearing my gift, and I will be excited to select another gift from the treasury. I have been assisting your Liponie. He is artistic with an inner vision that is a far different scope than anywhere my mind would travel. It is quite amazing, the vision that he has."

"I think he and Tonas almost came to blows over my shoes. It was so funny."

"We are all aware of this. It was charming in its way and yet, you have brought out something in my dear son. He is careful of you. You see, my other children and their dear ones create for themselves whatever they desire. It is not like you would need someone to be walking behind and ahead, to carefully make all perfect and to guard. So to watch my son being your protector has been sweet. He did believe that, of course, you would wish to be with the bare feet. It was a mistake—and yet, it was so delightful that he should have been so adamant about you."

"He stood up for himself."

"He stood up for you. Oh, may I say, my dear, your gown is exquisite. It is, of course, a creation of Liponie."

"Do I have any flowers anywhere on me?"

"Yes, you have them in your hair and on the side and in the back. There is a spray of beautiful crystals across the front and down your gown. At the waist, where the crystals meet, the cut of the material begins to drape downward in that beautiful flowing manner that he has created for you. There is a bouquet of tasteful flowers there as well. Not big clusters, which would have been lovely as well, but small. He has miniaturized them quite delightfully."

"Liponie has been so helpful. It seems like every time I'm with Tonas, there's just so much to do. I really want to be able to spend time with you and Emmon. I haven't managed that so far, but sometime I will."

"We are eager for this in the future as well. We hope to have you in our lives forever, my dear."

I am almost in tears to hear her say this. "That's definitely a possibility. I'm trying to be careful what I say to Tonas, because this part of me that's talking to you has not yet evolved to where I want to be. Do you understand what I'm saying?"

"I do. I truly honor your care in this. Tonas is someone who, when he gives his heart, he gives it fully."

"I know that. The last thing on Earth or in the universes I want to do is to hurt him in any way. That is my biggest fear."

"I will tell you this, as a mother. Even though it would take one thought to transform the pain of that separation, as I know my son, he would carry that pain of separation with him for the ever. And so, I am pleased that you are holding your dedication until you are in assuredness."

"Thank you for understanding and for talking with me today. Please give my regards to Emmon."

"I will take Tonas aside for a moment, with your permission. I wish to tell him how much I am in love with you. Of course, he was concerned about our talking of such as this. I already see it in his eyes! He is concerned that I have scared you away. I must assure him that we two have an understanding. You are a mother, you understand."

"Yes, I do."

"Farewell."

#

I ask to speak with one of the Folgor dancers and hear, "It is my distinct pleasure to be here on this vessel. It is also my pleasure to be dancing periodically. We have our full troop here."

"Oh, good!" I say. "What is your name?"

"My name is Dosh, but everyone calls me Doshie."

"Doshie, how many people are in your troop?"

"We have thirty-one dancers."

"When Esthra told me you dance on your fingers, I thought, how can they do that? Can you tell me a little bit about how it is possible?"

"I am assuming that you do not dance on your fingers?"

"Oh, no."

"I am in jest," Doshie says, chuckling. "Obviously, this is unique."

"Yes, you must have exceptionally strong fingers—either that or you're very light."

"Oh, no, it is all balance. And, of course, we dance in the most synchronicity. We are as if musing to the music. We move our minds into a flow. It is much like a stream of thought, and so, as one thought, each of us move in synchronicity."

"Are you roughly my size or smaller?"

"I don't know how rough it would be."

"Are you approximately my size?"

"Ah, I see what you mean. I'm looking up at you now. I'm at your shoulder."

"That gives me an idea of your size. I'm hoping that I can come visit you on your planet sometime and see you again. Do you think that would be possible?"

"Of course, we would be greatly honored. We will have a spectacle simply in your honor."

"Thank you for speaking with me. I will let you go back to your troop."

"We are grateful that you have selected us," he says. "You have honored us."

# # #

As Tonas speaks to me he sounds a little disgruntled. "My mother is so protective of me. Did you notice this, my dear?"

"I understand because I'm a mom."

"Please don't listen to a single word she said."

"Oh, no. Now wait a minute."

"Do not listen to the singlest of word. I want you to feel easy in my company."

"I do. And also, Tonas, I don't want to cause you any pain. It might be harder on me, I think, than on you, to be a source of distress to you. That's why I've been careful about what I say to you. This part of me—the part that's speaking with you—is not as evolved as you are in the way of the heart connection and knowing what that can be. And so, I'm a little bit hesitant when I talk about my feelings for you, because—although I think they're moving into the new—they're still kind of in the old Earth way of being with someone who's special. I want more than that. Do you understand what I'm saying?"

"Indeed, you want what is available everywhere in the non-dual."

"I've never experienced anything similar to the love that you have described, except the love I have for my children," I explain. "I know that there's even more than that. I'm glad you're so patient."

"And may I say this to you? If it is your desire to only, and I say this 'only' not to diminish, to give me your heart as much as you have in this moment, it is enough for me. Of course, I want more. I want the whole apple pie."

I don't feel like there's anything I can say now to address his statement of desire, so I simply ask him, "Did you pick apple or cherry?"

"Oh, we have both. There was no reason to be scrimping."

"I should probably say something to Esthra. Is he here?"

"Let me see what we can do."

# # #

Esthra says, "Yes, I am here, my dear."

"Do you know what Nosheeah, the Atlantean woman, said to us?"

"Yes, let me translate. She said to you that, 'You greatly honor her and the full lineage of the soul, and that, as an emissary of your time, you are leading your people into the dimension where they will at last meet you. When that day comes, you will step up to her and you will know her.' It is true that when you are on the 10th dimension, you will meet with them. They exist in that dimension, my dear."

Tonas says, "You were a success. You were a glorious success and you still are. Are you leaving?"

"Can I leave a part of me here?"

"I believe that is the answer. It would be disappointing for you to leave."

"I'm just going to intend that part of me will be here for the party."

"Simply forget to use your transporting and I will hold your hand—unless we are eating pie."

"Be sure I sample everything. Farewell, Tonas."

"Farewell."

CHAPTER THIRTY-TWO

June 22, 2014

Tonas informs me that we are a celebrated couple and our party is a success.

"Have we danced yet?"

"We have danced and danced and danced," he replies. "May I share with you that you are a lovely dancer? I have learned many dances. The grand ballroom waltz is the one that I believe we dance the best together. You take your train up with the little loop around your wrist and it carries the sweep of the tail of it. It is absolutely magnificent."

"Oh golly." As I say this, I'm thinking of the Regency era romance novels I used to read.

"It is quite magnificent. Our guests are enjoying the foods and all of the different rooms. We have different orchestras and music in each room. Of course, the Folgors are dancing. They are amazing all those in presence who were unaware of them. Many guests are wearing their gifts."

"I'm so glad the Folgors are appreciated."

"Officially, I was enjoying the beautiful neck piece that was made for this one particular woman. She is not of this dimension. Her eyes sparkle like diamonds and, of course, the jewels of this neckpiece were shining back as if mirrors to her eyes. It should be quite a delicious expression for her."

Somewhat slow on the uptake, I realize he could be speaking about me. "Do you mean me? I hope so."

"Yes, I am speaking of you—although you are from this dimension. Because when you are with me, you are from this dimension."

"I feel like I must be less in some way when this part of me speaking to you now is not there," I admit. "When I took my consciousness away from here yesterday, I went in and swept the kitchen floor and vacuumed the carpets. It sounds so lovely here, but it's not really *real* for me, Tonas. I want it to be more real. When I move back to my house, it feels like I'm not at the party, even though I *am* there."

"It makes sense, of course, that it would feel as though you needed to do something as different from this as possible, in order not to feel that separation and longing to be more present. I can see why you went into the stages of the labors, for it was easier for you to do something completely different than to imagine what is happening here and being unconnected."

His insight surprises me and makes sense. It's comforting to know that he understands me so well. "I was aware of a flow of conversation with you last night when I went to bed. Is one of your brothers there?"

"Yes, three of them are here."

"I know I met one of them. I couldn't catch his name, but I remember thinking, this must be Tonas's brother—so at some level, I was able to connect with you. These thoughts were just flowing through my head; I had to not focus on them completely, but just let the meanings come to what you were saying."

"You connected with my brother, Birone."

"Please say his name again."

"Birone. And the other two are longing to meet you. They are longing to be in your presence. But I will never leave them alone with you for long…"

This strikes me as somewhat ridiculous, but I find myself laughing anyway as I tell him, "Oh, you are funny."

"These are unattached in their hearts and they are open in their relationships. I am cautious around them—for they are just as beautiful as I, of course."

This is interesting, but not something I really needed to know. "Don't worry, Tonas. You are the one I'm waiting to see. Has anyone approached you with any suggestions about the next work to do?"

"It has been mostly conversations about the celebration of

what we have been instrumental in up to this point. It might be interesting to have a gathering after the event for those who would wish to stay and be, perhaps, part of an enclave of individuals to give strategy. Would you be interested in this?"

"That's a great idea. I believe the people of Agartha would be key in the next strategy, because of their feet being on the Earth. Shiva is the only one I know in that group. Please speak with him about who would be good to include."

I strain to listen for the sounds, the music and joyful conversation, of the party going on just out of my reach.

"Tonas, how many people are at this celebration anyway?"

"Ah, I knew you were going to ask this. There are twenty thousand, one hundred and three."

"Oh! Holy smoke! You did have to make this ship big, didn't you? It's a good thing the solstice wasn't another month ahead, because we might have had fifty thousand people here."

"You are correct."

# # #

Tonas remarks that they haven't seen Jill Marie. I tell him she has been in touch with me, and she said she hasn't been able to get out of the room where the men are.

"That's because I locked all the doors," he says.

At first I believe him, but quickly realize he surely must be joking. "You're kidding, right?"

"Yes, I am what you call 'kidding around.' None of the men want to leave your friend."

"That's no surprise to me. She's lively and funny."

As I'm thinking about Jill Marie perhaps beginning a new relationship, I realize there are some other things I want to know about the emotions Tonas has experienced. Thinking there's no time like the present, I inquire, "Do you experience anything like jealousy?"

"No, why would I? Protectiveness, yes, as my mother intoned."

"I was in a serious relationship where the man I was with did not want me to stay in touch with any of the male friends I knew before I met him, so I discontinued my connections with those men. Like I said before, I'm not used to relating to someone who doesn't experience all the not-so-nice things we experience here. For example, I really want to give Liponie a big hug before the ceremony is over—but I am not sure how you would feel about that. Without him, I know we would have had a good party, but I think the touches he added were extra special."

"Indeed, you are correct. I had wonderful ideas, and yet my ideas quickly became quite small in comparison to his vision."

"He has such a genius for this."

"He does indeed, and he certainly made some wonderful clothing for you. I could not have conceived of these beautiful costumes. All are wondering what you will wear tomorrow. What could it possibly be? How could it be more magnificent?"

"Could we have Liponie with us for a moment?"

"Yes, I will call him over."

Liponie's immediate response is, "You know I am never far from you, my dear."

"I was just speaking with Tonas about how, without you, we would have had a good party. But with you, it is a magnificent party. The touches you added put it over the top. I don't know if this is proper protocol, but I want to give you a big hug."

"It will put me in celebrity!" Liponie responds, sounding delighted. "We will call everyone around to witness. Come, my dear."

"You're a little shorter than me, aren't you?"

"I can be taller."

"I'm going to put my arms around you and give you this big oomph of a hug. Here we go."

"Oh, my dear, I feel that that is the best hug I've ever

received."

"I'm so glad I know you. I can't believe that I've only known you a short time, because I feel like you're just the best. It's wonderful to have you on our team."

"It is most delightful for me as well. I believe that your Tonas is watching us very carefully."

Both of us snicker. "Thank you from all of my heart for everything that you've been and all that you have done."

"This has been my great pleasure, my greatest of pleasure."

Tonas tells me, "I believe I have felt my first jealousy."

Even though I believe he is teasing, my heart sinks a little and I say, "No..."

Then he adds, "I felt as though I was wishing to have this hug."

"Well, I would like to give you one. Can I do that?"

"I think it is important; everyone is watching."

"Where are we now?"

"We are in the grand ballroom."

"Are people dancing or just sitting and talking? What are they doing?"

"There is a pause in the music because you stepped in. So now may I have my hug?"

"Okay. Ready? I almost feel like leaping into your arms."

"Come, my dear. The hug of my life."

"Mmm."

"Mmm, you are like a feather in the wind. It is always enough just to be with you."

I let Tonas know I will be back tomorrow and ask him to consult with Osiris about people we can strategize with about assisting Earth's evolution. Tonas suggests Commander Ashtar and also his father, Emmon.

"Is there anything else you want to tell me before I go?"

"I must kiss your fingers." Whispering the next words, he says, "I will whisk you into this side room. Ah, there are others.

Every room is taken. There is no privacy on this ship except in my bed chambers, and I would refrain from bringing you into that space at this time."

I'm curious about what his chambers are like, but it doesn't feel appropriate for me to pursue this subject. At least, not until I know my own heart.

Changing the subject to one I'm more comfortable with, I ask Tonas if people really like their jewelries and the orchids.

"Oh, my dear, it is a new innovation to have such gifts!" he says. "This is an Earth celebration, and so there are the foods and flowers of Earth, there are the stones fashioned into beautiful jewelries, there are the drinks and music of Earth and, of course, we do have the Folgors. It was an important idea. Even your beautiful gown today whispers of peacock."

"Liponie told me about it."

I answer a few of Tonas's questions about peacocks and then tell him I'm going to go.

"Farewell, my dear. But it is a silliness to say farewell to you. You are still here with me."

CHAPTER THIRTY-THREE
June 23, 2014

The CEV announce that they are in presence.

"Good morning. What would you like to tell me today? How did things go the other day when we did the work?"

"The history books of all reaches of space and time are rewriting, my dear."

I heard what he said, but I can't resist asking him to clarify.

"The history books—the story of humanity's history—is being rewritten now."

I'm still not grasping what his words actually mean, so I ask for more explanation.

"Indeed, much of what was applied moves backward and forward and anchors in the present. What occurred in the past streamed forward, breaching through the entrance of the 3rd dimension. Now there is much that is, as you would say, rewriting in the past outward into all dimensions of Earth, following the threads, reaching beyond Earth's atmosphere into the other realms of space, out into the other worlds that you connected with your many eggs in the past."

I try to envision this as he continues explaining.

"All are affected by this that you applied. And so, dual worlds everywhere are being transformed in the past and in the present; the future is being reformed constantly by the reforming in the past, the cycles moving forward, rippling forward from the past. Each of the worlds of duality that exist throughout all that is in physical—including even different universes than the one that you are about—is re-conforming."

"This is beyond anything I could imagine would happen."

"Some of the ninety-four million threads that were part of the application affected the threads that you and Tonas laid in foundation in all the dimensions. Do you understand that these threads are affecting the cycles of the universes, rewriting the past? Time is moving faster now toward the completing on all other realms, and Earth is the guideline. Do you understand?"

"I'm trying to, but it's difficult. I'll have to sit with this awhile, before I can begin to comprehend it. I'm honored that Tonas and I were able to play a part in this work."

"The momentum leading to that final culmination point is affected as all individuals of many universes, many worlds, many star systems throughout the everything are each—in their own timing—evolving free of the images of their past, moving from duality. The vision all are holding is that within the three hundred and fifty year cycle of Earth, all in existence will meet the same focus. This is a grand endeavor."

I agree with that statement completely, but I have so many questions. "What do I do next?"

They suggest a waiting period to allow the new evolutions to reach their maximum potential.

"What do you think would be the amount of time that it would be best to wait—or is that something we can't know yet?"

"It is in our determination that three minutes is long enough … That was a joke."

Laughing, "You're getting really good at this!"

"Indeed, we are collectively laughing."

I'm sure they are, but he says this with such a serious voice.

"Were you able to enjoy any of the festivities so far?"

"We are aware of this; we are aware."

"Good. I'm going to be speaking to a few key people at the party about what we can do next. What do you think is the time we need to let people move forward?"

"Let us wait seven days and reconvene."

"That sounds good. I'm really honored to be working with you."

"It is our pleasure, it is our gratitude, and it is our excitement. If I had hands, I would clap them."

"I'll clap for you!"

"Clap for all of us."

# # #

Tonas makes himself known. "My dear, I am waiting."

"Here I am."

"I must tell you that it is different when you are here speaking to me, as we are now. And yet, I must say there is no difference in my heart between *you* and the 'you' that has been here constantly."

"Being there all the time makes me feel a little fuzzy here on Earth, like I'm not quite in synch."

"Yes, of course, I am sure of this."

"Tonas, you have no idea of what we did. I was just talking with the CEV and there were additional threads in what we planted the other day. All of the dual worlds in every universe are rewriting their history."

"To what end?"

"To be able to evolve in synchronicity with Earth. The work we did is so significant, I can hardly grasp what they told me about it."

Tonas asks if we are still going to have a meeting. I tell him yes, and he lets me know he put Osiris in charge of selecting the people to meet with.

"Can we have him with us?"

"I will call him. He is somewhere else, and I am sure he has a large group of people all around him. He is a celebrity here. People follow him from room to room, just to be in his presence. I am tempted to do the same, only it is important for us to be hostess and host, and so I am not a groupie. Osiris is approaching us now."

"My dear, I am at your disposal."

"I'm sorry to take you away from the festivities."

"Ah, there will be more of this. I doubt that this will end as of your midnight. These are what you would consider to be party extravaganza followers. This is one that will be talked about for the longest of time, perhaps even eternity."

I relate to Osiris what the CEV told me about all the dual worlds rewriting their histories, and, of course, he already knows. He adds that the futures of these worlds are rewriting themselves, and they haven't even happened yet! I realize that's true. When you change the past, you change the future.

Osiris agrees with the CEV that we should wait for seven days before doing any "tweaking" of the work, adding that will leave the way open for miracles. He does suggest that, if we draw everyone at the party together, perhaps they could assist with a divine focus of the outcome of the work.

"That sounds good to me. How do we do that?"

"We can draw all," he announces. "I have the clout, as you would say, to bring all of the instruments into silence, and all of the dancing to still, and I shall do so now. Those who are in presence, hear me well. There is, as you are aware, a vision of Earth rising from its positions now, along with all of the threads leading from each of the dimensions and the waves created from it in its evolution. Though Earth may appear a lowly position, they are in inspiration to rise most delicately and in their own timing to the 25th dimension."

I can't hear the telepathic response, but I can feel it.

"This one here—she is an Earth being, as you know, and she is choosing for this to be of her reality. And, of course, this is a defining moment. It is in her right to make this defining choice. It is in her right to request from each of you a vision that joins her own. And so, I will leave you now to listen to the voice and the vision of this one who has the right to make this request of you. I know that you are greatly excited to gift her in recognition of all the gifts that she has given to each of us throughout her incarnation. And, of course, you are wearing her beautiful bangles—so it is time for everyone to make a contribution in return. Not that you must be convinced. My dear, they are ready for you. Please go forward. They can all hear you."

I wasn't prepared to speak to this group. I thought Osiris would be the one doing the talking, but I realize he's right. It is my place and privilege to do this, so I send out a quick request for guidance and begin.

"Thank you again for being here. I'm requesting your assistance in expanding my vision for the Earth's gentle, graceful, masterfully divine progression through the dimensions. Recently, Gaia told me to, 'Bask in the glory of all the dimensions.' That's been a little bit of a challenge for me, because I've been so eager to reach the 8th dimension and begin a more conscious relationship with my friend, Tonas. Also, of course, I want to enjoy the wonderful abilities of manifesting and having fun changing my body with a thought, as well as all the abilities available in that dimension."

I can feel attentiveness and a sense of expectancy radiating from the audience.

"I've seen pictures of the majestic trees that used to be on Earth. I've always been fond of large trees, but we don't really have anything that can compare to those forests of antiquity, the streams that flowed so clearly and beautifully, the animals and the buffalo herds that were happy in their realms.

"I have a strong connection with Native Americans, and they have always been special to me. I'm wishing for a restoration and maybe even a grander version or vision of what the Earth was and can be. It would include a restored connection with nature, with the devas and fairies that we don't have, that *I don't have* ...

"What I'm saying is this: I don't know that my vision is as big as I want it to be. I've been kind of stuck in releasing the quagmire—this is one of Liponie's favorite words—the quagmire of the past that I grew up in. I'm not going to dwell on that because I'm moving forward and enjoying those moments in my day when I feel more divine.

"We come into our bodies and get stuck in all the challenges of living on Earth. Those of you who have had an incarnation here know what I'm talking about. I'm wishing to move forward easily and gracefully. I want to chat with Shiva and Sekhmet. I want to grow orchids in Florida and then teleport to Santa Barbara and enjoy the French toast at my favorite restaurant there. Doing these kinds of things will, hopefully, show others the possibility of leading magical, joyful lives.

"As the days pass—and I become more adept at hearing, seeing and visioning—I welcome those of you who have an affiliation, especially with the academy, to connect with me and to inspire me to have bigger dreams and bigger visions. Thank you for your assistance today and all the days that are coming."

# # #

Osiris asks our audience to vision all that exists and to witness the non-dual worlds that many of them chose to incarnate upon, reminding them to be grateful for the opportunities they've had on those worlds. Then he asks them to picture the dual worlds everywhere and to vision with me a graceful evolution for Gaia as she moves from the 4th dimension. He also requests that they vision all of the dual worlds matching, in their own timing, the evolution of Earth as she moves toward the 25th dimension. "Hold the vision of this progression, my dears, and hold the vision of this dear one, that she will have the prize she has requested from you."

"Thank you," I declare, with gratitude.

"Indeed, if there is nothing more that you wish of me, shall I restore them back to their festivities?"

"Yes."

"You are now restored back to your festivities. We are in gratitude. You see, all were stilled and focused on your words, my dear. We all are dedicated to assist you."

"Thank you, Osiris. You may return to the festivities, too."

# # #

"Tonas, what does your ship look like?"

"If you were to take the pie pan from the cherry and take another of the pan from the apple pie and put them together, you would see that this is a close interpretation. You would see that this is crystalline."

I remark that crystalline pie pans create an interesting image in my mind. He says his ship is beautiful and I agree to take his word that it is.

"Tonas, I've got to get Liponie to help me with my musical abilities."

"You are magnificent in your virtuoso."

"That's not translated to here. I need to start practicing soon, because the orchestral season starts in August, and I haven't touched my violin since our last concert."

"Ah, but later today you will be playing."

"Oh, I will?"

I've been experiencing incredible things on this dimension, but this news is really a shock to me. I begin to feel panicked, although I try to stay calm as I listen to Tonas continue.

"Yes, indeed."

"I'll be playing my violin?"

"It is arranged."

"What will I be playing?" I ask, hoping it's something easy and familiar.

"I have not put my nose to that question. I have simply allowed myself to be the instrument of creating another room and it has to be a room large enough to encompass the full measure of each to be in a seat."

My panic is heightening as I ask Tonas to find out what I'm going to be playing.

"The piece is *Paganini Caprice*."

I am speechless for a moment, then disbelief spurs me to protest. "Oh my God, Tonas! Those are too difficult!"

"It is the number twenty-four. Is this difficult?"

"They're *all* terribly difficult, and I've never played any of them in this reality."

"Ah, I understood from Melchizedek that you are ready, and that he has been playing and practicing with you."

I am so unnerved by what Tonas has told me that I start blathering about Paganini to take my mind off the fact that I'm going to be playing an impossible violin solo.

After I run out of things to say, Tonas tells me Liponie created a special violin just for me.

Liponie says, "My dear, I have created for you the most prestigious instrument. It is what I would consider to be even superior to that of your famous violins of the world of Earth."

This is so fascinating, it momentarily takes my mind off the fact that I'm in hot water. Maybe with a violin like Liponie could make, I won't sound too bad.

"Wow, Liponie! Does it look like an Earth violin?"

"Of course, my dear. It was created on Lyra."

"Oh Liponie. Oh, I may have to hug you again."

"Hmm! Most excited I am for another hug! Let me tell you that this violin was created for you; it is intuitive. It will follow what you wish the sounds to create. It has a cerebral interface."

This is sounding much better. Maybe I won't make too big a fool of myself. I really do have to talk with Melchizedek, though. "Liponie, you astound me at every turn."

Liponie assures me that I am ready to perform, which helps me feel a little calmer—but I'm still going to talk with Mel. The other news Liponie shares is that there will be special fireworks shooting off as a grand, you know the word, *spectacle* above the crystalline ceiling of the ship. And the Joy Star will be right outside the window, watching me and shining brightly.

#

"May I speak with Melchizedek for just a moment?"

"Yes, my dear, are you excited?" Melchizedek asks. I tell him I'm more terrified than excited and that the caprice is an extremely difficult piece. He assures me that, with my magnificent violin and the cerebral interface to assist, it will be a simple piece to play. He adds that this was the piece I selected!

"I hope this interface is going to be transmitting, or whatever it does, as I move forward, because I haven't played my violin for a couple of months."

"We are transferring over for all instruments, my dear. This is part of the project. You've asked for my assistance; I am using all measures to meet your highest potential. This cerebral interface—I hope this is the correct wording—is linked to your mind, you see."

"It sounds like something I'll really enjoy."

"It links to your brain and, of course, it links to the full measure of your fingers, arms, and everything that your mind brain directs. The song will be in your mind and in your heart, and from the heart the music will play. From the brain/mind, the direction from the heart will guide the bow. It will guide your hands, your fingers. It will guide your body as it moves to the music. You will become as if fluid."

"All right, thank you so much."

"I'm glad that you are pleased."

"I am, very much so. Is Tonas still here?"

"Humph, I don't believe you could tear him from your side."

#

"Are you excited about your recital?" Tonas asks.

"I'm more overwhelmed than excited."

"Liponie has an exciting finish for you. As the last note is still ringing in the crystalline dome above, we will have great fireworks bursting in the sky."

"If he's doing it I know they'll be fantastic. Tonas, you know what I think about? As wonderful as these fireworks will be, I think about how it would also be wonderful if you could be with me and enjoy some of the things that I do here on Earth."

"We have a lifetime to experience these things. I will perhaps one day wear blue jeans for you and we will ride horses together."

"Oh, Tonas, I want to do that!

"It can be on other worlds."

I've been curious about creatures Tonas has seen on other worlds, and so I ask him if there are dragons.

"There are other worlds with dragons, yes. And there were dragons of Earth, indeed."

"What planet has dragons?"

"Oh, there are several. In Earth's history, they were creations of those silly initiates of the ancient academies. They were so hilarious in their creating. They would be in competition with each other to see which one of the dragons they created could make fire shoot longer and farther from its mouth. It was actually funny; we all have seen visions of this. I did not witness it personally, but I have seen a projection of it."

"Will I get to see dragons?"

"Of course. There are many universes for us to explore, and you may even choose to explore them without me. You might rise to that great awareness and then, ah, tire of me."

"Tonas, I'm not sure what the future is going to bring. It doesn't feel like that will happen, but I can't make any promises. I *do* think it would be lots of fun to travel with you. Here, I enjoy traveling by myself, because people want to do different things than I do. But I don't think that would be a problem for us. I'm not sure when I will consciously come back to the party."

"My dear, may I offer you some unrequested advice?"

"Sure."

"Take a few moments to feel yourself standing beside me. You are a vision in this moment. You have not asked about your gown."

"What am I wearing?"

"You are wearing the deepest of turquoise."

Tonas also tells me that my gown is short and daring. When I comment that I must be ready for some fast dancing, he tells me the dress will not get in the way of my legs. The gown he's described is not something I would have worn, even when I was young. What is that part of me thinking?

We haven't done any fast dancing yet, although there will be music for dancing jitterbug and the Chicken. I've never heard of a dance called the Chicken, but Tonas says they are prepared for anything and that later, we will dance the twist. I love twisting. I tell him, "That was shocking to me the first time I saw it. It was so unlike any dance I'd ever done before. Yeah! I like to twist. Thank you, Tonas!"

"Ah! Never thank me again! You have given me more than I could ever give."

"I don't think so. Without you, we wouldn't be able to do this work."

"Oh, there is always a way, when it comes to a genius like yourself. You would have found some way. Your passion is so deep."

"Working with you is the best way."

"I agree, my dear."

#

More conversation reveals that Liponie's jewelry gift for Tonas was deep green cuff links. Those are so elegant. This was the perfect gift, in my opinion. Thinking about elegance, I ask

Tonas if he knows what a tuxedo is. He tells me he thinks he does because he has watched the cartoon *Tennessee Tuxedo*. I advise him that a tuxedo is distinguished formal clothing that men wear here and suggest he watch some Fred Astaire movies to see what one looks like. He promises to do research.

"I'm going to say goodnight now."

"Oh, it is a mistruth, my dear. You are in my arms now. I have my arm over your shoulder—very protective, of course."

CHAPTER THIRTY-FOUR
June 24, 2014

"Esthra, I want to chat with you about a few things. To manifest the things I'm thinking of manifesting, I'm going to need money. Do you have any thoughts about that?"

"In the history of humanity, there have been many who have been attractive to abundance. Solomon was a king of ancient times in this world, and he was someone who could attract prosperity to himself."

"I've always been fascinated by him," I say. "Where is he currently?"

"He was assisted to ascend. This is one who, I believe, would be of value because he was human. I know that the great Osiris would be someone who would be of assistance, especially since he is training you to direct the forming of elements. And yet, I continue to ponder what it must be to be human and to be the greatest in attracting prosperity. That is why I mentioned Solomon."

"Is he someone that I could speak with?"

"Certainly. He was assisted to ascend."

"Who assisted him?"

"You, my dear."

"Oh, gosh … Oh, Esthra! Okay, I'd like to speak with Solomon for a little bit if I might."

#

"I am Solomon. This is quite interesting."

"It certainly is. I've been fascinated by stories about you for many years."

"Ah, I have been fascinated by stories of you."

This startles me. I can't imagine how Solomon would know anything about me, but he continues to speak, so I quickly bring my attention back to what he's saying.

"You may call me Jedidiah."

"Jedidiah is a wonderful name."

"I don't wish for you to call me King Solomon; it is so unfriendly."

"All right. Esthra tells me that the stories are true about you having the temple built."

"It was the holy temple, my dear. It is one of my greatest achievements, I believe. And, of course, it was built in Jerusalem. You are familiar with this?"

"I've been there."

"I know this. Your energy in that space has left a mark."

"That's interesting. I'm finding out lots of surprising things lately. I'm searching for assistance with creating abundance."

"In money and properties?"

"Yes, and in relationships. I've been involved in several business ventures that are not giving me the income I would like to have, so that I can do some of the grander things I'm visioning."

"Your mind must be fully aligned with the vision. Do you have husbands, my dear?"

"No, although I'm in a relationship with a man named Tonas who is an Ashtar Commander on the 10th dimension."

"That is an interesting long-distance relationship."

"It certainly is."

"It was my suggestion that, if you were to bring a husband with great wealth into your life, this would be the fastest way. The other way is to claim as your own this great wealth, the prosperity. I sense within you that you have a lesser vision of what is possible for you. It was easy for me, being the son of David. It was simple for me to fully immerse with the belief that I, of course, could create something even from nothing. For you, you have the vision that something must be created from something."

"Yes, I'm having grand ideas, but I don't see a way to get the funds to afford to do them. That's not going to help me move forward."

"I was wise, and yet I was ruthless. I would not recommend this as a path for you."

"No, that wouldn't fit me at all."

"It would not fit who you are. And it was what was considered to be the most graceful means for someone to own everything. And, as you are likely aware, I was not the first born—and yet you are, I believe."

"Yes."

"And so, let us instill within you the rights of the first born, so that within yourself you are holding that vision of, not only the first born, but the one who is to inherit."

"But it's not like I'm from a lineage of wealthy people—or at least, that's my perception."

"It is the energy of this that I wish to instill within you."

"Oh, well, I'll take that."

"We are in agreement that it is not in your liking to become ruthless, and you have told me that your sibling is already in his position."

"Yes."

"The Rite of Inheritance, the energy of that, will assist you because it holds that birthright foundation within you. It holds you upright as if you had the greater staff in your hand. And, of course, it would not be in your interest to be ruthless, as we mentioned. I have a sense that your SVH is about to become more well-known in the next months. This will offer you opportunities and choices."

"What I really want to do is model to the world what the divine life, the life that we're moving into, looks like—with the ease of living, the perfection of the physical body, the joy of traveling, and the master abilities that are our birthright."

"I see. You wish to share this vision, but first you must feel it."

"One time in my life, I had the sensation of what it must be like to be a queen. I felt a vibration of absolute divine sovereignty and 'queenness.'"

"Ah, yes."

Speaking of queens reminds me of the stories I've heard about Solomon and the Queen of Sheba. Our conversation has been so pleasant, I am emboldened to ask, "What about the stories of your involvement with the Queen of Sheba?"

"This is legendary."

"Was there any truth to it?"

"Most assuredly, I was attracted to her trade routes and then to the root of her being."

"So it was a grand romance?"

"It was a connection of heart."

"That's what Tonas tells me he feels for me. I haven't been able to feel that yet for him, but I'm hoping I will."

"And may I say, I had wives and concubines, and yet none of them held my favor as much as Sheba. When you find the one of your heart, it is important for you to take measure of this. I was not as wise as perhaps I could have been, for I would have had no need for any wife but her."

"Thank you for sharing that with me."

"It is a matter of heart."

"I appreciate your candor. I still haven't fully grasped this inheritance thing that you're talking about."

"That is because you have not received it. It will be my endowment."

"All right then. How do I go about receiving it?"

"I will convene with Osiris, for he is wise and he is still incarnate. It is something that I can bestow upon him to gift you."

"Thank you so much. I want to meet you in person one of these days."

"You will, when you ascend—or perhaps we will meet in your higher dimensions."

"Where do you exist now?"

"I am in the ascended temple at the top of Sinai."

"I've been there!"

"Yes, I know."

"I loved St. Catherine's Monastery there. The energy was magnificent."

"It was impossible for me to leave, for this was part of my kingdom. It spread far and wide."

"I appreciate your assistance with the gift of inheritance."

"It is only right that I should bestow upon you, for you have been the bestower upon me. You have my continued and forever support."

#

Tonas sounds unsettled as he greets me and tells me he has been waiting. It seems no one is interested in leaving the party and since I'm wearing an extraordinary gown, everyone is gathering around to witness it. Wondering what Liponie has created, I'm told it is a beautiful, flowing gown that makes me appear as if I am a mermaid.

Tonas adds, "It has been exciting for me because you are barefoot."

I'm laughing as I tell him, "I think you have a foot fetish."

"It is possible. You always wear such long coverings. Yesterday was a delight for me to see you in your skimpy wear."

"I had no idea it was as skimpy and daring as was described to me."

"It was adjustable, my dear."

I remember, with a feeling of trepidation, that my recital has come and gone. "How was my violin playing?"

"You continued playing the same song for many audiences.

It is playing in my head even as we are speaking now. And the fireworks! Oh, they were beyond amazing! And your star, my dear, became so bright amongst the fireworks that it was as if she was part of it. She made herself colors, you see. It was such a grand spectacle."

"I told you I love the fireworks; I'm glad they were beautiful and that you enjoyed them."

Tonas informs me that Osiris has been selecting individuals for our meeting which will take place in another part of the ship. Everyone else will have an opportunity to listen in, since it is important to have their added assistance. We move to the meeting room but before we enter, Tonas has a suggestion concerning my dress.

He diplomatically suggests, "Perhaps you may wish to wear something a little less festive—a little more serious?"

He's probably right, so I ask him for a recommendation. He tells me that I am always beautiful in a flowing gown of gold. I didn't know I'd ever worn a flowing gown of gold, but obviously I manifest it because he says, "Thank you, that honors me. Let us enter now."

Then he tiredly adds, "I think we can dispense with the trumpets. Thank you, Liponie."

Addressing the group for the meeting, I thank them all for being here and then ask, "How many people are in the room, Tonas?"

"At present, there are thirty-one in the room. There have been more additions to the party, my dear. It is more than twenty thousand five hundred, so we have gained somewhat in participants."

###

"May I speak with Osiris just for a moment in privacy?"

He tells me, "Come, my dear, we can move out into the hallway. We will ask all those crossing through to give us privacy."

"I was just visiting with Solomon."

"Solomon the king?"

"Yes. He's going to give you something for me called the Rite of Inheritance. He tried to explain it to me, but I didn't understand it. He said that was because I didn't have it yet."

"Let us move over here, as others are joining the council. Yes, I have this endowment for you. It makes sense for you to receive this endowment from me simply because it is impossible, of course, for you to receive this from Solomon. He is ascended, you see. There are rulings that even I must follow—but this has been offered to me as a gift for you. May I place my hands upon your head?"

"Yes."

"I will place one hand over your third eye and one hand over the crown of your head. Tonas is moving us into the 6th and 7th dimensional framework. It is important for this to be applied in your current dimension."

"That makes sense."

"We draw upon the universals to bring into the installation of your presence the endowment of the Rite of Inheritance. That which insures your right of birth, that which instills within you the confidence, the magnetism, and the energy of assuredness. It is done and it is so. We may be returned back to your dimension. Feel your energies at this time; do you feel much surer?"

"Well, maybe."

"If you had said 'No,' I would have suggested you wait until there is a time for this to have settled in your dimension. Your 'maybe' gives me great hope for your acceptance now. Let me share with you how you may utilize this if you are interested."

"Yes, definitely."

"As you stride through life, imagine what it is like for a human who bears the Rite of Inheritance. There will always be something that you are ready to step in to claim, and so that energy becomes magnetism. It magnetizes other opportunities, because you are written to be the receiver. Do you understand?"

"Yes. This doesn't take anything away from my brother, does it?"

"Your brother is not here to receive such an endowment."

"He's not the first born, but he has what you're talking about—that successful moving forward in the business world."

"I believe that he has possessed this, of course, being the first-born son."

That settles my mind about receiving this rite. I say, "Let this take effect and see what happens."

"I love how you have used the wording, the take effect. Let us move back in to the council."

"Before we do, let me tell you that you put me on the spot just a little bit yesterday when you said, here she is and let's hear her vision. That's been a challenge for me, Osiris, to see the big picture and even the bigger picture. That's why I asked people to help me be more glorious in my imagining the possibilities for the future. Do you see my dilemma here?"

"Until the true vision of purity is revealed, there could be smaller visions that are less supportive shared between you of the academy," he replies. "There are individuals in your academy who believe that, as soon as you move into the 7th or even the 8th dimension, you will no longer have legs, that you will be pure energy. They don't understand that you are pure energy *now*."

"Understanding when and how our bodies will change is somewhat confusing."

"I exist within the non-dual higher dimensions and I have a physical body. I have, well, it is blue blood—and yet it is blood. I have a heart that beats in my chest, I have lips and I consume that which pleases me. It is a fantasy to imagine that, all of a sudden you are acting as though you are ascended, just because you are in a higher dimension."

"But the higher dimensions have so much more to offer."

"The value of the higher dimension is in the purity of the focus, the ability for what you desire to be instantly manifest, and that there is no more suffering, no more the need for conflict. There is no need to be without a physical form for, indeed, it is the physical form which gives the pleasure of the experience. I am sure that those like Sananda and the others who have ascended are pleased with themselves—and yet, I don't believe they would enjoy one of your cookies as much as I did."

"I'm glad you enjoyed the cookies."

"We should return. The group has grown to forty-seven, my dear."

"That sounds like a good number."

"It is indeed."

As Osiris and I re-enter the room, Tonas says, "May I say that you look lovely! Your costume today was divine."

"Thank you."

"It was an inspiration to all of the females."

"Can I say a couple of words to Osiris, and then maybe ..."

Osiris says, "It is important for you to be the focus of this meeting. We all will give ideas, of course—but this would be a useless meeting without you, for it would be all in conjecture. No action could be applied."

# # #

As I address the meeting members, I begin by reminding them why we are here.

"Yesterday, I asked you for an expansion on that which has begun in a somewhat small fashion for me. Recently, as I was chatting with my guide, Esthra, I suddenly started babbling about the new house I'm going to have. I got really excited describing many rooms, exquisite construction, grounds with big trees, the perfect location for my orchids to grow and people to help me with them, a stable for horses, sculptures on the grounds and a lotus pool, in honor of Isis. I kept thinking, where are all these ideas coming from? It was wonderful to be able to think expansively like that. I am not used to thinking that way in my current reality, because I would have difficulty paying for any of those items.

"The majority of people on Earth have to work for a certain amount of time to receive a certain amount of money. Many people are on a subsistence income and some not even that. There are homeless people here who sleep outside under bridges with cardboard over them in the winter to keep warm. People are working at jobs they don't like because at least they get money to buy food for their children.

"I hope that gives you an idea of the difficulties many people face with accepting and allowing abundance.

"Perhaps the people representing Agartha would be most helpful in assisting us to move forward since they have a foot on the Earth. May we hear from them?"

"I am Tria of the high council at what you call Agartha. Greetings, my dear."

"Greetings."

"Tria is my designation. It is, of course, true that what we have to offer you in our support has great measure of weight. When you bring to us a concept and vision for what you wish to create, we have the necessary allowances that give us the pleasure of supporting these projects. Earth itself is encoded with all that is necessary to create the balance that you can vision, and even beyond that, to what you have no concept of being possible. And yet, it is the smaller vision that is held by most of the species of Earth. It is the survival rather than the living."

"Exactly so, Tria."

"The new vision of plenty is one that we are committed to assist you in achieving," Tria continues. "We cannot give you the concept. You must bring it to us and then we will join you in the focus for that upliftment."

"There are many that are agreeing," Osiris tells me. "This is the next step, for one of the greatest steps in learning to manifest is to vision that it is possible."

"Yes, some of what I talked about today is the foundation for it. People have programming and belief systems which are disempowering. They see what is and don't feel they can move beyond that. I've done a lot of work on that myself, and I still have some of those challenges, although not as many as I used to have. We can't push people into their passion. They have to believe that they can flourish when they follow their dreams. I don't know how to help them know that."

Tria continues, "Allow me, my dear. Your first position is to hold the vision of freeing survival forever from *your* consciousness, and instead, take upon yourself the new, focused vision that everything is at your disposal to create—for that is the truth and shall be the inheritance that you achieve upon entering the higher frequencies of the 7th dimension and further on. This is all waiting, at your disposal.

"And so, as you bring the enclave of your academy fellowship into collaboration of releasing survival and accepting the full presence of the right of birth, then each of you may put your thoughts together of how you can, individually and collectively, hold the greater vision of the full measure of success in creating a world that is free of struggle—for it is an abundant world. It is a world that speaks to the heart and the heart is the conduit for the creating."

Osiris adds, "I believe we have completed this gathering for this time. We will reconvene; how many of you will be remaining until the Monday? Ah, no one intends to leave. All wish to remain and be of support. This is a gift to us as well as to you."

###

Tonas says, "Come, let us leave. Ah, Liponie, he is tiresome with those trumpets. Whenever we enter a room, the trumpets blare. I feel as though I am ready to jump out of my skin. He is doing what he believes makes you happy so, of course, I am accepting of this—and yet, please, you must ask him to stop."

"Yes, I agree, it's enough with the trumpets. Liponie, let's have a little more soothing music, please. Would you mind?"

Liponie asks if I am displeased with him.

"No, but I think we can dispense with the trumpets until the last ceremony. It's a little startling. Some gentler music would be nice."

"But I wish for everyone to know when you are entering a room! It certainly brings their attention to the door."

"Can't we play something that would be less startling?"

"I will make an announcement that whenever they hear the sparking of the bells, it will be you entering."

"I like that idea, Liponie. Thank you."

Tonas sounds relieved. "My gratitude, my dear, for I am never far from you. The trumpets were quite shattering to my calm."

###

I decide to check with Melchizedek about my violin performance. He assures me it was perfection. That is a relief to hear. We chat for a moment and then I realize that what I would really like to be able to do with my violin is to improvise, to play music that has never been written.

He tells me that ability "is what you might consider to be the greatest crown of this piece that we have in your cerebral interface connection. When the energy of your playing joins with that of the mechanism, you will follow that energy stream with such delight. It will carry so that you are inspired. I believe that this is the time for you to take this tool—though it is made of energy, like all things—and to feel the realness of it and how it will affect your life. That is when you will improvise."

In the course of our conversation, we discuss options for my violin playing and Melchizedek reminds me that I have three hundred and fifty years or so to pursue my desires. When I really contemplate that amount of time, I realize that even three hundred years and fifty years might not be enough time to experience all the possibilities that I'm beginning to become aware of and opening up to.

I mention to Mel that Osiris hinted at some kind of divine voice that I'm going to be able to access. "What he said, to my understanding, was that it is a resonation, vibration, or tone of speaking which comes from my heart and speaks to the hearts of others.

"Part of my vision includes speaking to people," I tell him. "I'm not exactly sure what I'm going to be speaking about, other than my love for the Earth and encouraging people. I don't want to feel that I'm trying to convince people of anything. I just want to be able to say what would be of most benefit, whatever it is. Can you help me with any of this, Melchizedek?"

"I have just had an idea that will help you step into the conscious stream of infinite truth," he replies. "It will begin to allow the vibration of truth to be held in your voice and words." He adds that it is the energy of my goddess presence that captures the stream. "Can you gate to Mt. Nebo in your current dimension? I will assist you there."

#

I go to Tonas to tell him I'm going to leave for a little bit.

He says, "This is so important for you. I understand and support you completely."

But as I start to leave, he says, "Ah! Excuse me. I had to put my finger up, for I knew Liponie was drawing perhaps a next surprise. He is what you would call a *handful*."

"That's what it's like when you have children, Tonas. At least, that's what it's like here when you have children."

"He is incorrigible."

"I'm going to see Melchizedek."

"Yes, I witnessed; I am so excited for you. I wish I could be a part of it but I will wait here for you."

# # #

Melchizedek suggests that we gaze out now upon the Sea of Galilee.

"I've been here."

"We are aware of many things about you. I selected this place specifically because of this. This cross before us only means the energy of cross—there is no energy of death, or any kind of suffering attached to it."

"Thank you for saying that."

"Now, if you will, stand up against the cross. I know this is quite an interesting concept, but I wish to draw upon the energy of the cross, for it is a universal energy that brings into completing the sweetest balance."

"Yes, that's been my understanding of the vertical and the horizontal."

"It is most delightful. As you stand, you do not need to bring your arms up, my dear. You are not Jesus."

This makes me laugh and say, "Correct!"

Melchizedek poetically guides me to draw energy from the Earth and the cross and allow this energy to flow outward into the water of Galilee, the sky and then back into the Earth. He then asks me to take the universal energy that is drawn to me into my heart and become one with the vibration of truth and the flow of that stream that carries my thoughts and my words out into the world.

He finishes by instructing me to, "Draw upon the endowment of presence that all that shall come from your lips—from the beating of your heart, from the thoughts of your mind—shall carry the vibration that can be heard, that will carry the sensibility that can be understood, that will carry the vision of what can be. And we are complete with this. There is no buffet afterwards."

"You're funny. Thank you for your assistance."

"It is my great honor to be of assistance."

CHAPTER THIRTY-FIVE

June 25, 2014

Tonas says, "My dear."

"I just can't stay away. It's no fun having a party and not being there."

"This is a song to my heart. "

"I have a request."

"I am at your disposal."

"I know you're busy, but can you watch some Fred Astaire movies?"

A note of panic is in Tonas's voice as he exclaims, "Wait, wait! I think I said this wrong. Do not dispose of me!"

"Oh, no, I wouldn't do that." Thinking this reassurance would be enough, I attempt to go on, but he is not satisfied.

"It is a wording, I think, which is incorrect. I am at your disposal; I have said it more than once. I am very concerned. Please do not disposal of me."

"I won't, Tonas, I promise. It's just a phrase that means you are ready to assist me. I have no intention of disposing of you!" This seems to satisfy him, so I continue. "Can you and Liponie watch some Fred Astaire and Ginger Rogers movies?"

"I will research it immediately."

"They were a wonderful dancing couple."

"Ah, like us."

"Yes, well, I hope so. He was the most graceful man, and in some of his movies, he wore a tuxedo. Remember when I was talking about those, the other day?"

"Yes, I have not had the opportunity to research yet."

"I know it's an Earth thing and you're not an Earthling, but I think you would look magnificent in a tux. This party is about Earth, you know, and it would be fun to dress in those kinds of costumes. I'd like for Liponie to make me a gown or two that are similar to the beautiful ones Ginger Rogers wore. I know he will want to put his own touch on it, but still it would be more of an Earth style."

"I would enjoy wearing for you the clothing you describe."

"The other fun thing is, I know that Osiris likes marshmallows. Those are little, puffy, white foods we use on Earth for different things. I would like for him to be able to taste s'mores."

Tonas doesn't know about this treat, so I describe how to make them. This makes me wonder how I can make one for myself. I live in the city and I don't have a fireplace; I suppose I could use the little blowtorch I have to melt the marshmallow, but the thought of doing that feels ridiculous.

Continuing my explanation, I say that it might be fun for people to take part in making their own food by roasting their marshmallow to the perfect degree of toastiness. Tonas and I discuss other foods that would be simple for our guests to prepare, and he suggests we could have workshops to teach them how to make things.

I'm thinking that we will need to teach them how to use their own implements, but Tonas points out that the really important aspect of all this is that individuals will be using their hands to create something.

I keep forgetting that these beings just *think* things into existence. They don't generally even use their hands. So I surmise that going through the motions of actually, for example, making a peanut butter and jelly sandwich would be a novel experience.

Tonas states that, "We have offered many varieties of ice cream, but this has not been something that they understood they could dip for themselves. Perhaps we could add this to the workshop as well, for individuals to make the ice cream sundae."

Of course, I have to add a description of how to make banana splits, and then Tonas says that he will need to find different clothes for people to wear, since they are dressed elegantly. I'm inspired to mention picnics to Tonas, and begin describing how to have one. This suggestion inspires another of our comedy routines of misunderstanding.

"How about picnics. Do you know what a picnic is?"

"I have not completed that research. Where do you find the nics to pick?"

"No, you put the foods, drinks and all the utensils you will use to consume them into a basket. A blanket is nice to take, too. You go somewhere that's a beautiful place in nature and spread out your blanket—or you can sit at a table—and eat."

"But where do you find the nics?"

"Picnic is just a word."

"But if they're going to pick it, we must give them the opportunity to find them."

I didn't think it would be so difficult to explain something that, to me, is commonplace. I attempt once more to define picnic.

"A picnic refers to putting food together and taking it somewhere."

"Ah, we are not picking something like berries, as you explained to me. Ah . . ."

Finally, we reach an understanding concerning picnics!

As our conversation continues, I suddenly realize that Tonas has frequently been telling me he will have to do research. I've been so excited thinking of things to eat that I just kept plowing on.

I finally come to my senses and tell him, "You don't have to have things just as I've described. We just want to let people have fun putting things together. There's no failure, no way to do it wrong. If you miss something, I don't care. I'm just throwing ideas at you to have fun playing with."

"Ah."

"Do you understand?"

"Yes, of course. I think it is exciting to consider individuals having this opportunity to create foods. It will be quite an extravaganza!"

"I'm going to be back tomorrow and the next day— because I just can't stay away."

"Oh, delight!"

# # #

Esthra greets me with the fateful words—"I am at your disposal"—that Tonas was so panicked about uttering.

"Esthra, I was talking with Solomon the other day. I loved meeting him and he happened to mention the Queen of Sheba. He had a connection of heart with her, but he let it slip through his fingers. Is there something I could do to help them be together?"

"I think this is something you should ask Solomon himself. He is the one who gave you that information. I am curious about your Tonas. He has heard me say, over and again, 'I am at your disposal.' He was quite frightened, was he not? He does not understand the wording."

"Yes, he was saying, 'don't dispose of me.' It took a bit of explaining to convince him I wouldn't."

"He had a clear understanding in an instant that he was in trouble. That is endearing, of course. Do you wish to speak with Solomon?"

"Yes."

# # #

Solomon says, "Again we have this meeting, my dear."

"Hello, Jedidiah. I'm meddling a little because I was stricken when you talked about the Queen of Sheba. I wonder if there's any way I can assist you to be with her. I don't know if any alliances or relationships are of interest where you exist, but if they are, I would like to help."

"We have known, from the beginning of our meeting, that there is a time for us to be together. This will, of course, happen in the Fifth Realm, when we make our transition. When I am in that realm and re-structuring the story of my incarnation, I will experience—as she will—that we make our stand and claim one another."

"Oh, good."

"There is hope for us, my dear, and your romantic heart …"

"I know. Can I do anything in the meantime? Can you visit each other? Is she in a temple somewhere?"

"Ah, the dear one has chosen to be in the Fifth Realm."

"All right. Then I'm not so sad that you aren't together."

"Already she has recreated the reality for herself. You are dear."

"I just wanted to see if I could do anything. I'm glad that you've got it figured out, so carry on."

CHAPTER THIRTY-SIX

June 26, 2014

Tonas welcomes me and says that things are progressing nicely.

"Hello, Tonas. First of all, I'm sorry for dumping all those ideas on you yesterday."

"I have met the challenge."

"Jill Marie says the ice cream was delicious but she has a few suggestions for you. I just can't get used to the idea that you all get to think of what you want and it manifests. Here, we have to physically do things—put it together, dip it, or slice it, and that's not how you folks are used to doing things."

"Ah ha! And yet, this is the most exciting part of the experience for them."

"Can you have someone in each area to demonstrate what to do for new people who come?"

"What if we have a projection of the creation of some of these delicacies?"

"Yes! People would say, 'Oh, that's how you do it,' and then they could dive in and experiment on their own. I want to make sure people know there's no one perfect way to do it."

"Are you sure?"

"Yes, because here everyone has individual tastes; some people don't like banana splits, or they don't like chocolate ice cream. So if you have a demonstration…"

"I don't believe it!"

"It's true. Jill Marie doesn't like chocolate. Maybe it's different there; maybe everybody likes everything. I want to encourage experimenting."

"Well, this is quite an extravaganza."

"Did you figure out how to have hamburgers and hot dogs?" This was something I had left to Tonas to create, since I know they don't kill animals in this dimension.

"Certainly, we made a version of these from a delightful substance that is made from a root from Sirius."

That doesn't sound too appealing to me, but it's probably delicious, so I move on to my next item. "I'm sure you have foods from all different cultures, like Italian and Mexican foods."

"Indeed, we have a presentation of the cultures. I want you to know there are individuals who have spent three days in the food room. They have not left. They are consuming everything, just to experience it. Food is the most delightful experience for so many."

Three days in the food room astounds me. Tonas explains that holding the spade and lifting the foods onto their plates is a unique experience for everyone.

"I just realized that last night, and it's mind-boggling to me. That's just how we do it here, you know."

"It is an action experience."

"Yes, right."

"I was surveying earlier this morning and it was interesting to watch an individual holding an apple. She observed the apple and she seemed to think it was quite pretty. She had no vision of how it could be eaten, and so I showed her the vision of placing it in the mouth and biting, taking out the big bite. These, of course, are part of visions that you can see in the research."

"It sounds like you've done a wonderful job."

"Ah, it has been a delightful challenge for me."

# # #

"Are Earth's animals part of the spectacle, Tonas?"

"I wish for you to know that Liponie has created a room to display the animals of Earth's seas. He also has a section with the full experience of an individual from the beginning of the first cell leading through the dinosaur age and the development of different species of animals, the plant life, and the birds."

"That was ambitious!"

"Oh, and there is a full complement of the species of plants. He created another section that has been designed to show the different minerals. Liponie has out-manned himself. He truly has. He has created a true celebration of Earth."

"I am so impressed."

"I am impressed myself. I thought it would be simple to decorate a little." We both laugh. "My vision was small next to his."

"Does he have anything that shows the development of a human?"

"This is not news for us. We are well versed on the creation of the human. As you might know, those who are of your affiliation of the ancient academies created many of the animals of this world, the fish, the birds, and much of the plant life. It was part of their studies, you see. I understand that there was a lot of creating and improving upon those animals, birds, plants, and different creatures from their own worlds that they were recreating—or improving upon, let us say."

# # #

"Tonas, I have something I would like for the people here to assist me with."

"I'm sure they will be most willing. Perhaps we should include Osiris in this, for it is he who commands such attention."

"Could we have him join us, please?"

"As before, when we made the communication available to all who are here on the vessel, I'm sure we can arrange this through Osiris."

Osiris makes himself known. "This is quite an event, my dear, and it became even more exciting when I found the marshmallows."

"Well, there was no one to demonstrate how to toast them

and assemble the s'more. Jill Marie came over last night and gave some instructions as to how to make that dessert."

"Oh, I will make my way there immediately."

Before he can leave, I say, "I spent quite a bit of time last night sitting and thinking about what I want to claim. I'm claiming the Earth as my realm and I have a page of ideas I would like assistance with."

"Ah, those here would be most willing; let us bring the consortium of them together. Of course, it will be difficult to bring those away from the foods; perhaps we can make this available to them. We are ready; you may speak and they will hear you."

I gather my thoughts for a moment, and then address the group.

"I spent some time yesterday deciding what I would like in my life. I'm going to share my vision with you, and I am asking your assistance in manifesting it or something even grander. I am asking for your blessings, inspirations, encouragement, and assistance for all people(s), organizations, and companies who wish to assist Earth and her inhabitants. This includes, but is not limited to: inventors, scientists, innovators, entrepreneurs, visionaries and teachers who are developing new methods, products, and technologies, farmers who grow organic produce, places that sell it, and people who buy it as well as companies and people who make organic, safe, effective, environmentally friendly products."

I know it's quite a list, but I continue my request, to be sure everyone will receive as much help as possible.

"Please assist in whatever ways are most divine and for their highest good all my past, current, and future students, customers, clients, friends, family, my sons, mom, dad, my brother and his family, teachers, mentors, associates, and anyone who wishes to support or help me in any way that is divine.

"I am choosing to model to the world what the divine life—

the life that we're moving into here on Earth—is like, with the ease of living, the perfection of the physical body and the gifts of master abilities. I choose to radiate encouragement, love, prosperity, wisdom, humor, and joy.

"Specific areas that I feel our country, and perhaps all of Earth, needs assistance with are: commerce, education, government, arts, science, and health. That's a big list. I would appreciate your assistance with any or all of it."

Osiris speaks. "I call upon all of you now to join me in a singular focus to support this delightful one, a focused individual who is elevating through her own heart and her own desire and through these actions the destiny of each of us. We will continue to hold this vision for you. Of course, as you achieve these elevations, we will continue to hold that vision even beyond that point. If you reach the pinnacle, it is not that we release our support of you. We will continue, for you are a part of us."

"Oh, thank you! Thank you all."

He asks me, "Is there more? We are open and ready to receive. If you have more, we will listen. Not one of the guests here has even considered leaving this great party. I believe that this ship has now exceeded its size by two thousand measures."

"Oh my gosh!" His astonishing statement is another glimpse of how impossible things are an everyday occurrence here. I hesitate for a moment before sharing my personal vision, worrying that maybe it's not really appropriate to do so. But then I gather my nerve and begin.

"I do have a vision for my next home, which I am in the process of refining. I have shared some of my vision with my guide, Esthra, the other day. I would be glad to speak about that also."

"We are your audience, just as we were when you played your beautiful concerto," Osiris says. "As you played your beautiful music, we have been your most focused guests."

"Here on Earth, the mindset has always been, you have to

have something to create something. Solomon told me that he knew he could create something from nothing. I know that's the visioning of what you want and then allowing the universe to manifest it for you, with ease and grace.

"For most of my adult life, it never occurred to me to dream about a life much different from the lives of my parents or peers. I wasn't in a 'survival mode' type of life, but I was deeply in the rut of a view of life that was only slightly better than the way my parents and grandparents lived.

"When I finally spoke to Esthra about my dreams and desires, it was like a floodgate inside of me broke and they started pouring out. Once I started speaking, I wanted to send out to the universe the most magnificent vision of abundance that I could possibly imagine. Here, then, is the beginning of my vision."

At this point, I go into a detailed description of all that I wish to manifest. I know from the business training I've received that it is important to be specific, but my intention also is that I will be open to the universe providing an even more magnificent and expanded version of my desires.

After I speak at length about my vision, I explain, "The reason why I am spending so much energy in creating this vision of a home and lifestyle is because I hope to shift a major paradigm that is held in the collective consciousness on Earth.

"We have not been taught, nor have most of us experienced, that life is infinitely abundant and that we have the capacity to tap into that flow of abundance at any time. Instead, our collective beliefs support a mindset of lack.

"I have been told and shown, over and over again, that abundance is free-flowing and that it is our birthright. I am choosing to embrace that teaching and to demonstrate to others that the universe is eager to provide for me, *and for them*, whatever we desire. An abundant, joyous world is our *true* inheritance."

Osiris pauses only a moment before addressing me. "I wish to assure you that all of us have pledged to do everything in our power to assist you to achieve and surpass the dreams you have shared with us today. You are our dear Joy, and we treasure you more than you know."

#

I feel relieved that I was finally able to express one of my major concerns about the society I live in. I can't remember when I have addressed a group with such passion—perhaps never. It takes me some moments to regain my composure, but finally I am able to ask Tonas about what we've been doing.

"Tonas, have we danced yet? Have you worn your tuxedo?"

"I am saving it for later today."

"I'm glad Liponie made you those cufflinks. I think they're dazzling."

"I am creating a new sensation, for this is not considered to be the normal dress, you see. I believe that all will wish to experience something like this."

"The gowns that women wore in the past were so elegant and refined. I always think that an attractive man in a tuxedo is really glorious. Even men who aren't so good-looking are gorgeous in a tux. Thank you for humoring me. I just want to be consciously here with you."

"Indeed, you have never left—and there will be a time when you remember this."

"I hope so. I want to spend all day there, and it's impossible at this time. Can I ask Liponie something really quick?"

"Of course, he is ever at our side, my dear."

"I'm going to say farewell."

"Oh, I am blessed that you never 'farewell me' all of these days."

#

"Liponie, how are you thinking about my list of impossible things now?"

"Hmm, I am impressed, my dear. Since you have presented me with this list, you have advanced tremendously simply in the vision of what you can create. For me to witness you in the presence of these great ones, defining these realities as if they were, of course, the simplest thing for you to have achieved—it is as if the mountains have moved. I am, of course, doing what I can."

"Thank you."

"It has been interesting to watch you change your mind. Those things you listed do not seem quite as impossible, I think."

"No, not so impossible."

"And so, I must tell you that there is much that I have been applying already."

"That sounds good to me. Can you tell me what you've been doing?"

"I have been doing what you might consider 'miracle moves,' my dear."

It seems that he's not going to give me any details, but I'm glad he's doing something, so I say, "Oh, I accept that, and I thank you for whatever it is you're doing."

"It would be difficult to pull me away from this project, because it is something that has caught my imagination. And though I have magic, I must say that it is you sparking the magic in my mind and in my heart to create with passion. And, of course, you give me an incentive to inspire even more so."

"I accept. Carry on with your magic. Can I chat with Melchizedek for just a moment before I leave, please?"

"We must find him. I am sure he is with the foods. Ah, and here he is."

# # #

"I am over the whelming. I am overwhelmed, my dear. Overwhelmed is a new verbiage. It is an Earth term that you are aware of?"

"Yes." I love the variations on the English language that these beings come up with.

"I must say that you were the highlight with your playing."

"That's one of the things that's so exciting to me—my new violin and being able to do what you're saying."

Mel—I feel like calling him that to his face, but I haven't had the nerve to do so yet—tells me that people want me to play more music on my violin. I wonder how much I'll need to practice and he gives me some great news.

"If you know the song, you can play it. You don't even need to know every note, because the music will come from your heart."

This gives me a great idea. I mention some music that I consider "fiddle music," which is still played by a violin but is more like what old-timers would play—foot stompin', hoedown-type music that people could even dance to.

"If you'd enjoy playing that music, this will be arranged. You know, you are the star of the party. There is nothing more exciting for all than to have your presence here, and to have you accompany them is delightful."

I know Mel is telling the truth, but his description of my party activities are completely unlike my mode of operation at any party I've attended as an adult. Usually, I'd hang around for a little bit, munch a few party snacks, chat with a few people I knew, and then leave early. It's difficult to grasp that I'm the star of a party as magnificent as this one is.

"Do you think people would like to do square dances and stuff like that?"

"There has been instruction here for the other dances, so it would be simply another instruction. Tonas is shaking his head up and down; he is listening intently, my dear. He will never fail in bringing what you desire into presence."

"You see, the thing is, I don't want him to think that he would ever fail in anything. I need to tell him that."

Tonas says, "My dear, thank you for this."

"Tonas, I want you to know, from all my heart, that no matter what you ever do—now, in the future, or till the end of time—you will never fail me."

"This is my focus."

"No, you're still not getting it. No matter what you do—even if you don't think it's perfect—it's never going to be a failure."

"You are accepting."

"Yes, no matter what happens, it's going to be wonderful for me."

"Ah, this is a tremendous gift."

"Tonas, I want you to be as carefree and light-hearted as I'm feeling when I'm with you."

"And yet, you are still in duality."

"I know, but I'm feeling marvelous and I don't want you to feel like you've got to have it just exactly like I said."

"But to make you happy gives me pleasure."

"Yes, but if you don't, I'll still be happy. It's all perfect. The thing is, if you make a 'mistake,' think how much fun it will be correcting it."

"You have an interesting vision."

"Don't you think that would be just right? You are supposedly not fallible; we've been fallible here on Earth and we make mistakes. We say, 'Oh, that didn't work. We've got to try something else.' My life has been full of mistakes, more than I could ever count."

"This is in no way dampening my passion to bring you your heart's desire, but it does endear you to me even more."

"Having fun and playing is important to me. The work is the

play and the play is the work."

"Ah, you are fun."

"I'm glad you think so. All right, my consciousness is going to leave. I'll talk with you tomorrow because we're going to be doing important work with Tria. I know that she heard what I had to say today. Perhaps some parts of my vision will be able to assist us tomorrow evening with our group meeting."

"Do you wish to have the meeting broadcast through the vessel?"

"I think it would be helpful to enlist the aid of others. That's all I have for now."

"I am grateful, my dear. This helped me beyond measure."

"Farewell."

"Farewell."

CHAPTER THIRTY-SEVEN
June 27, 2014

"Ah, my dear, you are back! And you have never left."

"Hello, Tonas. I have a list of music I have jotted down for you here."

"I do not read this language."

"Oh, you don't? This is English." This is a challenge I had not anticipated.

"I do not read English, and yet it was well chronicled for me with all of the movies and the popcorns. Jill Marie gave me a full breakdown and a building-up as well."

I take a moment to savor this "Tonasian" expression … "break down" and "build up."

"Can you get someone to decipher what this says? Because I thought you might like to listen to one of the songs I enjoyed when I was in college. It's called 'Barefootin'.'"

"Yes, of course."

"Can someone read the list for you?"

"Certainly. And I have understanding that Jill Marie will be back several hours from now. I must report that I have seen the *Wizard of Oz*. I have witnessed this cinema and, of course, you sat beside me most cuddlingly. I put my arm around you. We ate candies and we enjoyed the popcorn."

Cuddling sounds like so much fun. I sigh as I take a moment to imagine what it would be like to actually feel his arm around me. Then I remind myself to be patient, because that *will* happen.

# # #

This morning, an awareness of a desire I've briefly contemplated over the years came strongly into focus for me. I ask Esthra to join us in order to share my new goal with him.

"Esthra, this morning I thought about something that has me

the most excited of anything I've ever visioned—and here it is. I want to be able to afford to purchase all of the land of the farm where Sheliah's garden exists. I'm going to share this with everyone at the end of the party. Do I need to meet with you every time I add to my list?"

"Simply convey your desire to me."

"Okay. See, I'm still wondering if you really hear what I am sharing with you during my 'normal' day."

"We have the impression, my dear."

# # #

I decide I'd better check on Liponie. He says that he is creating a whole section of cooking class.

"Oh! I probably should attend."

"This evening for the dinners, some of the greatest of masters are cooking for those who will be dining with us. We are making spaghetti and we are also making what you would love to consume for yourself. It is much like the sweet potatoes and we are using the marshmallows and some of the brownest of sugar. This will be quite delicious. Listen, I have discovered something simple. If you make it sweet, our guests will eat it all day and all night."

"I was worried about that, because I love sweet food. I was thinking about all the desserts and how maybe we need to have other foods. We're going to have devil's food cake and angel food cake."

"This is a bit hilarious."

"I think so, too."

"I believe you are the hit of any party, my dear, the top hit."

"I'm not used to that either, because I was never one of the 'in crowd.' I was shy and I definitely was not one of the people who were popular. It's strange to be a hit now."

#

Now feels like a good time to ask Esthra if there's anything he can tell me about blocks I might have to manifesting the vision for my life I've been working on. He promptly mentions that I have a fear of and resistance to work and that I have a belief that work is what I must do to create wealth. I feel dismayed, because I immediately know he's right. I really don't like the idea of work.

"Luckily," Esthra adds, "work is not necessary for you to create the realities you desire."

We discuss some of my other work-related beliefs—you've got to work hard to succeed, and it's the struggle that makes things worthwhile. I judge people who inherit wealth instead of working for it. "I have been afraid to buy a lottery ticket, because I might win. I want people to be able to do what I do to succeed," I say.

He wisely tells me that people must find their own way. I have been coming to that realization, also.

#

Before I leave, Tonas informs me that I played my violin for an exceptionally long time yesterday. Curious as to what music I'd been performing, I ask Mel to join us.

I'm delighted to learn that not only did I play Dvorak's *Romance;* I played some fast and fun reels and jigs. "There was much revelry," Mel says, "and there were musicians from different worlds who assisted you with the songs that required accompaniment."

It's an odd feeling to wish I could have heard myself play those songs.

CHAPTER THIRTY-EIGHT
June 28, 2014

Tonas says, "Oh, delight! May I say that your face completely changes when your conscious essence sparks within. I know in an instant that you are back with me."

"I look really different?"

"Yes, it is a different spark within you." He pauses before saying, in a conspiratorial whisper, "We have a surprise for you."

"Oh, what is it?"

"Take my hand. Liponie and I have a grand surprise for you. Now open your eyes."

"Oh, you're so funny, Tonas."

"All right then, I will describe for you. We have created a permanent space within this vessel that is called the Joy Room, and it resembles the greatest of environments for orchids everywhere of Earth. Look here! It is the Venus Slipper Orchid that you told me makes your heart sing."

Trouble is brewing, because I do not know what he is talking about. "What is it again?"

"The Venus Slipper. Ah yes, you have told me that you enjoy the Calypso."

Finally I voice my concern by saying, "I don't know what you're talking about when you say the Calypso."

"You have told me that this is an orchid from Finland and it is called the Venus Slipper. I immediately made sure this was the one. There is the Spider Orchid. There are many of these orchids that you are most pleased with. Have I displeased you?"

"No—but I don't know of these orchids. I've never heard of the Venus Slipper. You say it's from Finland?"

"You told me it was from Finland."

"Some part of me must have that information, but this part doesn't. I didn't even know there *were* orchids in Finland. I'll look it up, though. I must love the orchids, because I told you I did." Suddenly, tears come to my eyes. "I feel like I'm being left in the dark. It's frustrating, Tonas."

"Oh, this will not always be so, my dear," he reassures me. "Let me describe what we have created. This is a grand exposition, as if it were the same environment where the indigenous of these orchids grow. It is quite beautiful, and … when you can see it, you will appreciate the spectacularness of it."

"I appreciate your generosity in creating this for me. I may have to move my bed in here."

"It was the idea of myself and Liponie. He is a little confounded at the moment, because he thought it was going to be a big surprise for you. I am, of course, transmitting a consciousness to him that this is part of your development that is soon to be."

"How many different kinds of orchids do you have?"

"There are many thousands, and there are many of them of the hebrids."

"The Hebrides Islands?"

"Ah, I am sorry, the word is hybrid."

"Yes, I know what hybrids are. Oh, darn, now I really want to see them!"

"This will be a delightful carrot for you."

"Tonas, there are so many carrots there now, I'm surprised your ship can even fly."

"Ah, we are all your carrots."

"Thank you so much for your thoughtfulness."

"It is our pleasure. The Joy Room is here for you when you wish to be in the energy of this. We got this idea when we walked into the room full of orchids that you are gifting to the individuals. We thought, 'Oh, it must happen for you.' It will always be here."

"Thank you both."

#

Osiris joins Tonas and me for a strategy talk and I ask him to listen as I speak with Gaia.

He says, "We will summon her immediately. She is embodied into a glorious female. It was important for her to be embodied, of course. To show up as a planet would have been too much."

Laughing, I agree that would have stretched the ship a bit.

"And of course, without legs, how would she get to the buffet?"

Gaia asks me how she may be of assistance.

"I am asking for your ideas for assisting all the indigenous peoples of Earth—the aborigines, the Native Americans, the Eskimos, and especially the Seminole tribe. Esthra tells me that, because of the cell phone towers, they are really struggling to feel their connection with you."

"Yes, indeed, and we are aware of your long association with these tribes of indigenous. It is important to assist them."

When I ask Gaia what she can do, she offers to amplify her energies to their heart connection. "Because this connection is part of their culture, it is not manipulation to set what was once into what is continuous."

I'm thrilled about her offer. To my mind, this should help restore the deep connection these people must have felt for Earth in earlier times.

She explains that she will begin amplifying her heart connection from a point sixty years ago, because that was when technological interference began increasing, along with an increase in tarmac, bitumen, and cement, which are also deterrents to connecting with Earth's energies.

"I've spoken with many of the Native Americans about a vision of what is coming and the return of the purity of the Earth," I tell her. "I've been trying to communicate to them about the restoration of the buffalo herds, the land, and the vitality of their existence, which was sapped by our culture."

Gaia responds, "We are moving more readily to the restoring. I have a presence on all of the Earth dimensions leading up to the 10th dimension, and I am fully present within that dimension. On the 10th dimension as well as on the 8th is where the restoration begins fully; on that 8th dimension, there is the purest of waters. The species that have been eradicated are restored there."

"That is wonderful news. I'm going to ask the whole assemblage to assist with radiating blessings and love to all the indigenous peoples, and also anyone who has that love of the Earth—for example, people living in the country or on a small farm often have a sense of closeness to the Earth. Hopefully, we can amplify your connection for all of these people.

"My sons grew up in a city. They don't know what it's like to live close to the Earth. They have their jobs, cars, and video games. If the people of Earth who do have that loving connection with you can feel it even more strongly, I believe that's one of the major things that will assist us to move forward."

I have a plan for her suggestions. "Now that I've made the request, perhaps we can add what you come up with to whatever the CEV is going to give us."

"Indeed."

"Thank you, Gaia. Is Esthra standing there?"

"Yes, he is energetically beside you as if a hump on your back. He is everywhere that you go, you know. I will leave you with this thought: I am emanating to the hearts of the indigenous. You will leave this with me, my dear."

"Thank you so much."

# # #

Esthra has an interesting tone of voice as he remarks, "I am now a hump on the back."

"Do you think what we're going to do for the Native Americans will be enough?"

"This will be a good start. As their spiritual leader, it is possible for you to add some nuances. These will come to you, I know."

"Did you find out who I was talking to the other night?"

"It was a collective of the Seminole. There are elders who come together and create in a circle around the campfire. They smoke interesting tobaccos and make open spaces within their consciousness, which allows them to transmit a collective voice. There were nine of these."

"I could feel myself inside one of them. It seems so odd to say that, Esthra. I was emphatic about whatever I was saying to the group. I reminded them I'm there for them, I guess."

"Yes, it is important for them to continue receiving your heart-felt connection with them, for it is something that has never ceased for the full extent of Earth's history. You are a transmitter from this time, and yet your communications are timeless. Do you understand that the higher part of your consciousness is linked to a greater knowing presence?"

"Yes, I have a sense of that. I'd like to be able to access and accept more of my higher knowledge. I walked into this beautiful room that Tonas and Liponie had designed for me, and they were telling me about all these orchids that I was supposed to love. I'd never even heard of the orchids they described! I disappointed them, I think. It's getting more frustrating for me, Esthra."

"I can feel your frustration. I know that, the more elaborate your gathering here becomes, the more left out you feel."

"Right, I'm missing the party of the century. I'm thinking of all these wonderful things to do, but I'm not experiencing them!"

"Ah, you must believe me—you *are* experiencing them. There will be a time when all of these memories come into your consciousness as if you were here in full presence."

"I would rather have that be sooner than later."

"Yes, of course. I was with you making the connection with … I don't know what to call it … this arbory? It is a space that is probably as big as a village. You will be pleasantly surprised. And in this place, your flowers will never wilt or be of sadness. You will visit and be aware of the place soon. I have no doubt of this. No doubt of it at all."

"It's just that *your* time frames are not anything like *our* time frames."

"You have become a different person from yourself already, in three months of your time. Imagine what will happen in another three months."

I think about that for a moment, and then I realize I can't even guess what I will experience tomorrow—let alone what I will be like in three months.

# # #

"Hey, Liponie, did you have a chance to make me a viola as well as a violin?"

"Oh my goodness!"

I'm delighted I could surprise him with anything, and laughing, I say, "I got you on that one!"

"Ah, you are in trickery! You are most trickery! Yes, of course, I will accomplish this. It will be required that I must make another journey to Lyra. It can be done quickly. I can have this for you for your concert tonight."

Two of the viola pieces I'm thinking of playing are written for a string quartet. Liponie tells me that the musicians remaining who could play that music with me are from Lyra. And they are currently playing music from *American Bandstand!*

"Oh my gosh!"

"Ah, it was your Tonas who gave me the idea. There is twisting, yes. And of course, there are individuals who are joining in on the fun."

"That does sound like so much fun! You guys are brilliant. Thank you, Liponie."

"It was quite exciting for me to have been with you at the arboretum—but I am aware that this has been a faulty attempt. Please do not feel it was in any way designed to cause you displeasure."

"I know that. It just sounds so lovely; it's like the place of my dreams. I want to touch, smell and see the orchids there so badly."

Tonas chimes in with, "Don't listen to him, my dear. He is wishing to take all the burden of this mishap. I was the one who threw the focus toward this creation. I know that you will love it, for you love it now. I watch you walking through it and you touch the flowers as if they are your dearest babies."

"Well, that's how I feel about my orchids here, so I can't imagine I would feel any less appreciative of the ones there."

My longing to fully explore this new gift is too intense to continue. "It's time for me to go, Tonas," I say. "Farewell."

"Farewell."

CHAPTER THIRTY-NINE
June 29, 2014

Tonas says, "You are back."

"I know, but I have to leave, because I'm not feeling right. Esthra says my energy body has been here maybe two days too long. I'll be back tomorrow morning to finish the work."

With great sympathy, Tonas says that I must take care of myself. "While you're gone, I will do research," he says.

We bid each other farewell and I gate back to my house.

#

I begin to consider another issue that's been on my mind. "Esthra, I feel like I have cleared many of the issues relating to my financial abundance. But as layers are cleared and blocks are released, something else pops up to work on. I feel that there is a struggle going on for me in my relationship to abundance, but I'm not even sure the struggle is mine."

"One of the imbalances that affects the whole of Earth is the belief that someone else owns the money, and that it is from them that it must be extricated," he explains. "The government owns the money. The power magnates own the money. The banks own the money—and it is a struggle to get it from them."

"Do I also have a fear of losing money? Am I afraid of the responsibility of having money?"

Esthra tells me no. That's good to hear!

"Then please give me a hint about monetary issues I do have."

He relates that we are moving toward a time when something can be created from a particle of light. Money, in the near future, is on the way out. So it is almost as if I'm waiting for that time when I can manifest with my mind.

Esthra adds that, "You have always been manifesting with

your mind—and why wait? Why not create as much as you desire of everything that you desire, right now?"

"I'm doing my best to be open to receiving money so that I can fund the experiences I am dreaming of doing in this dimension."

"You are open to where the streams are flooding to you," he says. "Now you must be ready to collect that which flows into your treasury."

"My main concern is that there are no blocks to that flow."

"You are most dear. I believe that it is your time. It is your time, and there are many avenues. We will simply light a few of these for you."

"Thank you, Esthra."

# # #

The CEV speaks: "We are in presence."

I greet them and relate the information Gaia shared with me about how she is going to amplify her heart connection with the indigenous peoples. Then I ask them to add anything they can to assist any part of this work.

"It is a worthy endeavor. It is through those of Agartha that the Atlanteans could assist."

"Can we go farther back than sixty years?"

"Why was the year sixty selected?"

"That's when more of the communication ..."

"Ah, technology."

I tell them what Gaia said about concrete and cell phone towers and about my attempts to encourage the Native Americans with visions about what is coming.

"I would like to connect people with the knowing that better times are coming, and in fact, that better times *are here*."

The CEV says, "It is, of course, understood that the concrete, the dirt, the waters, trees, and buffalo are all comprised of the same essence of being that is foundational in all that exists. It is one element of essence that is found in the tarmac, the cement, and the technologies. People simply have disengaged from the recognition of their true essence."

"I hope we can assist them to recognize that again."

"We will ponder this in our collective ponder."

"Do you have anything for me to do before the work tomorrow?"

"We would like you to focus on bringing balance to your body. Your body is out of balance."

"I know. It's because my energy body stayed too long on the 10th dimension."

"You can rebalance easily. It is important for you to know that there will be a time when this will not be an issue."

"I hope that time arrives soon."

"You are building your stamina."

"Thank you for speaking with me today. I always enjoy our visits. I will talk to you tomorrow."

"It is our pleasure."

## CHAPTER FORTY

June 30, 2014

Back on the ship, I ask for an audience with Commander Ashtar. Immediately, Ashtar informs me he is present.

"I'm excited to talk with you," I say. "I have gifts from some of the galactic councils that I believe will assist Earth. Also, I know that perhaps others of Earth have worked with you in the past, so I used SVH to recalibrate and uplift all of that work to be of the highest in effectiveness. But I'm not sure how to give you what I have."

Ashtar answers that it might be possible for him to receive something through the Council for Earth Vigilance. "I am intrigued by your thinking, for many have brought information from transmissions that I have made through them, not all in the greatest of clarity."

"I thought you might have something additional to give to me that I could take to the CEV," I say. "I got what I could in the way of systems and principles to help the different areas of our existence, but if you have something from the fleet you could give me to present to the CEV, I'd like to take it to them."

"Would you like me to join you in your communication with them? For it is my will to bring these things directly to them?"

"I would love that."

"It would, I think, be a bit difficult to describe to you all and to offer these transmissions."

"I think that's the best idea," I say. "Can we hold hands and just go there?"

"I am considering all that has been in the past," Ashtar says. "There have been many of your years that I have been of service to Earth. There is a lot, my goodness; we are talking about many years. I am assuming that you have a means for this."

"Well, we can move through time."

"Ah, the SVH, yes indeed. I am somewhat familiar."

"July fourth, which is only five days from now, is America's Independence Day."

"This would be the perfect of days!"

"I want to claim independence in all areas that would be of benefit."

"Yes, I have pondered on the possibilities. I believe I can transmit to this council. The Fourth of July, ah, this is the day of the fireworks, correct? They can be seen in all dimensions."

"This is my favorite holiday," I reply. "I love the fireworks."

"I think we should involve Osiris in this project. I believe that it might require some of his nuance. He has many visions for Earth as well."

Ashtar continues, "I wish for you to know that your Commander Tonas has received a commendation. This has been exciting for him. I am sure he would wish to tell you in private, but we are all proud of him and all he has accomplished through his connection with you. He has cultivated a relationship and has given you the means in which to take us all into a new level of connection with our support of Earth. And so, of course, he has been rewarded for these accomplishments. He is now a High Commander, which is quite a feat of accomplishment for someone his age. He is the youngest of our fleet."

"That's wonderful! He certainly deserves it, because he's very dedicated to Earth. I can't wait to ask him how he feels about the promotion. Did you enjoy the party, by the way?"

"Oh, I'm not willing to leave yet."

"I've not been here as much, because I got too fatigued to stay."

"Yes, we were aware of your absence."

"You're welcome to stay as long as Tonas doesn't kick you out."

"Now that he has the bigger pants, we will see," he said, chuckling. "I will tell you now that I will remain until this Fourth of July so that I might be present for our new project. We will have this be the great culmination. This will be the cherry on your ice cream sundae that we all now enjoy. We are now all addicted."

"Well, join the crowd, because I love ice cream, too."

"Delightful. I think you and I will continue to talk for years to come. We will have this opportunity when you are more readily able to commune with me in person. You have an open invitation to my ship, my dear."

"Thank you. I'd love to tour it."

"Perhaps Osiris has something to offer."

Osiris speaks out, "My dear, you are at it again!"

"I know!"

"Mmm, you are in the midst of something quite grand. I can feel it already."

"Earth is my sandbox, and I want people to be playing in it who really love the Earth."

Osiris replies that it will be a little while before that is possible. "There are still some people 'schlepping around in the muck.' They don't know it is muck. But perhaps we can show them through the work we are doing."

He congratulates me that I chose to carry the templates to them by placing them in my heart. If I had brought them otherwise, he says, they would not have been as effective. "That which you embrace, you can choose shall be within the presence of that realm that you exist—if one can rise to meet that level, of course. I am in agreement that it is in the highest form for us to connect with the council. If each of us could take one of your arms, Commander Ashtar and I will allow you to take us."

"I just love my escorts!"

"Yes, indeed. We will come in with great power and form."

"My intention is that I will gate you two lovely beings with me to the CEV. Here we are."

#

The CEV speaks. "We are in presence. We are in vigilant presence. Greetings."

"Greetings. I have two wonderful beings with me, Osiris and Commander Ashtar."

"We are honored, of course."

"I also have templates from different galactic councils to assist in upgrading several of our systems on Earth: commerce, education, government, justice, divine marriage, religion, technology, and divine communication. As a little bit of an aside, I am specifically requesting additional assistance in the department of healing the money systems of Earth. Are you familiar with what Earth is currently experiencing in this regard?"

"It is quite, I do not have the word ..."

"Barbaric?"

"No, I would not say that it is barbaric. I would say that it is as if child's play."

"Esthra pointed out to me that we have a mindset that there is a limited amount of money, and that other people have it and we have to get it from them. This we do by either providing a service for them or giving them something that they want so that we can get something from them."

"The word I was searching for is 'archaic.' There is a more advanced system of simply directing creation energy into form."

"We're moving to that—but I'm not there yet."

"Are these templates that you possess within your presence?"

"Yes. I wonder if more could be added to them."

"We read that these templates are defined for several dimensions. This was wise. We will put the profile together for you and add more."

"Can you assist me to release the 6th dimension?"

"Shake your foot." They pause for effect. "That was

comedy. You are also requesting that we assist to amplify and imprint those templates into the 4th, 5th and 6th dimensions, correct? They exist in the 7th dimension so you have no need for insertion there."

"I understand."

"We can use the threads that you have imprinted into those dimensions. The installations can be activated in those dimensions with Tonas. Ah, this will be an excellent exercise. You will have great support. What is your input, Commander Ashtar?"

Ashtar telepathically connects with the CEV and delivers the information about all the past transmissions he has been involved with that have assisted Earth.

The CEV responds to the commander's transmission. "We understand. Is there more for you to add, Osiris? We receive this clearly. We have pondered your earlier request, Joy, and we have some exciting news. We have made you a special egg that will assist your indigenous."

"They are so close to my heart. Thank you for remembering."

"It will assist all sentience of Earth, and yet it is focused for your indigenous, the animals, those that fly in the air, those that swim, the plants, the waters, and also the air itself. May we extract a copy of the templates now?"

"Yes, please do so."

"We are ready. We have your parameters, commander. All that is brought forth through you, for all of the two thousand years of your presence formally linked to Earth, we shall hold in vigilance. Joy, you are capable of placing yourself in positions in time. In those positions in time, it is possible for you to make connection and receive the templates, the encodements, the upgrades, and all that Commander Ashtar and his fleet of commanders have done to support Earth. Since it is more than two thousand years, you will need to spread yourself widely through the time lines."

"Wonderful! It sounds like fun."

"For the maximum benefit there must be at least one other than you. Perhaps the commander? They are his transmissions, after all."

"Oh, that's a good idea, thank you."

"You may apply that which is for the indigenous from the 10th dimension, connecting to your 4th, 5th and 6th dimensions. The templates we offer you in this golden egg are the upgrades you have asked for. These will shine most brightly onto all of the sentience of Earth. These upgrades will fuel that which is of your vision. Before you leave, we would like you to know that there are six hundred and twelve orbs waiting for you."

"Oh, thank you for reminding me."

# # #

We load the orbs in our baskets and arms and I gate us all back to the ship.

Osiris comments, "I believe this was quite productive. It is delightful to watch you in your works, as always. What shall we do with all of these orbs? Perhaps we could draw all of our guests that are still in presence, and they could amplify. They can all be sent out at once, I am sure."

"That would be good."

"Ah, Tonas is excited because he likes this action with you."

"I know. We can hold hands."

When Osiris asks me what we are to do with the orbs, I realize I'm not sure. He checks with the CEV and tells me they are to be transmitted out to all the dimensions where we placed the threads. He adds that everyone on the vessel is watching and that there is "no pressure."

"Not with this new High Commander I'm working with. Hey, congratulations, Tonas!"

"My dear, it is all through you, of course. It is all through your great gift to me."

With exasperation, I reply, "Oh, come on."

"It is the gift of your presence, of course. Take my hand." Whispering, he says, "All are watching, so we will do our best works." In his normal voice, he tells me, "The orbs are floating between us, and, of course, we transmit from this dimension into all dimensions of Earth and outward into everything. Yes?"

"Yes, I agree—with my lovely friend and High Commander here."

We have done this procedure so many times that it flows quickly and gracefully for us today.

I feel a little woozy after sending out the orbs, so I ask for assistance from Osiris. He instructs Tonas to put the ship in three dimensions—the 4th, 5th and 6th and tells me I can simultaneously send individual transmissions into each of those dimensions.

I copy the templates so that I have three sets that are exactly the same. Then I take them to the Agarthans in the center of the Earth. I feel the templates begin to open and dissipate through the 4th, 5th, and 6th dimensions with the Agarthans assisting to amplify the dispersal. The energies move through and out of the Earth, out to the grids, and then through the threads to the all and the everything.

When I ask how to implement the gift the council gave me for the indigenous people of Earth, Commander Ashtar speaks. "There have been many years where our presence has been not as constant, and yet growing more so over the last three hundred years. There are positions within the Earth's atmosphere and the energies connected that lead back to the times of Jesus, who was one that received our transmissions. Does this surprise you?"

"A little bit—but it's wonderful, because I was with him then."

"Your abilities astound me, my dear."

"I just found out the other day that one of my incarnations was as John, the Beloved."

"Ah, now I understand. I was thinking that you were teleporting to this place. I know you have the ability, for we rode with you on the energy threads and ribbons of light that took us to that council. It was quite liberating."

"I'm glad you enjoyed our trip."

"It was delicious, of course."

Osiris informs me that he added upgraded transmissions from other councils that have been assisting Earth.

"You are right after my own heart, Osiris."

"It is most expansive."

"It's going to be great on the Fourth of July!"

"It will indeed."

Osiris speaks again. "What else would you wish to do? We've got everybody watching and holding this energy for you. Is there something else that you would wish for their support?"

I pause for just a moment. "Several things, actually. When I was talking about the indigenous people, I was actually specifying all the Native American tribes, the aborigines, the Eskimos, and people like that. We were going to use the Atlanteans to funnel back assistance to the Agarthans, to assist Gaia for those peoples."

"Ah, everyone is listening. Give them your greatest desire list and they will comply. I'm sure of it."

I relay some of the work we've done to assist the Native Americans and explain Gaia's offer to amplify her connection with the hearts of all indigenous people. "I wish to assist all these peoples in the most magnificent, divine way with knowledge and enhanced awareness of their connection with the Earth," I say. "I also ask for your assistance in helping them feel and know the new Earth that is coming, the vision and the hope of that—the restoration of their lands and the buffalo, the forests, the waters, the animals and the trees."

I remind myself that thousands of people are listening. Although I can't see them, I can feel their presence.

"Gaia says the animals and other species that are now extinct will be coming back," I say. "I'm a little nervous about the dinosaurs, but I guess they're going to be the divine version of dinosaurs. I don't know the details of all that yet."

I try to summarize my request in a way that everyone present can understand. "Help the Native Americans, and all people, to feel again their connection to the Earth, and to be encouraged in their lives, so they know that their current situations, however hopeless they might seem, will change and are changing for the better. Help all of us to feel the easy, graceful, and sweet paths that are opening to us as we evolve.

"We all are chosen peoples. We all have the love of the Earth and we can feel that. We all know that this new Earth is here and we are moving into it. That's my vision."

Tonas says, "My dear, this is a beautiful vision indeed. Ah, it is an honor to be of association with you and all you represent."

"Thank you. I would like for us to focus our intentions and our energies on doing that for the Earth."

#

Isis asks if she may interject. I immediately agree.

"It has been a delight for me to witness and to be a participant of this party," she says. "I wish for you to know that the event has created a sensation throughout the expanse of everything. That which you hold in vision for you is a *commitment* for us. It is not a momentary agreement, for we take this very much into our hearts. We dedicate ourselves to support what you have visioned for us now."

"Thank you."

Osiris asks, "It is the New Earth, is it not? This vision?"

"Yes, but I want to keep expanding the vision. I know it's

even more glorious than I've been able to imagine."

"Indeed! Imagine all of the species returned. You will be picking flowers or smelling them endlessly, forever, for there are many that have been extinct."

# # #

"I hope you've acquired a taste for champagne," I say, "because I want to give a toast on Friday to many individuals. Maybe Tonas can research toasting?"

Tonas says, "We have had the toast. Liponie has informed everyone. There has been the baking of the breads, then there is the toasting, and then, of course, there are the butters and the jams. We've had the toast."

I giggle. "This is a different kind of toast. It's one where you pour champagne—or any drink you choose, but we traditionally use champagne—into a glass and we raise it high and say, for example, 'Here's to all of you, I give you my love and thanks for your assistance today.' And then we all take a sip of our drinks. It's a ceremony to commemorate something important."

"Ah, it sounds even more lavish and lovely. I will tell you that waiting for the toast to pop up was such an excitement for everyone. This one sounds even more exciting. A new kind of toast."

Who would have thought that these people would get excited about waiting for toast to pop? I can just picture them peering into the toaster to watch. How endearing.

"Yes, this is a new kind of toast. I will be speaking with you again on Friday. I would like to release everyone except you, Liponie, Melchizedek, Osiris, and Isis."

"Certainly, my dear. They have immediately honored your request."

# # #

Liponie is laughing as he says, "I am so sorry; pardon me." Then he whispers, "It was interesting to see Commander Ashtar exit and to have me remain. It is quite delicious. I am in the know."

"But I would like for him to be here, too!"

"Oh, I will call him back. It will give him great pleasure— but it was delicious to feel his great esteem for me, knowing that I remained. He has returned."

"Commander, I didn't mean to dismiss you! Thank you for returning. I would like to have a small group, you that are present as well as any of your recommendations of people you would want to join, to meet on a regular basis and keep facilitating this work. Osiris, I'm sure you know of people who are key, people who would be essential to help us continue moving forward. Also, members of this smaller group could communicate to the other people we've been meeting with. However you want to envision that, I would love to have that be our council. Perhaps we can call it the Joy Council. And Gaia would be important, too. Do you have anything to add?"

Ashtar suggests adding Jesus, which I think is a good idea. I ask for a recommendation of one of the Atlanteans, and he recommends Aconna Shareeah, who is a high-ranking official. The Agarthan he names to join our council is Tria.

I suggest Osiris add a few people, and he tells me, "I think this is a good idea. It will give us opportunity to bring information together. When we do not have something like this, many ideas can move aside as time moves, you see. So do we all agree to call this the Joy Council?" Osiris questions.

I immediately agree.

"I believe this is the best name, of course."

"If nobody else has any suggestions," I say, "I would like to speak with Tonas a moment before I leave."

#

"They have left us, my dear," Tonas says softly.

"High Commander, ooh."

"I am elevated to High Commander. I wear the big boots now."

"Do you have little epaulets you wear on your sleeves?"

"Oh, it is certainly known. My parents are of such excitement. It was announced early, as you would say, in this morning."

"How exciting."

"It was indeed exciting. Of course, there was great celebration. It was most delightful because Liponie was *in the know*. I was not in awareness of this. It came as a complete surprise to me."

"That's even better!"

"Liponie made an excuse and told me that there was a new flavor of foods I must inspect. He said that he had made a whole section for this food. It was quite elaborate, and he was concerned that it was too much. I told him, of course, that he had our complete support—but he insisted. It was quite exciting as I moved into that vision and everyone was in presence. The size of the room was gigantic, and I was led to the highest point. The commander himself gave me the elevation."

"Oh, Tonas!"

"This, of course, was transmitted to every vessel in the fleet."

"Ooh!"

"Yes, it was most exciting. My parents were in the know as well. They were on the stage, as you would say. I was most honored by everyone and their accolades. And, of course, what they were most accolading about, my dear, was all that has been accomplished since you. Since *you!* This was not an elevation because I made a good party. It was an elevation because of all that I have had the privilege of doing since I've been in partnership with you. You are aware of all that has come about since we began our work together."

"It is marvelous."

"I mean, every single individual—every plant and every rock—is linked to a continuum that will unify. It will be synchronous. And I was just following your directions. I want you to know that it is my deepest affection for you that brought me the greatest joy. It is a great honor for this elevation. And yet, really and truly, my heart is beating poundingly in my chest because of the deeper connection that we have made through these months. In these months, my dear, we have grown to a much deeper friendship."

"I know we have."

"Soon, you will see my face. You will touch my face and feel your hand on it. You will feel me kiss your fingers. That will be first."

I feel somewhat shy about pursuing this line of conversation. I have been working on clearing my relationship issues with men, and I do trust Tonas. So I decide to take the plunge and tell him, "I really would like with all of my heart to *feel* your lips on my fingertips."

"I will hold your words in my heart until this is a reality for you."

"I have a serious request for you, Tonas. I want you to take full ownership of your part in all this work."

"But how can I do this?"

"Because you're my partner in it."

"Ah, without you it is not possible."

"Well, without *you*, what am I going to be doing?"

"From what I have come to know of you, there is much that you accomplish."

"Perhaps you are right—but I have chosen *you*. I'm asking you to fully embrace your importance to me in facilitating this work. There is an expression in the game of baseball that might be fun for you to consider. You'll probably need to research. Pretend you have the bat in your hand and what I'm asking you to do is 'step up to the plate.'"

"I held a plate in my hand just this morning."

"This is a different kind of plate. This is a plate in baseball."

"You confuse me sometimes, dear. But I will not fail you on the champagne. I will research immediately."

"All right. I'm going to say farewell right now, but I'll be talking to you soon. I may zip over tonight."

"Oh, if you do, you will be excited. Liponie has made you a gown that is of the pure crystals that ring. They are the tiniest of beads. When you walk, when you move, they will sing."

"Please give Liponie my deepest gratitude."

"I will be happy to do that, as I am grateful that he has made a gown that would excite you so."

"I *am* excited to wear it. Farewell for today."

"Farewell, my dear."

CHAPTER FORTY-ONE

July 3, 2014

"Esthra, can you recommend a fairy to talk to and maybe add to the council meeting tomorrow?"

"I would say Sheliah," he responds. "She is one that you are familiar with, for she spent much time with you in the trees of your youth. My dear, you feel different. The clearing work you recently did to focus your energies was good. You feel less pulled."

"I still would like more clarity about my work. I'm beginning to love the idea of appearing before people and speaking about what the New Earth is going to be like. Can you make any suggestions about how to commence that?"

"It is truly to take the steps. Each time you have an opportunity to speak, you simply do so—if it feels comfortable for you. As you build your communications, they become more expansive. Some people are simply not interested in anything except what they are doing. Do not allow that lack of favor and passion for what you are discussing to color the topic. Do not take it personally, for that is a disservice to you. Your message is an important one. If someone cannot hear it—that is a loss to them."

"Would it be of benefit to talk with Sheliah now, or should I wait until tomorrow?"

"It is important to invite her to be on the Joy Council—if that is what you wish—rather than to assume she will be present."

"Thank you for that recommendation. May I speak with her then please?"

#

Sheliah says, "Greetings." Her voice is bubbly and high-pitched. It sounds as though someone very small is speaking.

"Hello. Thank you for speaking with me. Do you know my guide and friend, Esthra?"

"Ah, yes. He was in the presence of our garden many years ago. And you have been in this garden as well."

"Was I there when I was little?"

"Yes, we shared the same garden. I live where you lived. You have climbed our trees."

What Esthra had told me about spending time with her "in the trees" when I was little, hadn't really registered with me. But now that Sheliah reminds me of this, it hits me at a deep level and I begin to cry. I tell her, "Yes, I used to like to do that."

"You are fearless."

"Are you still there, or are you at another place now?"

"This is our garden," she replies. "This will always be our garden. You do not come to this garden anymore."

"I know. I became afraid of climbing trees."

"Ooh, don't be afraid. Don't be afraid."

"Sheliah, I have something important for you to think about. I'm working with Osiris, Gaia, and other masters of light to assist the Earth, the Native Americans, and other indigenous peoples of Earth."

"We know of the indigenous," she says. "These others, we are unaware of them."

"Do you know the people of Agartha?"

"Yes, we know of them as the people of the inner Earth."

"They are part of a new council called the Joy Council."

"Oh, what a name of joy! This is so lovely. We enjoy love and joy."

"We've been meeting on an Ashtar Command ship on the 10th dimension."

"It is above Earth?"

"Yes. What dimension are you in, Sheliah?"

"We have a range that we can exist within. It is as high as in the 6th dimension as well as the 4th and 5th."

"I would love to be able to include you in the work that our council is doing to assist the Earth and especially the people who love her. I would like to involve you somehow."

"Can you think about your plan so that I may hear it and assimilate?"

"Okay, I'll think about it."

"Ah, we will be over the joyed to be a part of the council you speak of. This opportunity gives us greater leverage to help. We may bring the crystals as well?"

"Yes, anything you think would be of assistance to the Earth."

"There are many of us here in this garden."

"Select who or what you think would best represent your peoples and the Earth, and then come visit us or talk with us tomorrow."

"But we cannot leave our garden."

"Can we communicate with you?"

"Yes, you can—and the crystals."

"I'll figure out how to do that tomorrow."

"You have a worthy plan. These indigenous lived in our garden before you, but they were made to go away."

"When you say the indigenous, do you mean the Native American peoples like the Seminole, the Sioux and the Cherokee, or are you talking about other peoples?"

"I am speaking of the human that has lived on the land for many thousands of years. They are very connected to the Earth. They are Indian."

"Those are the peoples I'm most wishing to assist, along with all of Earth."

"They are beautiful people. They have been driven from our garden. They are away from here now."

"How can we reconnect them with that feeling of your garden?"

She pauses briefly. "Hmm, we will help."

"Gaia will help, too."

"Earth? Ah, of course she will help. If we could have the energy of the Indian back on this land, it would be so lovely."

"I think they would like it, too."

"The rabbits are still here."

Sheliah says this so sweetly, I am even more charmed. I feel such tenderness for her and realize how much I have missed her.

"Are there other animals there?"

"Yes. Yes, you must come back to our garden! It is your garden, too."

"I don't know how to do that anymore."

"Ah, can you take off your shoes and walk on the dirt? Then we can feel each other. I can feel you when you come to our garden."

This touches me, and the tears well up in my eyes again. My voice is thick with emotion, but I manage to say, "All right, I will try that."

She tells me, "Don't be sad. Don't be sad. It is a time for joy. It is a beautiful world and it has such great promise."

All I can manage to say is, "Okay."

"Yes, you will come. Will you climb a tree?"

"Maybe, but I'm bigger now."

"If you climb a tree, I will sit next to you."

"I'll look for one when I come."

"Don't be sad."

"All right. Thank you, Sheliah."

"How did you know of my name?"

"Esthra told me your name."

"Ah, the angel told."

"Yes."

"Ah, bring him. Bring him, too."

"He always comes with me wherever I go."

"Oh, this is the answer then. Yes, be happy."

"Goodbye, Sheliah."

\# \# \#

Esthra asks me if I am in distress. I reply that I am, because I just realized how much I miss this fairy and the place where she lives.

"Sheliah is not the high fairy," he explains. "She is one you witnessed as a child. That forest, the land that you wish to bring together, is where she exists."

"I know now."

"She would be pleased to know that you have this plan. I'm sure that you will share this with her—or perhaps you have already?"

"I didn't talk about it today. She was telling me about her garden. How big is her garden? Is it the whole Earth?"

"It is the area near your father's land that you wish to compile and make a restored space. The fairies are ageless. Sheliah has known many thousands of years of human beings, and yet I'm sure she remembers you."

"Yes, she said that I can connect with her by taking off my shoes and walking on the Earth. And if I climbed a tree, she'd sit beside me."

"She will indeed do this, I am sure. This is good advice she gave you."

"Connecting with her has brought up many emotions for me, Esthra. I realize it's not just her that I miss. I believe I'm mourning the loss of my childhood innocence and the close connection I had with the Earth during that time. Every year before I started school—and as soon as it was warm enough to do so—I spent my days running around barefooted on the pasture and woods where her garden is. I take frequent walks in the parks around my home now, but it's just not the same. I am also reminded about many awful fairy stories I have been exposed to

357

in my life."

"What kind of negativity could ever be said of a fairy?"

"There are many stories that depict fairies as mischievous and evil. For instance, some say they steal children or force you to stay in their kingdom if you eat food in their land."

"Well, I'm glad we've had this conversation. I can dispel your fears. None of this that you speak of is a truth, for fairies are the keepers of the land—so much so that they have gifted their lives to support the Earth. Sheliah inhabits a specific region which encompasses the area that you wish to reconnect with. This is why I selected her, for you have already had acquaintance with her as a child."

"I never wanted to leave that area when my dad bought another place. But, of course, I was just a child, and I didn't have any say in what happened."

"Will it be difficult for you to step onto that land now?"

"It's not my property, so I really shouldn't. We are not supposed to trespass on private property."

"Perhaps the new proprietor would give you permission."

"I don't know who the owners are, but I will find out. I will need to know them anyhow, since I plan to acquire the land again. Is Sheliah the one to connect with tomorrow? Are there other fairies we could involve?"

"Perhaps it's best if you bring this one who is familiar with you."

"But she said she couldn't leave her garden."

"Oh, I did not think about this. But her consciousness can be reached."

"We shall do that then."

# # #

Tonas is happy to see me. "Ah, my beloved, we are waiting for you. Come, come."

"Hold on a minute," I tell him. "I've been wary of coming back to where you are as I don't want to go *woo woo* again."

"I think that was simply a matter of your overstay."

"I'll stay here until the meeting tomorrow. How does being a High Commander affect you? You probably can't just go traipsing off across the universes now because you have duties and things you need to do, correct?"

"I will be even more free to do these things."

"Oh really?"

He reiterates, "Even more so."

"I thought you would be less free with more responsibility."

"Hmm, I think not, my dear."

"Well, that would be good—because I think I've got an itch to travel."

# # #

"Tonas, I have an idea I'd like to share with you, Osiris, and Commander Ashtar."

When we are together in a council chamber, Ashtar asks, "How can I be of assistance, my dear?"

"I just proposed to Tonas ..."

"Ah, we are delighted. We know that you will be happy together!"

Laughing, I say, "Oh, you are so precious. I think that after this party tomorrow, I don't want it just to end. I know there are universes and people who would still like to know more about Earth and perhaps to assist us. I would like for Tonas to have, if possible, an embassy in his ship, so people can visit and learn more about Earth. Perhaps they can even give us ideas about how to assist us. This ship could be a liaison between Earth, all the wonderful ships you have, and all the other worlds that exist. What do you think?"

"I believe that this is an innovative idea with great merit.

This would be as an education, correct?"

"Yes. They could learn more about us, and I could learn more about them."

"There is no dimension or universe that is unfamiliar with Earth, yet it is difficult for these individuals to come to a true understanding of the uniqueness of Earth and the species of human."

Ashtar seems to mull over these ideas for a moment before he begins generating ideas of his own. "We could have a whole section of this vessel set into the themes of Earth itself, just as you have offered us this experience," he says. "We have seen— peered with our little, what you might consider, visioning scopes—and witnessed Earth. Yet to actually experience Earth things hands-on was quite genius. It was a delight and still is for all of us."

"I'm so glad everyone enjoyed it. Will the ship stay in its expanded form?"

"I believe the ship can quarter fifty or sixty thousand beings at a time, with instructors teaching about Earth and about humans from their beginnings to their present stage. The instructors can lead the students through visioning what can come in the future of time."

"Would Tonas approve?"

"I am sure the High Commander is accepting of this. I can see by his smile and his doting looks upon you."

I return Tonas's smile, then focus on Ashtar as he continues.

"As you can imagine, there are many thoughts coming into my mind—and yet *your* thoughts seem to be so unique and drawn to an even more intricate vision. This is because it is your world. Your world is being affected by the works you have done, and a thread of your world touches everything that exists. Even the rocks of dust that are floating in the atmosphere of space are connected to Earth. Let us call this school an Academy of Enrichment—shall we?"

"That sounds good to me," I reply. "I don't want to lose contact with the twenty thousand beings who have been on the ship. I know they are going to go back to their own lives, but I've so appreciated their assistance with the work that we facilitated. I hope that we can somehow continue to receive their assistance without disrupting their lives."

Ashtar laughs. "I believe you are assuming this connection has been casual for them. It has not. I wish for you to imagine that there is nothing that could pull the hearts of these individuals away from the focus of whatever you are choosing in any endeavor. You have their hearts, my dear."

"Thank you for telling me that. This work is so important to me."

"Keep one thought in your mind that you benefit from their presence, and they will amass again."

"Where will they meet?"

"It must be defined by you, of course—because you are the one with the clever ideas. Perhaps the Earth's Moon?"

"Oh! All right. We can talk more about how to do that when we have our meeting tomorrow."

"But the Academy of Enrichment, my dear—that can be created right here."

#

I switch gears and tell Ashtar, "I reconnected today with a fairy named Sheliah that I knew as a child, and that's why I'm still a little choked up. The fairies are going to give us their assistance for the indigenous people. During the course of our conversation, Sheliah told me that, although the Indians had left long ago, the rabbits are still in her garden."

"Rabbits are noble creatures. And they are so fluffy."

It was all I could do not to giggle after he said this. I never expected a man who commands the entire Ashtar fleet to appreciate rabbits for being "fluffy."

# # #

Since I don't know how to enlist the aid of the fairies, I ask Gaia to join us. She speaks to say she is at our beck. "Hello, Gaia. We want to involve the fairies in assisting the indigenous peoples. I talked with Sheliah today, and she said they can't leave the land. I don't know how to involve them in this process of work we're doing."

Gaia explained, "They are in a dimension that is closed from the dimension that you exist within, and yet shares much of the presence of the Earth as well as the foliage."

"Can you think of ways they can assist Earth?"

"The fairies support all of the elements of Earth, including the grasses, the trees, and all that grows—and the crystals, of course, as well as all parts of the dirt, the rocks, and even the water. They are not the overseers of the water, and yet they call upon it to draw into the life of everything in their presence. They can call upon the rains."

"Maybe it's not possible to involve them directly but I wanted to see if we could. Sheliah mentioned something about her Earth crystals."

"Crystals are powerful mediums for directing energy that can move through all dimensions, as you might know."

"Can you work with them to do something about that?"

"Yes, I will work with this Sheliah."

"Thank you. Bid farewell to everyone for me, Gaia."

Liponie asks, "Are you most excited? We all are."

"I have a little request. I hope you'll have time to do it before we drink our toast."

"Little or big, I am ready."

"I'm realizing that I can always count on you … and that's refreshing. I'm assuming that everyone has a champagne glass, is that correct?"

"The instant that you are wishing for them to have it, they will have the glass in their hands."

"This is the inscription I would like to have on the glass."

"Inscription?"

"Yes, writing on the glass."

"Ah! But first, my dear, you must know this information. I have created glasses which are tall and unique. They are the shape of my crystal bells and are as a sweep upward, like your calla lily. Now, we have procured the Dom Perignon from your dimension of Earth. It was a bit difficult. I made the purchase myself. We have the Dom Perignon, although we had a bit of discussion. Some thought it should be Cristal. I thought the name was lovely, but Dom Perignon is something that is quite an ancient name, as you would say. It is something that I have been aware of in some of my exploits of Earth, so it was special to me to use this brand. Go ahead, dear, tell me what you wish."

"Here's what I want written on the glasses, 'To_____, a member of the Joy Company, with Gratitude and Love from Tonas and Joy, July 4, 2014.'"

"Ah, this is a lovely idea! It will be taken care of. Would you like it to be in the purest of gold? I can place the wording in gold?"

"Yes, that would be nice. I think maybe some people have left, but I want to make sure everyone gets one. Can you see to that?"

"This is the grand finale," Liponie says. "There are some musicians who are still here."

"If they've been here but left, is it possible to give them one also?"

"We can easily find them."

"That way, they have a little memento."

"As if they need something to remember this," he said grandly. "This event is emblazoned within their hearts, my dear. They are quite excited and I am so excited. I will put these letterings immediately."

"Liponie, *you* are emblazoned in my heart. I just cannot tell you how special you have been in helping with everything. You made miracles."

"We are good working together, my dear."

"And the food fight! I was a little bit trepidatious—that's another word for your vocabulary—about all these glorious people having food fights. Jill Marie tells me they were howling with laughter and really enjoying it."

"It was one of the highlights for many of our guests," he says. "Of course, they have never experienced anything like it."

"There's been a lot of that happening. I wanted to give you a little chance to prepare. I'm going to be leaving for a while. I would like for you to have Osiris, Tonas, Gaia, and Ashtar when I come back to the ship for a pre-meeting before we talk with everybody."

"Of course. And may I say that we have great works to accomplish together in the future."

"Oh." I have too much to do right now to ask him more about these great works, and I know he probably wouldn't tell me anyway. Still, I'm going to try to see if I can sneak some information out of him in the future.

"I am most honored to be of service to you."

"I really do appreciate your work."

# # #

The CEV says, "We are in presence."

"Hello. It's Independence Day, and a big celebration, so I'm wondering what you have for me."

"We have taken your considerations deeply into our hearts and have fashioned for you an embellishment that will enhance all that you have applied," they say. "It is a golden egg that is encrusted with crystalline which will allow the energy transmission to all worlds from the heart of Gaia."

"What is its purpose?"

"It will amplify and magnify. Envision a computer that is capable of doing great things in the beginning of the development of computers—and then view the modern day computer. This embellishment offers Earth an increased ability to expand beyond its current range of development by enhancing the transmissions from each of the dimensions. It holds the vibration of that 8th dimension that you are in most delight to achieve."

"That is great news!"

"Indeed, it is a gift to you more so than any. It is a gift to your heart, and of course, when you apply the transmission of this into the heart of Gaia, it is a gift from you to her, also—for we know you love her so."

"I do."

The CEV inform me that this embellishment will especially assist those who feel a connection with Earth to have easier passage to the higher dimensions. They add that I am to transmit the information in the egg out from the center of the Earth.

"This is the best gift ever."

"And it is the best gift ever to us as well, to Gaia as well, and to all who are ready. It is even a gift to those who are unsure that there is a journey. This gift, my dear, we must place within your hands. It is possible for you to have the support of those great ones, yes?"

"Yes."

"It is acceptable to bring this embellishment into their company, and for them to witness it and even to touch it. Their touch will enhance the contents of the egg and assist them to focus their attention for the activation. Please bring this to your grand spectacle, which we have been witnessing. We are in gratitude for your invitation to be of conscious connection."

I try to clarify exactly where in the Earth I am to place the egg. They are unable to tell me the location, but suggest that since Gaia is to receive the gift, she should be allowed to define where she wishes it to be placed.

"All right. I'm going to be back. I know we have many more wonderful things to do together. Thank you for this magnificent gift today."

"It is our gratitude."

"Do I have the egg in my little hands here?"

"We have placed it within your little hands."

"It feels so wonderful."

"It has a tripod that it can be placed on, so that you are released from holding it while others touch it."

"Good idea. I will do that when I get back to the ship. Thank you very much."

"It is an honor, my dear."

# # #

Gaia, Ashtar, Liponie, and Osiris are with Tonas as he welcomes me back.

"Here is the egg from the CEV and a tripod for it to sit on so that people can touch it," I say, after greeting them individually.

"Ah, everything is always so special that you bring into our awareness," Tonas says. "Perhaps you would wish to have it in the grand ballroom? People are gathering there."

"Let's wait and take it when we go out."

"I have extended the grand ballroom to hold all participants."

"Did Liponie tell you about the toasts we're going to do?"

Tonas tells me they know about the toasts and agrees with me that Commander Ashtar should be the one to announce the Academy of Enrichment at some point during our gathering. I suggest we should ask the Moon for permission to construct the building for our future council, and I am informed she was honored to be chosen and has already given permission.

I mention that it would be nice to construct a crystalline structure. I should have known that Liponie already has designs for a half dome made of purest crystal with views in all directions.

"I need not to micro-manage this because you are all so wonderful," I say, partly as a reminder to myself.

"Liponie will be offering you the opportunity to accept these designs. He thought it a bit premature."

"I would like the Moon, you, Commander Ashtar, and maybe Osiris to go over them. You have my permission to do whatever you feel is the most wonderful thing."

"We are dedicated, my dear. There is nothing more important in our hearts and minds. We have simply been waiting for you to go forward. Liponie also wishes to supply a christening of that space, once it is complete; he is already preparing champagne for this. He has taken over part of the ship to acquire all that he needs for such an endeavor."

"Do we need to do that today, or can it be another time?"

"We can do that at some other time. Today, everything is about the culmination."

# # #

"Tonas, what would you think about every non-dual world having an Academy of Enrichment?"

"It can be imagined. It would be the greatest academy of every world. It would be the most sought-after. Each one would have to be quite large. There would be many lines of waiting."

"Does Commander Ashtar think that would be a good idea?"

Ashtar chimes in, "My dear, I am inspired by you and this idea. Let us, of course, create the first one, for it will be of the history that this ship was part of our fleet."

"Yes, I agree."

"And that it will be of this High Commander. It will be special that it shall be this ship, this beautiful vessel. And then, once it is involved, we will accept only one participant from each of the worlds, no matter the universe. The position will be most eagerly prized."

"I would imagine so."

"Once it is complete and we have it in function—then, of course, these can be easily replicated. In fact, with you now inspiring me even further, I can see that each world might have as many as would accommodate every citizen of that world. There would be many satellites of these throughout the regions of each world, each system."

"Fantastic!"

"Everyone is aware of Earth and the human species and how it is evolving to enrich us all. So certainly, this would be a great wonder."

"I think that's all for the pre-meeting," I say. "The egg that I have is an embellishment for all the things we have done. Gaia, can you read what's in it?"

She asks to hold it and I hand it to her.

"This is truly a gift to us both," she says, meaning her embodiment as Gaia and her existence as the Earth, "and to all parts of us. It connects us even more intimately with the many threads that you have put in place in the dimensions, the connection points between us and all that exists in the fullness of all. This is an amplification. It will beat as if with my heart. Ah, there will be much pulsing of sweet joy. You have done a great service for all of us."

"We're going to take it into the main room. The CEV suggested that everyone touch it, because that would enhance their abilities to contribute to the application of the egg. Before we do that, were we able to involve the fairies in any way with this celebration?"

"Yes. In fact, it is through me that they will be a part of these festivities," Gaia says. "They will be able to support through me. This will be an additional amplification, for the fairies are designing the paths for the elevation amongst all that lives within the Earth and the atmosphere, as well as atop the Earth. Everything that lives and breathes and grows is of their realm. It is important for them to be a part of this work today."

"I'd like to be more involved with them in the future. Is there a queen of the fairies?"

"There are several. There is a queen for each region. This Sheliah that you have engaged has opened up the conduit for all, every of those kingdoms and all of Earth that are of those fairy kingdoms—as well as the crystals. The fairies transmit to me through the crystals to be a part of this exceptional gathering and the work of support for the planet."

"Thank you for figuring out a way to make this work."

"It is through this egg that the fairies will receive amplification for that which they bring forth. They are inhibited from supporting much assistance to the human. Through the elements of Earth and also that of the animal and plant kingdoms—the birds, the crawling ones—it is through these that Sheliah and all the other fairies of their kingdoms will support the amplifications of individuals who are in readiness to move to the higher dimensions."

"This will assist the indigenous peoples also, is that

correct?"

"My dear, the indigenous are so deeply linked to the Earth. Earth is linked to every part of us," she said, again referring to herself in plural, "and it is through this connection that they will be elevated. Do you understand?"

"Yes, but I also know that several of them felt like they had lost their connection with you. I was wondering how we could help them with that."

"It is the collective of them that will be raised. They have their own collective consciousness. It is associated with all of the others, the greater collective. And yet, they have their own transmissions that are within a band that is of energy that their hearts can feel. It is through that and their connection to Earth that we will help to raise them."

"Very good. How many fairy kingdoms are there on Earth?"

"There are many thousands."

"So there are thousands of fairy queens."

"Of course."

"Are there fairy kings?"

"No, there are not. There are no male fairies. All are female."

That surprises me. There go all the tales of fairy romances. Hmm, a little idea settles in the back of my mind for later.

"Sheliah has a message for you she would like to transmit. Would you like this to be within the group or in this present now? I believe she has a great message."

"I want to hear what she has to say, but I wonder if all of the beings in attendance should hear it also."

"I am in concert with you on this."

"Can you ask if she would be okay with everyone hearing?"

"She is hoping to have her words heard by all."

"Anybody have anything else before we enter into the room where all are assembled to witness this transmission?" I ask.

Tonas says he believes we are ready. "It is a far distance

from where we are. We will simply transmit there." Tonas pauses and then says, "Ah, of course, there are the trumpets again."

I feel like giggling, but I refrain. Liponie is irrepressible.

"My dear, you may place the egg-shaped item on this tripod in the midst of the room. May I present the great and the glorious Joy! She is here now to address all of you."

I start to speak and Tonas says, "Oh, just one moment. They are making clapping. This is an Earth custom."

Humorously, I reply, "Yes, I know."

"Thank you. If you will all be of silence now." Whispering, he says, "Go ahead, my dear."

# # #

I take a breath and begin. "Welcome to our final day of celebration. Gaia is going to implement this beautiful golden egg—but first, one of my special friends from when I was a little girl would like to speak with us today. Her name is Sheliah, and she is a representative of the fairy garden where I grew up. Sheliah, you may speak; I'm eager to hear what you have to say."

Sheliah begins by saying, "I am greatly honored to be in your presence, energetically transmitting through our beloved queen, Gaia. I speak for all of us of the fairy kingdoms in wishing thank you and gratitudes to all of you, all of you here that are holding the greatest vision for our evolution. We are grateful and we are inspired by this one, Joy, for she is great. She is one of the greatest human beings of Earth, and she is here to ask you always for assistance for us, for our collective of the Earth. We know that you will give her all of your hearts and support us. For this, we wish all of you to have presents of something that is of our gardens."

She pauses, and I can sense excitement from the crowd as she continues. "We have brought you each a crystal of great importance, for it resonates with the energy of our garden and of our whole Earth—and, of course, our love and gratitude. We wish for you each to have this. This grand, pretty man—Liponie—has for each of you that which is to be offered. He is now transmitting into each of your hands these beautiful crystals. And, of course, we have a special one for you, Joy."

She says my name with such tenderness that I begin crying while saying, "Thank you."

"It is very special. It is shaped like a heart and it comes from our garden."

I am crying even harder as I thank her again.

"Yes, it is for you. Everyone, look at this one, our Joy. She is so tender. How easily she is brought to tears. Please be careful with her. Thank you."

I have to stop to compose myself before I can adequately acknowledge her gifts.

"Oh dear ... thank you, Sheliah. Thank all of you of the fairy kingdom, and thank you, Gaia."

I gesture to the golden egg on its tripod. "This egg that you see before you is a gift from the CEV for Gaia, and Gaia is going to have the say-so in where she and I put this in her soil. Before we do that, Gaia, can you explain to everyone a little bit about what this egg does? Everyone needs to touch it before we work with it."

Gaia asks Tonas to move the egg throughout the room, so that all may reach their energy and touch it. "All could stretch their energy to this point, and yet I think it might be important for this to be brought into their presence while we speak about this new implement."

As the egg is circulated, Gaia continues. "I wish also for each of you to be holding the vision that this beautiful Joy has held in her heart for the evolution of her world, for she is one of a small number who are holding, literally, the vision of the evolution of all of us of the Earth moving through the stages to the 25th dimension. If you can, when holding and touching this implement, see the pathways of grace and sweetness that will assist in our swift evolution.

"It will be easy to connect with all of your beautiful worlds, for you are of the non-dual. Your assistance will help those of the dual worlds in all universes and dimensions of the everything, to have the amplification of these threads from this implement assist in drawing all of the worlds together in the pinnacle point of our fulfillment on the 25th dimension, so that all may culminate together."

Gaia goes on to explain that each of the crystals that the fairies have gifted to everyone in attendance contains an encrypted message that will allow the recipient to connect with and assist the area of Earth it came from.

Gaia offers her gratitude to the peoples who exist within her (the Agarthans and others), the angels, all who have been guardians of Earth, the Ashtar Command and those from other worlds who wish to be of service to her. She invites all of these beings to come onto her in the 4th through the 7th dimensions to assist in the development and evolution of those of Earth who are awakened or soon shall awake.

Gaia explains that Inishimora will become an embassy vessel that will offer programs "to assist in the greater understanding of the whole of Earth, our cultures, our desires, and that which makes us in the greatest of happiness through our laughter and joy.

"You have experienced so many gifts in these days," Gaia concludes. "This is indeed the party that all will feel within their heart forever, for never has there been an opportunity for so many to know Earth, to know us as you have in these days. This, my dears, gives you a new insight as to Earth and how you can assist. You are welcome. Our arms and hearts welcome you."

#

"That was eloquent and wonderful to hear, Gaia. Thank you for sharing your thoughts with us. Has everyone had a chance to touch the egg, Tonas?"

"Not quite, my dear. Perhaps we can do the toast while the remaining individuals are having the opportunity to touch. My father is taking the egg around. It is his great honor."

"Liponie, can everybody have a glass?"

As usual, he laughs and says, "Let me take care of this, my dear. If you all can put fingers out like this, for there will be manifest into your hands the most beautiful of crystal. It is filled with an elixir of great Earth delight called champagne. It will tickle your nose, and when you drink of it you will feel a great upliftment within your body, as well as the essence of your presence. Your aura will begin to change colors. You will enjoy drinking it, and of course, you may look upon this glass of great crystal and read the words upon it." Then he whispers to me to make the toast now.

"This is the way you toast—not the kind of toast that you pop up, but a toast to people you want to honor. You who are here can tell your children that you have assisted in the greatest celebration of Earth ever held. I like to think of all of you as 'The Company of Heaven.' You have an inscription on your glass which says: 'To You, a member of the Joy Company, with gratitude and love from Tonas and Joy, July 4, 2014.'

"Please raise your glass. I'm drinking to all of you who have assisted Tonas and me. I'm drinking to my genie friend Liponie, a true magician without whose help we could not have created a party this magnificent. And to the CEV for the wonderful gifts they've given us. To Tonas, my wonderful partner in this work. And to Gaia. Tonas, would you like to give a toast?"

Tonas asks the group to, "Please raise your glass once again. I wish to bring to your attention that Joy—my own beloved—gave us the opportunity to be a part of something that would not have been possible except through her compliance and the invitations she extended for us to join.

"I wish to offer this of the toasts, to my beloved Joy. To you, my dear, to you. We now drink the fullness of our glass, which has now been refilled by Liponie."

"Thank you, Tonas."

# # #

Tonas informs me that the egg has been brought back to the center of the room and he would like to touch it.

"Oh, my goodness, yes! Give it a big cuddle."

"I wish to touch it with my vision for Earth, my commitment to Earth. I wish for all of our hearts to join in this focus now, as my beloved takes this implement, which is sworn by Gaia to be the inspiration of the future. We are ready. What would you have us do?"

I first thank Emmon for taking the egg around and then I ask Gaia to tell me where to place it.

"Bring this implement into the center core of my physical presence, which is part of those three dimensions merging into the fourth, into the heart of the physical Earth," she replies.

I begin the work by going down into the Earth. When I am in position, I allow the Language of Light to flow through me to assist opening the energies that will facilitate this transmission. I also telepathically transmit the following description to the people on the ship.

As I place the egg at the heart of Gaia, I feel the energy of it flood through all of Earth and then out through her surface to touch upon everything that exists there. I sense the energy move up through our atmosphere, along the grids, and out through all the threads to all the dimensions and worlds. I can feel the egg pulsating with the heartbeat of Gaia as it sends out enrichment and assistance for our smooth, graceful evolution to the 8th dimension and beyond, to the culmination.

Addressing the group on the ship, I say, "Thank you for your focused assistance. I'm coming back to the ship now."

Tonas requests, "Please, hold the vision, all of you, of this day of liberty. Hold the vision of the journey that Earth shall make, that Earth is destined to travel. I have been forever changed and inspired by this. I know that everyone here is feeling the same. I can see from your faces that you are greatly touched. You can see the wisdom in your support of this world, and what it means to be a part of the grand evolution of Earth and its species. We are truly, in this moment, inspired to be in unity with all of Earth and to feel our hearts beating with her. We congratulate you, Gaia—and, of course, we celebrate you."

#

I suggest to Tonas that this is the best place to have some fireworks.

"If everyone will look please, your glasses are refilled. Let us look upward into the sky. Ah, we will move the Joy Star a little bit to the side. She always wants to be right there for you. Liponie, you may begin the spectacle. Oh, it is wonderful, my dear. I will make sure one day you can see every sparkle of this!"

Tonas continues, "I wish for you to know, my beloved is not aware yet, that every world that is in observance of Earth, has, I think you would call it a 'monitor' that displays this. It is easy for them to transmit and see within their consciousness, and yet there are great size monitors for those to witness this grand spectacle. These are only worlds of non-dual, for it is not yet time for us to bring into awareness those of the dual plane. One day, they will be ready to know, for this spectacle is of grand proportion. I wish for you all to know that this will continue for the next twelve hours. There will also be dancing, music, and much merry-making."

I'm feeling a little disheartened at not truly being able to see the spectacular display with my own eyes. "I'm going to see some fireworks tonight," I say. "Maybe."

Tonas immediately picks up on my frustration and says, "Oh, my dear, there will be one day when you *will* see all of this; I will make sure of it."

I do appreciate his consideration. After a moment, I decide that twelve hours of fireworks is an event worth waiting to see.

"Are you pleased with our gathering?" he asks.

"I am. You did wonderfully. You're always surprising me. You already anticipated much of what I was going to say."

"Did I rob you of a pleasure?"

"No, not at all! I was worried that I would have to do some things that I wasn't sure how to do. I'm glad that Liponie is going to design the building for the Joy Council."

#

"Liponie has completed your tree house."

"Tonas, can we go there and just talk for a minute?"

"Of course, they are ignoring us. They are looking up into the stars above, which pale into comparison with the fires working. Let us go. I am sure you will be pleased. Let me describe your treehouse. There is a bed in your sleeping quarters and it is oval. I thought this was a poor idea, and yet Liponie feels that it is most delightful to you. He has made a curved frame across the top, so that you will not fall out if you are to roll in your sleeping. He has designed with some of the most beautiful colors of the peacock. There are windows all around with no glass in them, for there are no insects. He has encouraged flowers to grow all around the outside of it and they will come in through the windows. It is charming."

"It sounds enchanting."

"Now, you are familiar with—oh, how do you describe it? Liponie put little pieces of wood together to shape beautiful chairs and a lounge with comfortable, puffy pillowings. The pillows are in the back as well as the front, dripping downward so that your legs will have comfort if you wish to bring your legs upward. He believes that this has something to do with laziness and I am not understanding him."

"They're called La-Z-Boy Recliners."

"I thought it was insulting, actually."

"No, because men and women like to get in them, recline, put their legs up, and relax."

"Liponie is innovative, for he has made it the size that we both can enjoy the comfort of sitting together, so that we may have intimate conversation. He has added strings that are as if a wall of threads of the crystalline which you love. Of course, walking through them will make sounds that will be quite melodious."

"Built-in music! How lovely."

"His vision for the sweet lighting that will illuminate is a flower that is not native to Earth. Many worlds have this flower, and it is most luminous. It is perhaps the size of five of your hands together across in a circle. It is all colors, and he has these positioned on the walls and the ceiling.

"He has positioned many of the crystals within so that, when there is no luminary, they will light as the stars. At first, he wished to have a crystalline cap for your house, but then he thought that would not be of privacy, you see. Even though there is no one who would be peering in through the light of the sky, it still was important to him that you would have your own space of privacy—and so he has created this cape with these beautiful flowers which have names on different worlds. On my world we call them Zahsharra flowers."

"I can't wait to see them!"

"When you are lying upon your beautiful egg bed—Liponie believes it is important for you to have this egg bed because of your great works, which is why he made it oval—and when the luminaries are quiet, then those that are crystal will begin to shine as if the stars of different universes. Wherever the vessel is, that will be the configuration of the stars. If you are somewhere with me and you are of the homesickness, then the sky will reflect the stars that are just above your Earth abode."

"Oh, Tonas, I think I'm going to cry again."

"He is an extremely gifted genie, my dear."

"I know."

"I think you are not accustomed to so much care being put into your desires."

"I'm not. It's incredible to me." I'm sniffling now.

"I believe Liponie would do anything for you, and you know that I would as well."

"I know. It's been a wonderful, remarkable day."

"I hope that it met all of your expectations."

"You have exceeded them."

"We will complete the party after the final of the fires working."

#

I am quiet for a moment while I contemplate what I am about to reveal.

"Tonas, over these past months, I have gone through confusion, excitement, joy, frustration, and a myriad of other emotions as we've come together in this great work. I respect you, and you know I don't want to ever hurt or disappoint you. But at the same time, I've come to realize that I need to embrace my now. I don't know the *future*, but I know my *now.*"

I can sense he is worried, so I hurry on. "Holding back my feelings for you out of fear that I will hurt you in the future is something I no longer choose to do. Tonas, I love you. I know— deep down—that I have loved you for a long time and that a part of me will always love you. My hope is that my love will deepen to match the love you have for me."

As always, as if reading my mind, Tonas's words release all tension and doubt I have surrounding my decision to be so candid with him. He simply says, "I know in my heart that it will."

MISSION PARTICIPATION DIRECTIVES:

The masters of light assisted me to make energy bridges so that you can visit Tonas and me on his spaceship. While you are there, you can participate in the transmissions we send to Earth from the 10th dimension. To do so, find someplace comfortable to sit and close your eyes. Intend to visit the ship on the date of any of the transmissions we facilitate, and feel your consciousness travel in time to transport you to the ship. (You may visit the transmission you select multiple times.)

To add to the transmission, simply hold a vision for the highest hopes and dreams for your life and for the Earth, and find yourself in front of the window in his ship that looks down upon Earth. Send the gifts for yourself and for the Earth into the orb that Tonas and I hold in our hands. When we send the transmission out, you can feel the energies of it waft their way to Earth.

Another suggestion is, before you go to sleep, specify a session you would like to visit and set the intention that you will remember your visit when you wake up.

I really hope to see you at the Summer Solstice Party.

GLOSSARY

A special thanks to Jill Marie for her assistance in articulating many of the definitions in the glossary of terms.

Angelic Rebirthing: This SVH process wraps you in an angelic cocoon of love and light that begins at your conception and continues through your gestation. During your gestation, the angels will sing to you and whisper of your greatness. All thoughts, words, and energies generated from outside the womb which hold less than the highest principles of divine love will be transmuted by the cocoon to establish a sacred foundation that will reflect a joyous beginning. At your birth, you will experience a welcoming ceremony attended by all the masters, angels, and guides that are aligned with supporting your evolution to higher consciousness.

Ashtar Command: A consortium of elevated non-dual masters that are committed to support the graceful evolution of Earth. From the 10th dimension, their fleet of more than eighty million ships, non-manipulatively assist all sentient beings to achieve heightened states of conscious awareness. "Our hearts are pure and our focus is always to honor the timing of all beings." Commander Ashtar.

Dimensions: Layers of space that interconnect with form and vibrational frequencies, defining the resonance of the fields they exist within.

The 4th dimension defines itself by the duality that exists as a constant within the resonance of the fields that are a part of its blended energy that coincides with the 3rd dimensional fields on one border and the higher vibrational energies of the 5th dimension on the other border.

Why choose to elevate to the 5th and higher dimensions? The payoff is heightened clarity, focus, and enhancement of natural abilities. These abilities would appear to be magical to someone in the 3rd dimension, just as flying in an airplane would have seemed magical and fantastic to someone just two hundred years ago.

Will this evolution happen for everyone, whether they step in to a specific path associated with an evolution to higher consciousness or not? The elevation of Earth as a world and each individual existing on her is a reality that will occur in its own timing, for all beings live to experience this great wonder. This can be said with great confidence, because it is the soul that is leading this journey, and all sentient beings on this world are living to evolve in their own way, in their own timing, and in their own flavor of experiences. All roads lead to the heightened states of conscious awareness.

Dual World: Dual worlds offer the opportunity for residents to experience the many flavors of duality. Light and shadow exist side by side, creating a space for peace and adversity to fuel experiences of harmony and free expression amidst discord and suppression. Earth is a dual plane of existence that is currently evolving to achieve the higher dimensional planes of non-duality.

Fifth Realm (short version): The Fifth Realm is an energy field of Earth associated with the 5th dimensional plane. This is the designated space for one's post-ascension expansion.

Fifth Realm (long version): The Fifth Realm is a dimensional presence that exists as a corresponding element of the 5th dimension. It was selected to be the new realm, because 5th dimension was a neutral space until the Atlanteans made their transition from the 3rd dimension into the 5th. In this leap, they introduced their duality into that space, which "muddied the waters." The 5th dimension could no longer be considered a pure, non-dual dimension. As a result, the previous realm of consciousness associated with the 5th dimension was left unexpressed, leaving it to be an ideal settling place for the new Earth. The Fifth Realm now exists as a realm of consciousness that supports the continued evolution of ascended and transitioned beings.

Though Earth is destined to evolve well beyond the 5th dimensional frame, the realms of consciousness and settling presence of the Fifth Realm will remain a constant. It is a new realm of presence born to house the next stage of the cumulative expansion of all that is.

Before the Fifth Realm: Initially there was a place of the after-life where peoples of Earth and other worlds transitioned to when they died. They "went to the light" and existed as energy, awaiting the next stage in the collective evolution of all beings. This realm of the after-life was very pleasurable, though some beings periodically chose to leave in order to become a "walk-in," which allowed them the opportunity to reincarnate into the body of someone already living, as a means to benefit individuals from a new soul entering their body. These walk-in experiences typically saved the life of the recipient and such actions were always sanctioned and implemented by Creator.

In the years 1999 through 2003, peoples from all over the world experienced a surge of awakening to their sacred path and purpose. One group of these beings is known as the 144,000. They and a secondary wave of 144,000 sleeping angels incarnated to be alive here on the planet during this time, in order to support humanity's individual and collective evolution. These evolving beings and a growing number of other awakening beings worked tirelessly to assist humanity and all sentient beings of Earth, though many times this work was implemented on a higher level, unbeknownst to them. As they went about their daily activities, these evolving masters joined Gaia, who lent 96 percent of her energy body to support the development of foundational elements that were dedicated to birth a New Earth Realm. This realm was to seat within an existing dimensional field of presence associated with the 5th dimension. From the end of 1999 to November 13, 2003, those that joined Gaia supported the forming of what we now call the Fifth Realm. The inauguration of this New Earth commenced the Golden Age of Light, which laid the foundation for our current Golden Rose Consciousness.

Grid(s): A matrix of energy that is like a record of the vibration, the story, and even the history of the planet and where it is in its evolution. Some grids will have a high vibration and some will be evolving to reach that level. There are all kinds of grids and energy lines; each of the dimensions has a system of grids. Some are specific, especially the "Harmony Grids." The network of energy lines around the planet are linked to other matrices of grids in our solar system and the cosmos.

My List of 30,544 Names: This is something I've been working on since January 2007. I spent hundreds of hours researching names of people who have died. They were people who were known for abilities and attributes I would like to possess. Sananda assisted me to incorporate only the perfected form of their genetics, abilities, and attributes that would benefit me. Now you know—I'm a compulsive list maker.
Nobel Prize winners: 439
Artists: 3,901
Olympians: 774
Authors: 2879
Geniuses, Alchemists, Kabbalists, Mystics, Wiccans, Zen masters, McArthur Fellows, Rhodes and Fulbright scholars, Hermeticists, polymaths and polyglots: 2,448

Gods of all cultures: 1,057
Templars: 268
Musicians, composers, conductors, troubadours: 3,656
Others including athletes, dancers, explorers, Native Americans, priestesses, famous couples, fencers, wealthy, ascended masters, Freemasons, archeologists, astronomers, famous women and men: 5,429
Philosophers: 4,995
Samurai: 1,246
Sufis: 362
Violinists: 2852
Grateful Dead (ancestors and friends): 238

Non-Dual World: Non-dual worlds are free of the resistance of duality. Everything co-exists in harmony with no adversarial roles to thwart perpetual states of focused conscious awareness. Andromeda, Arcturus, Sirius, and Lyra are some of the non-dual worlds of our universe.

SVH: The **Serenity Vibration Healing® and Enlightenment Technique** (SVH) is a personal empowerment tool that works at the transcendent levels to reform foundations of limiting beliefs and perceptions that are stopping you from reaching your highest ideal.

The foundation for this modality is Quantum Level Reprogramming, which is a reformatting tool that empowers the Creator to energetically release barriers and blocks that have seeded or built upon limiting beliefs and perceptions that are anchored in your experiences in this lifetime. These tools will also reformat genetic predispositions that have been activated into your reality and release limiting alliances with unbalanced beliefs that have been anchored into your life through its imprinting.

SVH is all about sovereignty, autonomy, and the freedom to

elevate your vibration and light quotient, free of the attraction of limiting experiences that have the potential to block your smooth, graceful, and expedient evolution to higher consciousness.

SVH is the premier set of tools to master the mind. It is the safest, most effective means for reformatting genetic and current life imbalance, as well as restoring harmony to the physical body and quieting the mind.

Walk-In: When a soul essence vacates its host body to allow a new essence to inhabit its space the new essence is commonly referred to as a walk-in. Through unexplained, divine means, the Creator aids the host body to continue functioning by assisting a new essence to carry forth the previous, amended or new purpose.

Here's a peek at some of the events in Book 2...

BLOSSOMING OF LOVE

The second book in The Adventures of Joy Chronicles offers you the opportunity to participate in a more active manner in your personal evolution as well as in the evolution of Earth. If you wish to pull up a chair at one of the Joy Council tables, you may choose to sit next to a famous figure from Earth's history and listen as they share parts of their stories, or, more importantly, their hopes for our new Earth. Witness exciting developments in the fairy realms, the return of many mythical creatures, and allow yourself to feel the magic that is part of life on Earth!

ABOUT THE AUTHOR

Joy Elaine lives in Bloomington, Indiana, in a house with crystals displayed on every windowsill. Instead of pets, she has over two hundred orchid "babies" in the greenhouse on her back deck. In the past, Joy devoted her time and travel to buying orchids and playing her violin in the Bloomington Symphony Orchestra and her viola in a string quartet. Now she dedicates most of her time to Joy Council work and writing.

Mailing list signup:
www.joyelaine.com

Purchase or read about Joy's books:
www.joyelaine.com

e-mail:
info@joyelaine.com

Blog:
www.joyelaine.com/blog

Amazon:
www.amazon.com/Joy-Elaine/e/B01N6G5JJX

Facebook:
www.facebook.com/joyelainebooks/

Goodreads:
www.goodreads.com/search?q=joy+elaine

SVH (Serenity Vibration Healing):
www.thejoyoflife.info

Made in the USA
Columbia, SC
07 November 2018